FitzRoy
of the
Beagle

FitzRoy
of the
Beagle

H. E. L. Mellersh

Mason & Lipscomb PUBLISHERS

to Margot, my wife

Acknowledgements

The jacket illustrations and of the FitzRoy barometer are reprinted by permission of the British National Maritime Museum, the picture of Wellington Harbour by permission of the Alexander Turnbull Library, the photograph of FitzRoy as an older man by permission of the Misses E. and M. Smyth, the portrait of Charles Darwin by permission of George Darwin, Esq., and the portrait of the Duke of Grafton by permission of the Governors of Milton Abbas School.

Quotations from Baron de Thierry's letter in Chapter 15 and from the FitzRoys' correspondence in Chapter 18 are made by permission of the Mitchell and Dixson Libraries, New South Wales.

Contents

List of Illustrations

Foreword

In one respect I am perhaps in an exceptional position to write a Foreword to a Life of Robert Fitzroy, for in 1934 I went to see his daughter, Miss Laura FitzRoy, in her London home, after I had been working on the manuscript of Darwin's diary on board *H.M.S. Beagle*. I remember well the look of her crowded Victorian drawing-room, dominated by a large white marble bust of her father,—a remarkable face, sensitive, severe, fanatical; combining a strength of purpose with some weakness or uncertainty, which can be more easily seen, I think, in his earlier portrait. I asked Miss FitzRoy tentatively whether the bust had ever been photographed? And I remember how her brisk answer was unequivocal and final: 'No, I should not like the idea at all.'

There were many pictures round the walls by Conrad Martens, official artist on board *H.M.S. Beagle*; and I could see that the book-cases were filled with tantalizing books which must have belonged to her father. But I had to restrain my eagerness to examine them, for she was aware of my especial interest in the voyage, and of my relationship to Charles Darwin; I knew that I was therefore somewhat suspect.

Yet she spoke of Charles Darwin openly and charmingly, and said: 'He was a great man—a genius—but I cannot help regretting he became so broad.' After a pause she added: 'He had been raised up for a special purpose,' again adding with a sigh, 'but he overstepped the mark. Yes, he overstepped the mark for which he was intended.' These words and a full account of my visit I recorded immediately afterwards in a letter which I still possess; after the lapse of thirty-three years I could not have trusted to a memory of her words.

As we talked she told me the following anecdote relevant to her father's work on weather forecasting. One Sunday morning when she was a young child living with her parents in their Kensington home—it must have been about 1860—she heard the bell ring, and ran downstairs to open the front door for them, as she thought, returning from Communion Service. But to her immense embarrassment on the doorstep in front of her stood the Queen's Messengers, come to enquire at the Admiral's house about the weather reports and storm warnings for the following day, when Her Majesty was intending to cross to Osborne in the Isle of Wight; Admiral FitzRoy had only recently instituted Weather Forecasts from the Meteorological Office. The charm of Miss FitzRoy's personality and her appearance in her white cap and her shawl as she told me this story, still remain vividly stamped on my mind. After my visit I felt that I could realize more fully how the intransigence of the *Beagle's* Captain could have been combined with an almost tortured sense of right and wrong; how righteous indignation and desire to punish was mitigated by his sense of generosity; and how compassion was near the surface, except perhaps towards himself.

Mr Mellersh has followed Captain FitzRoy through the less well-known episodes of his life after the return of the *Beagle* from her second voyage in 1836, through the tragic New Zealand episode, to a brief return to the Admiralty, when his nautical knowledge was needed at the time when the introduction of steam revolutionized the Navy.

But it is in his work at the Meteorological Office that his name will mainly be remembered. He can be called the father of weather forecasting; no one could value the need of storm warnings more than a captain of a sailing vessel who had faced for months on end the winds and waters round Cape Horn. The *Beagle* was equipped with barometers—an innovation at that time; with their warnings of coming gales and FitzRoy's consequent prompt action, he had probably saved the *Beagle* and all on board on more than one occasion. But it was not until barometric information from many different stations could be collated immediately by telegraphic communication that their information became more reliable; and this achievement FitzRoy did not live to see. Mr Mellersh points out how the humane, life-saving aspect of this pioneering work appealed to FitzRoy's deep human compassion.

Much has already been written on the scientific results of the voyage and of Darwin's opportunities and the use he made of them. Much too has been written, often with a prejudiced emotional bias, on FitzRoy's tragic experiment in taming the Fuegian natives he took back to England on the first voyage, returning them to Cape Horn on the second expedition after over two years' absence. In dealing with the long and complicated story of subsequent South American Missionary efforts, usually so weighted with emotional feeling on either side, Mr Mellersh is doing good service in telling the story with unbiased objectivity.

In this book Mr Mellersh gives the first full-length portrait of Robert FitzRoy, his aristocratic background, and the part he played in these many situations, his notable achievements, his failures and the tragic aftermath. The successes are recorded, with the conquest of incredible difficulties and dangers; the failures are here too, but they were noble failures, inspired by an ardent spirit in search of improvement of the human lot.

Throughout Mr Mellersh gives contemporary accounts of comment and criticism. In his use of references, both from *The Times*' leading articles, missionary societies' and other reports, Admiralty records, and in other contemporary publications, he reveals the reactions of the public opinion of the day, and adds another dimension to his work. It is with this full documentation of the contemporary scene that Mr Mellersh's portrait becomes the portrait of an era. In this unveiling of some of the public and private actions and judgments of one hundred years ago, can we avoid any comparable errors of today?

NORA BARLOW

Preface

IT IS one of the strange chances of history that the choice for the post of Naturalist on board *H.M.S. Beagle* should have fallen, against all likelihood, on Charles Darwin. Captain FitzRoy, whose idea it was to take a naturalist on the voyage, only made the appointment with some hesitation; Darwin nearly did not turn up for the interview. Even the chances that the *Beagle* should be sent on its second voyage were at one time small.

However, the chances fell that way, or, rather perhaps, the two young men's determinations led that way. Darwin's career must have been very different if he had not gone on the voyage. So must FitzRoy's.

Not only so, but the personality of each greatly affected the other. Darwin found his 'beau ideal of a captain' at first charming and then difficult, but in any case a most forceful and arresting character. It is likely indeed that FitzRoy would have made his mark in the world whether or not he had set out on his great voyage with a potentially famous person on board his ship.

FitzRoy has in fact suffered unfairly in that to posterity he has seldom been known as anything more than as Darwin's captain of the *Beagle*. This book is an attempt to right the wrong.

By good fortune I was shown and have been allowed to use the letters of FitzRoy's widow and her report of his last days. For this permission I am deeply grateful to his great-nieces, the Misses Smyth. Amongst the papers of his first captain in South American waters, Philip Parker King, was found correspondence concerning FitzRoy's governorship of New Zealand, and I owe permission to use this material to the Trustees of the Public Library of New South Wales.

For the great help and encouragement of Darwin's granddaughter, Nora Barlow, I am abundantly grateful, as I am, too, for the very practical help and advice of Mr Alan Moorehead.

To Mr Alfred F. Loomis, editor of New York's *Yachting* magazine, I owe guidance in maritime lore, and to Mr R. N. Richmond-Watson I am grateful for a view of the house in which FitzRoy spent his early youth. To my wife I owe patience and encouragement and a sounder judgement than my own. To Mrs N. M. Banfield I owe patience and efficient typing. Robert FitzRoy's varied career has left its mark in many places, and I can do no more than barely list the libraries and institutions, members of which have been so helpful to me:

The London Public Record Office; the London Library; the Meteorological Office; the Mitchell and Dixson Libraries of Sydney; the Maritime Museum of Greenwich; the London High Commissioner for New Zealand; the Ministry of Defence (Admiralty Library); the Royal Society; the Royal Geographical Society; the House of Lords (*Hansard*); the City of Liverpool Public Libraries; the National Institute of Oceanography; the Church Missionary Society; the South American Missionary Society; the Royal National Lifeboat Institution; the Library of the R.N. Hospital, Plymouth; the County of Essex Record Office; the Northamptonshire Archives Committee; *The Times*.

H. E. L. MELLERSH

BOOK 1

The Shaping of a Sea Captain

CHAPTER 1

Family and Tradition

ROBERT FITZROY was born on July 5th 1805 at Ampton Hall, near to Euston, in Suffolk, the country seat of his family the Graftons. He was the second son of the second son of the third Duke of Grafton, the first Duke of Grafton's father having been Charles II.

Ancestors are of account biologically, though it is dangerous for a biographer to pick out inherited traits. Ancestors are of more account as an immaterial legacy where a family has a strong tradition, and a family that had begun with Charles II and Barbara Villiers, and which had without delay produced some outstanding personalities, would be likely to foster a tradition sufficiently strong to influence even the second son of a second son. There is no evidence that Robert FitzRoy was a man who rammed his lineage down anybody's throat; and the only approach to such an occasion concerned in fact his mother's family.[1] Nevertheless he was a conscious aristocrat.

The first Duke of Grafton, 'a fretful spirit', was dead by the age of twenty-seven and had by that time killed two opponents in duels. He had a more legitimate claim to fame, however, loyally fighting, and dying, for his new non-Stuart king as an

---

[1] Quoted in Darwin's letter to his sister Caroline of 25/4/1832 and referred to in Chapter 10.

English admiral on his own ship, the *Grafton*, in action against the French off Cork in the year 1690.[2]

The second Duke was Swift's 'Grafton the deep, drunk or asleep', a very different character who became the indispensable Court Chamberlain to both George I and II. Though the perfect courtier, he had a quick temper, coupled with a healthy feeling of superiority. There is a tale that the Prince of Wales, later to be George II, having been inadvertently bumped into by Lord Grafton, remarked boorishly that you couldn't move for bastards. To which the Chamberlain replied, no doubt with great dignity: 'Sir, my father was as great a king as yours, and as for our mothers, the less we say about them the better!' That the Duke must have been referring to his grandparents and not parents no doubt did not destroy the point of the repartee.

The person of the next generation to pass on the title and to leave behind a memorable tradition was Lord Augustus FitzRoy, who, like his grandfather, was a sailor and died young. By the age of twenty-one he too had his ship, and this incident is told of him. Cruising in 1737 in the Caribbean, Lord Augustus with four ships under his command was ordered to give chase to an equal number of Frenchmen. 'And when the French commander refused to bring to, his lordship without hesitation gave him a broadside, which being instantly returned, brought on a general action.' No war had been declared; and after fighting for some time the two sides broke off and exchanged apologies, no harm being done except perhaps a little spilling of blood.[3]

The son of this bold and rash sea captain enters history by more than an incident, for he became for a while the acting prime minister when Pitt the Elder retired sick in 1767. This third Lord Grafton seems to have been a remarkably easy-going and unambitious man, preferring to retire to his mistress and his horses as soon as possible, and leaving no mark except an interest in the Unitarian form of Christianity and a mild activity towards the abolition of the slave trade.[4] No one, however, can be prime minister without leaving some fame behind him; and the young Robert FitzRoy, aged six before his grandfather died, must, whether he remembered him in the flesh or not, have been impressed by this famous FitzRoy. He must too have imbibed a little more of the then normal tradition of aristocratic families that if called upon to serve one's country one unquestionably did so, the fact of this particular example leaving behind a reputation of not having performed the task over-well being no doubt heavily discounted within the family.

After the unwilling prime minister, the Grafton family neither sought spectacular fame nor had it thrust upon them. Robert's uncle, the Fourth Duke, was content to be a slightly eccentric country gentleman, earning mild fame for once owning a Derby winner. The Duke's brothers continued to serve, however. Lord William joined the Navy, fought on the glorious first of June, and became an admiral. Lord Charles, Robert's father, joined the Army (after coming down from Cambridge) and saw service in Flanders as aide-de-camp to George III and became a general. For the rest he was an unexceptionable member of parliament, representing the electors of Bury St Edmunds for twenty-five years but never once speaking in the House. His son was to write of him as 'a farming, gardening, and fox-hunting country gentleman', who taught his son (no doubt amongst other things) to use the barometer as a weather glass.

In 1799 Lord Charles married a second time, his first wife having died after presenting him with one son. His second wife was Lady Frances Anne Stewart, eldest daughter of the First Marquis of Londonderry and so sister of Lord Castlereagh. These Stewarts were an Irish landed family living between the sea and the Mountains of Mourne. If sister were like brother, the lady must have been sensitive but self-contained and very highly strung; if Robert were to take after his uncle he would also be an indefatigable worker who did not spare himself.

Lady Frances gave birth to a son, George, then to a daughter,

4 Horace Walpole wrote maliciously that in the Duke's view 'the world should be postponed to a whore and a horse-race'.

Frances, and then in 1805, the year of Trafalgar, to Robert. When Robert was four the family moved across to occupy the 'hunting lodge' of the Grafton family, Wakefield Lodge, near to the village of Pottersbury, just within the boundaries of Northamptonshire from Buckinghamshire.

Wakefield Lodge would be a pleasant place in which to grow up into boyhood, very pleasant in the early years of the nineteenth century, when servants were servants and squires were squires. It is an imposing house, but not over-imposing nor over-large, a house of pale stone and Palladian style, built some thirty years before the Charles FitzRoys had moved there. There was a lake to sail in, there was a large park to survey, there was a ceiling in the salon to look up to, which showed in its moulding the royal motto, *Honi Soit Qui Mal Y Pense*, perhaps particularly appropriate for a family that had long ago forgotten any slur of illegitimacy, if it had ever felt it.

Robert only enjoyed the company of his mother for one year at Wakefield lodge. In 1810 she died.

With, therefore, a country gentleman father who had lost his second wife, with an elder brother and sister and a half-brother who was eight years his senior, Robert grew up. In the February of 1818, just eight years after his mother had died and while he was not yet thirteen years old, he entered the Royal Naval College at Portsmouth. With the careers of an uncle and a great-grandfather and a yet more distant forbear to inspire and support him, Robert FitzRoy began his own.

CHAPTER 2

Training for Command

'All zeal, Mr Easy.'
Mr Midshipman Easy, CAPTAIN MARRYAT

YOUNG Robert FitzRoy had ten years of training in front of him before, in the September of 1828, he took command of the *Beagle*, passing through the ranks of Volunteer-per-order, College Volunteer, Midshipman, Lieutenant, and Flag Lieutenant. It is a period to which he makes only very minor reference in his own writings. The Admiralty records cover it, but only in their very terse way. B. J. Sulivan, however, five years FitzRoy's junior, was destined to have his career, both at its beginning and near its end, quite closely bound up with that of his senior's, and in his biography,[1] while recounting his early years in the Navy, he throws considerable light on FitzRoy's. There are others too who, without mentioning FitzRoy, have told of the life of a boy who elected, or rather whose parents elected for him, to become an officer in the post-Nelsonian Navy and whose experiences must have been similar.[2]

[1] *Life and Letters of the late Admiral Sir Bartholomew James Sulivan, K.C.B., 1810–1890, edited by his son Henry Norton Sulivan* (John Murray, 1896). This begins as an autobiography, which however unfortunately is not continued beyond the author's transfer to the *Beagle* under FitzRoy.

[2] Commander Geoffrey Penn, R.N., quotes from these extensively in Chapters II and IV of his book *Snotty, The Story of the Midshipman* (Hollis and Carter, 1957), though he does not mention Sulivan's biography.

Both FitzRoy and Sulivan did what was in their time the less usual thing, in that they entered the Royal Naval College at Portsmouth. The majority of aspirants became so-called 'officers' servants' and imbibed all their learning in the more practical and even harder way, which was to go to sea from the very start; and, indeed, many conservative officers still favoured this way, looking on the college-trained boy with suspicion. Nevertheless, it was a way that undoubtedly gave more of the sort of academic training from which a serious-minded youngster could benefit.

Certainly the training at the Portsmouth College seems to have been intense. During the time of Sulivan and FitzRoy the head of the establishment was a certain Reverend James Inman, an unusual clergyman whose nautical tables were to become familiar to succeeding generations of naval officers and who, besides being a classical scholar, wrote books on gunnery and naval architecture. On paper at least, Inman's curriculum was frightening—even, one would imagine, to boys of the eighteen-twenties. The full course was supposed to take three years, and according to the syllabus the last two half-years covered the following subjects:

Fifth half-year—Fortifications, doctrine of projectiles, and its application to gunnery: principles of flexions and application to the measurement of surfaces and solids: generation of various curves, resistance of moving bodies: mechanics, hydrostatics, naval history and nautical discoveries.
Sixth half-year—more difficult problems in astronomy, motions of heavenly bodies, tides, lunar irregularities: the *Principles* and other parts of Newton's philosophy, to those sufficiently advanced.

In practice, however, boys were expected to pass out in two years or sooner if they could, and a medal was given each year to the quickest boy to do so, FitzRoy only being at the college for a little less than a year and eight months. It seems therefore that what Inman hoped to stuff into his charges and what he and his staff managed to stuff were not likely to have been the same thing. The actuality, as described by Sulivan, was formidable enough, though there was at least variety to help prevent mental indigestion. At the College there were, for the seventy students, three assistant masters for mathematics, while another reverend gentleman taught classics, history, geography and English. 'French was taught by a M. Creuze, a French *émigré*. We were also taught fencing and dancing. The forenoons were given to mathematics, the afternoons to French and drawing, the latter taught by a very superior master, Mr J. C. Schetky. There were also classes for naval architecture, which were taken by Mr Fincham, the master-builder of the dockyard. We began geometry with Mr Livesay; but no boy could get on unless he studied in his cabin and at the dining-room tables in the evenings. This some of the senior boys tried to prevent...The collegians were often taken round the dockyard, and shown the ships building and in dock, and, if the boys liked, they could attend the rigging loft to learn to strop-block and do many other useful things. There were also large barges to cruise about in to visit ships, and to take us to Haslar Creek on Saturday afternoons for cricket.'

Sulivan was a keen and hard-working student; and as FitzRoy was to be held up to him as an example, it is safe to assume that the latter was at least as keen and hard-working. Indeed, in spite of the reference to obstruction by the less intelligent seniors, for a boy to have been what later generations called a 'swot' does not seem to have been at all exceptional. A decade later a certain Astley Cooper Key, destined like both FitzRoy and Sulivan to become an admiral, is writing home: 'This last month I have second merit ticket, instead of first, which I got last time. I am what they call here five months before my time...I mean to try for a prize at the end of the half, for there is a prize for French, English, drawing, geography and mathematics...The drawing prize: as I do not draw one of the *best*, you know; but I think I have some chance (though not much) of the English, Geography, and mathematical prize. But nothing can be done without trying, so I will see what I can do.'[3] The letter goes on in the same candid strain, and if the college was breeding prigs it was in this case at least breeding both a successful and an unselfconscious one.

FitzRoy was specifically held up to Sulivan as an example when

[3] Quoted by Geoffrrey Penn as at Note 2 above.

the latter was nearing his leaving date. At that time candidates for promotion to lieutenant had to pass an examination which was held at the Portsmouth College. Said Inman to the young Sulivan: 'There was a collegian passing yesterday who won the first medal —his name is FitzRoy; and he did what has never been done before: in passing for a lieutenant he got full numbers, and I hope when you pass for lieutenant you will do the same.' Not long afterwards Sulivan was leaving the college and joining his first ship, the *Thetis*; and a few weeks later the man who had been set up for him to emulate was joining the same ship, as junior lieutenant.

That was in the Autumn of 1824 and after Robert FitzRoy had been at sea for nearly five years, having divided his time almost equally between being a volunteer on board the *Owen Glendower* and a midshipman on the *Hind*. Whether he met the disapproval of his first captain, as Sulivan did, at being a college volunteer, as opposed to a more ordinary and less academic one, is not known; but it is very possible.[4]

The life of a midshipman—using the term, as it often was, generically and to cover both ranks—has always been known as a hard one, and especially so in the early decades of the nineteenth century. It is possible, however, in righteous reaction on reading of the harshness of those times, to carry away in the mind's eye an exaggerated and distorted picture. These are the times of *Mr Midshipman Easy*,[5] and the reader of the adventures of that loquacious young buck, if he expects unrelieved brutality, will be greatly surprised. There is of course the bullying senior

[4] Pepys, in the name of FitzRoy's illustrious ancestor, had started the Volunteers, 'out of our Royal desire of giving encouragement to the families of better quality among our subjects to breed up their younger sons to the art and practice of navigation'. This had been at the beginning of a long war between the authorities and the naval captains, to stamp out and retain respectively a system of favouritism and nepotism on the part of the latter. By now the Portsmouth collegiates were the heirs to King Charles II's nominees: 'King's letter boys' or 'Volunteers-per-order', became *College* Volunteers, as opposed to *First Class* Volunteers on joining ship.

[5] Published in 1836; but Captain Marryat himself became a midshipman in 1806.

midshipman, the master with the chip on his shoulder, and so forth; but most of the officers in the story, both commissioned and otherwise, are essentially human in the best sense, kindly, humorous and understanding as well as sometimes stern disciplinarians. The experiences of a midshipman were not brutalizing.

They were however, toughening, to put it at the least. Whether as drill or punishment, the growing boy and young man must learn to be at home in the dizzy and swaying heights of the rigging.[6] His quarters were low, dark and cramped. His food was often unbelievably bad and he suffered frequently from the pangs of hunger, pangs relieved by the occasional invitation to the captain's table and the perhaps more frequent night-time foraging expedition, called 'cutting out', which, if hardly condoned, seems to have been tolerated as being a good breeding ground for initiative.

FitzRoy, seeing service during these years in Mediterranean and South American waters, does not sound at all unhappy in his only reference to them. In his description of the *Beagle*'s approach to Rio on the second voyage he digresses nostalgically to his first entrance to that glamorous harbour on the *Owen Glendower*. 'High blue mountains were seen in the west, just after the sun had set, and with a fair wind we approached the land rapidly. The sea was quite smooth, but a freshening breeze upon our quarter carried us on, nearly thirteen knots an hour. Though dark as any cloudy tropical night, when neither moon nor star relieves the intense blackness—astern of us was a long and perfectly straight line of sparkling light, caused by the ship's rapid way through the water; and around the bows, as far forward as the bowsprit end, was dazzling foam, by whose light I read a page of common print.' FitzRoy then goes on to describe the trouble 'we middies' had in trying to take readings from the

---

[6] There are authenticated tales of tragic results from midshipmen being ordered up into the tops. But there is, to my personal knowledge, an equally authenticated story of a boy who went up there because he enjoyed it. Unfortunately this also has a tragic ending: he went to sleep in a furled sail and fell to his death when the sail was unfurled.

quadrant with the sun almost vertical overhead and then a day's excursion in the beautiful harbour, when they discovered and landed on an island 'which seemed to me like an immense hot-bed, so luxuriant and aromatic were the shrubs, and so exotical the appearance of every tree and flower.' FitzRoy seems a sensitive and studious boy as well as a happy one.

When in 1824 FitzRoy joined the *Thetis*, just after Sulivan, the two young officers had four years of service together in front of them. Aged nineteen and fourteen respectively, they seem to have been drawn together from the start as two of the select but sometimes resented band of those who had entered the Navy by the more modern, technical and intellectual way. 'He was very kind to me, offered me the use of his cabin and his books,' Sulivan was to write in his autobiography. 'He advised me what to read, and encouraged me to turn to advantage what I had learned at college by taking every kind of observation that was useful in navigation.' Sulivan added handsomely that he attributed much of his own future success to FitzRoy's appointment to the *Thetis*, and called him 'One of the best practical seamen in the service', with 'a fondness for every kind of observation useful in navigating a ship.' Robert was obviously preparing himself seriously for his future career and also, though perhaps not consciously, for command of a surveying ship.

The job of the *Thetis* at this time, when not conducting troops to their stations or ambassadors to their posts, was to patrol the Cornish coast for smugglers. Such a storm-bound rocky coast may well have taught good seamanship, but the work can hardly have fulfilled the expectation of ardent hearts. Fortunately there followed a cruise in the Mediterranean, ending with a little excitement at Gibraltar. A gale having driven many merchant ships onto Spanish territory, the Spaniards proceeded to take possession of them and to land cargoes from them in order to recoup themselves for the customs duties which they felt were their due. The *Thetis*, with military backing, was ordered to right the matter. Cocked pistols and the display of force was enough to dissuade the Spaniards; but at least that was an excitement.

There followed a trip across the Atlantic to take Lord Ponsonby to Rio as ambassador, the diplomat and his retinue being obviously afforded every possible comfort and no doubt at the expense of the junior officers. Sulivan followed the example of the more experienced FitzRoy by being duly impressed with the exotical scenery. On the way home the action of their captain, Sir John Phillimore, had obviously impressed his officers. A midshipman had received a terrible injury to his arm and was in danger of losing it. The cabin lately occupied by Lady Ponsonby was given up to him, and the captain himself slept in a cot outside the cabin door, giving instructions that he should be wakened if the boy was suffering badly. 'I have known him sit an hour by his bedside, holding the arm with his two hands, trying to ease the pain.' It was Captain Phillimore on the *Thetis* who had taken the bold step of having the men's excessive rum ration of half a pint a day reduced to a quarter, a change which, though meeting with bitter initial opposition, became popular by reason of the improvement in other rations that went with it. Both Sulivan and FitzRoy made due note of the change for their own future action on the *Beagle*.

When nearing home from Rio it was a phenomenal storm that impressed Sulivan, as well as FitzRoy's ensuing action. Ordered up into the top, Sulivan was amazed to see that when the ship was in the trough of a wave the horizon was wholly obscured. This meant that the waves were sixty-four feet high. When he came down he told Lieutenant FitzRoy, and FitzRoy had to go up to see for himself.

On reaching Spithead the *Thetis* was paid off, but at once recommissioned. Sulivan, given the opportunity to transfer to a ship sailing for the Mediterranean, preferred to stay with FitzRoy.

Of the remaining year which the two men had together on the *Thetis*, two incidents only need be mentioned, and shortly: Sulivan—rather naturally since he was so young—does not give any of the insight into the character of his admired senior that Charles Darwin was to give.

The *Thetis* was now ordered to the South American station under Admiral Sir Robert Otway at Monte Video, and she departed with rumours of war with France in the air. At night in the Atlantic she met a ship who would not answer. 'Are you ready with the guns on the main-deck, Mr FitzRoy?' commanded the Captain. But in contradiction to the episode where Lord Augustus was concerned, there was no precipitate action, which was fortunate. The captain of the other ship, hearing English voices, managed to make himself known. An East Indiaman, she had failed to answer the hail because she likewise had feared the *Thetis* was French.

At Monte Video an even more exciting incident occurred. The Brazilians and Argentinians were at war, disputing the ownership of Uruguay; and both were anxious for the service of experienced British seamen, to the extent that they were constantly 'crimping' or kidnapping them. There was a certain Captain Pritz, a Dane, who, not liking the English and having for his favourite motto 'Remember Copenhagen!', was engaged in this practice for the Brazilians. One evening the captain of the *Thetis*, passing by the Dane's ship in his brig, was hailed by one of his own men. He promptly climbed on board, and, being met with a blank refusal to give up the crimped men, sent off his brig for immediate armed help.

How the captain filled in the interval is not stated. But in due course he was able to say calmly: 'I hear my boat's oars: you had better give me back my men!' FitzRoy and his barge crew appeared over the side, and Captain Pritz had the sense to see that discretion indeed took the better part of valour. Sulivan had managed to squeeze into the rescue party though he was officially on the sick-list; and FitzRoy had asked the senior lieutenant if he might push ahead because he was in the faster boat.

This episode occurred in April of 1828. Four months later FitzRoy, now nearly twenty-three, transferred to the *Ganges* to become flag lieutenant to the commander of the station.

In what ways exactly he managed to impress his admiral there is no way of knowing. It would be fair to say, however, that it would not be a particularly easy job. Sir Robert Otway had fought with Nelson at Copenhagen; indeed he had been flag captain to the commander and had done his best to prevent being sent the message to discontinue the action to which Nelson had turned his unseeing eye.[7] FitzRoy must have done the job quickly too. Less than three months later he was given his great chance.

Another officer, also of established reputation, was sailing in South American waters. This was Captain Philip Parker King, son of the first governor of New South Wales, who at the age of thirty-five had already become a fellow of the Royal Society and had made his name in surveying the Australian coasts. Now, with the *Adventure* and the *Beagle* under his command, he had for the last two years been surveying the coasts of the tip of South America. In October 1828 Captain King sailed into Rio harbour and reported to Admiral Otway. He had lost his captain of the *Beagle* under tragic circumstances and sought permission to appoint to the ship's command the lieutenant who had taken over from the dead man.

Admiral Otway ordered otherwise. He appointed Lieutenant FitzRoy to the command of the *Beagle*.

[7] See for instance page 442 of Carola Oman's *Nelson* (London, 1947).

CHAPTER 3

First days on the *Beagle*

HOWEVER deserving he may have been, Robert FitzRoy was undoubtedly lucky to have received the command of a surveying ship at the age of twenty-three. He must have been beside himself with delight. But there were sobering thoughts, in the contemplation of the toughness of his assignment. Here was a vessel engaged on a difficult survey under the leadership of an established expert, and its captain from whom he was taking over had just found the job so much too much for him that he had committed suicide.

The orders given to Captain King had been for 'an accurate survey' of the Southern Coasts of South America, from the River Plata round to Chiloé. The Plata Estuary lies at about 35° south, the island of Chiloé on the west coast at about 43°, and Cape Horn at about 56°. It will be seen therefore that the stretch of coast is considerable, in fact about 2,500 miles as the crow flies, if it flew through the Magellan Straits, and five hundred more if it went by the Horn, while if it followed every inlet along the coast, so fantastically indented from Tierra del Fuego onwards, the distance would be immeasurably increased. The job had to be done, it must be remembered, by two square-rigged sailing brigs; and that sort of ship has not the capacity to sail into the

wind of a fore-and-aft rigged ship, certainly not the manoeuvra-
bility of a modern sailing dinghy. There were to be innumerable
occasions, both on this first voyage under King and on FitzRoy's
second voyage on the *Beagle*, when the surveying work could
only be done from the small boats carried on the ships, and many
occasions, too, when sails on both ship and boat were useless, so
that, for instance, the bigger vessel had to be manoeuvred into
anchorage by just what that word means, the work of the human
hand, those hands pulling on the oars in the little boats. Sailing
in such waters also meant danger and anxiety and frustration, as
well as hard work. Often progress had to be sacrificed and a
retreat made to a safer anchorage already passed; often the ships,
on a lee shore amidst incalculable and unknown tides and currents,
and above a sea-bottom too deep for anchorage or too shallow or
rock-strewn for comfort, were in unavoidable and imminent
danger.

The coasts to be surveyed were also surprisingly unknown.
Magellan had discovered his Straits over three hundred years
earlier, Van Hoorn had rounded the cape named after him only
a hundred years later, and many famous sailors had followed.
Nevertheless, the South American coast, rather like Africa's,
had been regarded more as something to get round as soon as
possible on the way to the East than as of interest or use in
itself.[1] Recently however the position had changed. Sealers and
whalers were using these seas, and sometimes getting ship-
wrecked on these shores; and the British Navy, at the height of
its prestige, felt it its duty to establish a proper survey and to
present her findings for the benefit of the other nations of the
world.

The eastern coast from the Plata Estuary to Magellan Straits
would present no very great difficulties, nor any great satisfaction,
though there were rivers as yet unexplored. But the twisted tip
of the continent, which was Tierra del Fuego and a maze of
islands, was a very different matter; and the western coast as

[1] The Suez Canal was not opened until 1869 and the Panama Canal
in 1914. Not until 1859 was the first oil well opened, to cut into the
demand for seal and whale oil.

far north as Chilóe was almost as labyrinthine, and also rather
more rain-swept and wind-swept and inhospitable.

To Captain Stokes of the *Beagle* had been allotted the survey
of this coast. He had found it highly dangerous, insidiously un-
dermining of the health of himself and his men, and infinitely
depressing. All who went to these parts came away surprised and
saddened that the climate on a latitude roughly parallel with
London's should be so much colder and so much worse, and
using the same adjectives for what they saw and experienced:
desolate, depressing, sterile, repulsive.

Captain King was engaged on his second season's surveying
work when he sent the *Beagle* on the west coast mission which
was to end in its captain's suicide. He was meeting difficulties,
difficulties that were to face FitzRoy too and to which, as will
be seen, the latter reacted in a somewhat different manner.

There were some outbreaks of scurvy. Secondly, the native
Patagonians and Fuegians[2] had demonstrated their phenomenal
skill in the art of theft by stealing two of the ships' whaleboats,
those maid-of-all-work boats of sail and oar which the survey
ships carried and which were proving quite indispensable for
the work in hand. King's third trouble was that he needed a
supplementary schooner if he was to do his job properly and on
time, and he had been badly delayed by having to wait at Monte
Video for Admiralty permission to purchase one. By the time
that Stokes and the *Beagle* were parting company from King in
the Magellan Straits, winter had nearly arrived.

The *Beagle*'s course was across something over five degrees of
latitude, about 400 miles each way, and it took the ship mostly
along a narrow channel lying between great islands and rocks
which were by no means always marked on the old Spanish
charts which were her captain's only guide. Partly it must have
been the everlasting need for vigilance that wore Stokes down,
partly what he described with loathing as the sterile and repulsive
landscape, certainly the continued foul weather of gales and
incessant rain. The decks were awash, the men went down with
rheumatism and pulmonary troubles, and the sick list grew.

[2] Patagonians north of the Magellan Straits and Fuegians to the south.

Reaching the limit of their assignment they found a good shelter which they named Port Otway after their commander-in-chief. Here they were imprisoned by bad weather for ten days, a relief from pressing duties, but an enforced rest from which the captain at least was too ill and too worried to draw much advantage.

At length they were resuming their surveying work. An observation tent set up on the land had to be abandoned owing to the arrival of even worse weather. The sergeant of marines died. Staring at a rocky islet lashed by a tremendous surf, Stokes wrote hopelessly: 'as if to complete the dreariness and utter desolation of the scene, even birds seemed to shun its neighbourhood.' Then he was moved to quote, not the smooth cadences of Vergil, as Captain King was sometimes wont to do, but a stark line from James Thomson:

The soul of man dies in him.

Soon the loss of a boat and damage to another dictated a return to Port Otway. There Captain Stokes, on the advice of his ship's doctor, ordained a rest for his crew of a fortnight. But: 'every port along this coast is alike ill suited for a winter's residence, and it was only our peculiar situation that induced me to determine on making a short stay.'

With these words Captain Stokes's account ended. Soon, though the weather improved and good headway southwards was being made, he was shutting himself up in his cabin—there would come a time when FitzRoy would do the same thing—and paying little attention to the ordering of the ship, beyond giving directions to make delays that nearly caused a famine.

At last, well overdue, the *Beagle* reached her rendezvous with the *Adventure* at Port Famine[3] on the Magellan Straits and was duly welcomed back. Captain King, himself in command of a crew unable to shake off the scurvy, soon realized that something was very seriously wrong on board the other ship. He visited Captain Stokes, and found him at one and the same time

[3] So called from the death of the garrison of Spaniards put there by Sarmiento in 1580 in the hope of waylaying Drake.

despondent about his men ever facing up to another voyage and also talking eagerly but with a sort of fascinated repugnance of immediately renewing the survey. The next day he shot himself. He did not make a clean job of it, and the end was lingering and tragic. Having buried him with full naval honours, King and his two ships' companies made their way back to the Plata Estuary. Leaving the *Beagle* at Monte Video, King proceeded northward to report to Admiral Otway at Rio de Janiero, with the result already stated.

Such were the circumstances in which FitzRoy was appointed to the *Beagle*.

In fact these were already considerably more cheerful by the time that the *Beagle* had followed the *Adventure* up to Rio and FitzRoy had taken over command. A few days' dosage with Seville oranges, and a few days' sun and civilization in the Plata Estuary had worked miracles, both with scurvy and with coughs and rheumatic joints, and no doubt with the men's spirits too.

FitzRoy was allowed to take with him from the *Ganges* Mr Murray the ship's master, and also, on request, Midshipman Sulivan. He had before him the task of establishing good relations with Captain King, whose wishes for the *Beagle*'s command had been thwarted by the Admiral, and with Lieutenant Skyring, who would now have to be demoted back to assistant surveyor. That he managed it with the Captain is reflected in King's comment, perhaps a little cold: 'Captain FitzRoy was considered qualified to command the *Beagle*: and although I could not but feel much for the bitterness of Lieutenant Skyring's disappointment, I had no other cause for dissatisfaction.'[4] That he managed it even better with the demoted man is apparent both from King's acknowledgement that Skyring reacted with 'equanimity

[4] See page 188 of Volume I of the *Narrative of the Voyages of H.M.S. Adventure and Beagle* (London 1839). This volume contains King's account of his voyage, with extracts from FitzRoy's reports. It was put together by FitzRoy—and is referred to in future as the *Narrative*.

and goodwill' and from the fact that the two men were soon working together in obvious unison.

As for the crew, one immediate problem must have been to get rid of their feeling not so much of depression as of superstition: they believed that the ship was haunted by the ghost of Captain Stokes.

Here FitzRoy was unwittingly helped by his friend young Sulivan, for Sulivan was chief actor in an episode that was both absurd and, one must hope, salutary. Left on board an almost empty ship which was being hauled down and having her bottom scraped, Sulivan, on night watch, saw the door of the Captain's cabin swinging. In going to shut it his lantern went out. Then his companion thought he heard a man's breathing, then footsteps overhead. 'The ghost! It is coming down below! I slipped from my hammock behind the companion, and presently there appeared one naked foot on a step and then another. I pushed my hands through the open ladder and seized both ankles, when a voice above roared out, "O the ghost, it has got me!" '[5] It was one of the crew left behind when the last boat had gone ashore.

With the coming of the new year (1829), and something over two months since he had taken command, FitzRoy's real test began. Following the *Adventure* and King's supplementary schooner, the *Adelaide*, which ships had preceded him by a few days, he took the *Beagle* out of harbour and made south for the continuance of the survey. He began with a stroke of bad luck.

Both ships met a storm, a *pampero*, afterwards known as the worst for twenty years. The *Beagle* was a ten-gun brig of a type known in the Navy, not altogether affectionately, as coffins, from their reputation for turning turtle, and requiring, as Sulivan put it, 'careful handling and management of sail'.

The barometer fell to 28·5°. But FitzRoy was not so weather-wise then and did not take all the precautions that he might have done, a failure that was to stick in his memory and was to be confessed when years later he wrote his *Weather Book*. The *Beagle* nearly capsized, she shipped a lot of water, she was in

[5] Page 34 of Sulivan's biography, already referred to.

danger of crashing onto the rocks, and, worst of all, two men were blown down from the rigging and drowned. When she eventually joined the *Adventure* she was a sorry sight, with both topmasts and many spars carried away. Captain King, however, was in little better plight, with two whaleboats smashed in; and in his account of the affair there is no trace of censure. Repairs were made, the ships reached the eastern end of the Magellan Straits, and FitzRoy and Skyring were sent into the Straits with instructions to carry out surveying work in its unexplored westerly reaches. FitzRoy at last had an independent command and the job of winning the confidence of the *Beagle*'s crew and fully restoring their morale.

He seems to have succeeded in this task, first by providing his men with an exhibition of bold and dashing seamanship, and then by a process of trying them high and sharing their hardships and dangers.

The opportunity for the first came as soon as the *Beagle* reached the First Narrows of the Magellan Straits. These Narrows, with their complicated currents, sudden shifts of wind and forests of kelp, had been found difficult and dangerous by many mariners from Magellan onwards, and they had caused Captain King no less than a three days' delay. FitzRoy, his hand, admittedly, somewhat forced by the snapping of an anchor cable, chose to take a risk and shot through in a few hours and at night. Writing later (of the loss of his old ship the *Thetis*, for which its officers had been court martialled), FitzRoy provides his own justification: 'Those who never run any risk; who sail only when the wind is fair; who heave to when approaching land, though perhaps a day's sail distant; and who even delay the performance of urgent duties until they can be done easily and quite safely; are, doubtless, prudent persons—but rather unlike those officers whose names will never be forgotten while England has a navy.'

It was not long before opportunity came to try the second recipe for success. The Magellan Straits are no direct channel through the tip of the continent, but rather one of many channels through a maze of islands and peninsulas; and it was the job given to FitzRoy and Skyring to explore this maze as it approached the Pacific Ocean. Skyring's task was to sail down the already known Barbara Channel to see what he could see; FitzRoy was allowed to explore into the unknown.[6] He took his chance, pushing up northwards, discovering those two amazingly large balloons of water that lead out one from the other and that are known as Otway and Skyring Waters (connected by the FitzRoy Passage). Here it was that he tried his men high and where he shared their dangers and difficulties. In fact he led his men into them.

On May 7th he set out on the trip. It was designed to last a month, and he took two boats, placing himself in command of the whaleboat and putting Midshipman Stokes (no relation to the dead captain) in charge of the yawl. 'We were well provided', he wrote afterwards, 'with as much as the boats could stow, of what we thought likely to be useful during a month's cruise. Of water we took but little, trusting to the wetness of these regions for a supply. Each man had his clothes covered with canvas, or duck, well painted; and instead of a hat, every one had a "south wester" (like a coal-heaver's cap).'

How wet these regions could be none of this party of stiff-suited, shovel-hatted men can possibly have imagined. There were days so fine and warm that FitzRoy, enchanted with the landscape, was picking berberis fruit (to keep the scurvy away) and then bathing, while some of his men followed suit. But there were many more days when it rained continuously, the canvas suits were soaked, and sometimes, even, they found it impossible to light a fire. Then rain turned to cold, and FitzRoy noted that every morning his cloak was frozen hard over him. 'Yet I never slept more soundly nor was in better health.' One or two of the men who fell sick were treated efficaciously with port wine and wintersbark. There can be no doubt that FitzRoy was enjoying himself tremendously.

Having penetrated into the second of the balloons they re-traced their course, to see whether perhaps Otway Water so bent over to the East as to lead back into the Magellan Straits (which

[6] This trip is described by FitzRoy in Chapters 13 and 14 of Volume I of the *Narrative*.

in fact it nearly does). It was now that there occurred an incident which was to give FitzRoy the greatest satisfaction and an intimation that he had in fact won the loyalty of his men.

The two boats were sailing happily before a fine westerly breeze when with the frightening suddenness of these things the breeze turned to a gale that threatened to crash both boats onto a surf-lined shore. Mr Stokes in the cutter was instructed to keep one close-reefed sail standing and to risk clearing the dangerous shore. But FitzRoy in the heavy whaleboat decided that the only reasonable course for him and his crew was to turn round and row for their lives.

His boat was dangerously low in the now choppy water. A bag of fuel was reluctantly thrown overboard; their already sodden bundles of spare clothing were made ready for the same purpose of lightening the boat. Soon the sun set, and as darkness fell the wind grew stronger.

For five hours in all FitzRoy and his men rode out that storm, rowing and baling without cease, struggling to keep the boat continuously head to wind and conscious that failure to do so would result in their foundering. At last—suddenly and miraculously—the sea fell and the wind moderated. They were thankful to be able to get back to their camp of the night before—where eventually Stokes and his boatload met them.

FitzRoy's comment was as follows. 'No men could have behaved better than that boat's crew: not a word was uttered by one of them; nor did an oar flag at any time, although they acknowledged, after landing, that they had never expected to see the shore again.' The fact that many of the *Beagle* crew were to re-enlist[7] for the second voyage perhaps justifies FitzRoy in his paean of self-confident praise.

At the end of one month and a day the expedition was back, and FitzRoy was finding himself greatly relieved to discover all well with the *Beagle* and to be able to welcome back Skyring in the *Adelaide* on the next day.

The time for the rendezvous with King was now approaching.

[7] This is stated by FitzRoy on page 21 of Volume II of the *Narrative*, this being his description of the *Beagle*'s second voyage.

However, on hearing Skyring's satisfactory report of his trip to the sea by way of the Barbara Channel, FitzRoy conceived a new idea, which was that the *Adelaide* should be sent back into Skyring Water, there to make a much more detailed survey than he had been able to achieve on his whaleboat trip and to establish whether there might exist a new way out from it into the Pacific. Skyring was willing and FitzRoy felt that King would think it a good plan. The trouble was that King had made no specific order for further work by the *Adelaide* and would expect the ship to turn up with the *Beagle* at the rendezvous at Chilóe. FitzRoy therefore could not decide, 'without anxiety', what to do. Had he known his own character better he would perhaps not have bothered to be anxious. He sent Skyring back to the Water which was afterwards with magnanimity named after him; and Skyring did a thorough job and was not to be very late at the rendezvous; and Captain King was pleased. . .

As for FitzRoy, he took his ship out into the Pacific and speeded northwards up the coast to meet King at Chiloé. No enforced stops for staring at a sterile coast for him, no thoughts on a man's dying soul, but a ship, proved not to be a coffin in capable hands, flying with reefed sails before a south-easterly gale. 'We found the vessel scud extremely well.'

There was only one accident: 'by a moment's neglect of the steerage, a sea broke over the whaleboat, and carried her away.'

CHAPTER 4

A Loss to be Made Good

WHALEBOATS and Fuegian natives seem to have been almost an obsession with FitzRoy during his first command of the *Beagle*. Together they led to a highly personal action on his part, an action directly responsible for the fact that a second voyage of the *Beagle* was ever made.

First as to whaleboats. During a prolonged and pleasant stay by all three ships at the civilized little town of San Carlos on the isle of Chiloé, while some local surveying proceeded and the officers were busy putting their previous findings to paper, Mr May, the ship's carpenter, was engaged upon building a new boat to replace the one lost by the *Beagle* on her rapid sail to the rendezvous with King. Both commanders obviously felt that the loss of whaleboats had to be stopped and where possible remedied.

To the Fuegian natives FitzRoy reacted strongly. These most primitive and poor of aborigines, with their matted hair and wearing paint and grease more often than clothes, created typically a reaction of disgust, besides the more natural reactions of interest and pity. With FitzRoy the pity was uppermost and the disgust absent. He described them in perspicacious detail and was the first to start compiling a vocabulary of their languages.[1] In

---

[1] Number 15 of the Appendix to Volume II of the *Narrative*.

his first season before sailing up to Chilóe he had gone out of his way to meet several of them. He had sketched them;[2] he had prevailed upon one of them to wash the paint off his face so that he could see what it looked like underneath; he had let them listen to his watch and guessed from their awed reaction that they might believe in a Superior Being; he bought a mongrel puppy from them and then gave it back on witnessing their grief at parting with it. Soon on this second surveying season he was to be buying more than mongrel puppies from them.

It was on November 18th 1829, that FitzRoy received his orders at Chilóe for his second and last trip of the surveying expedition.

On this occasion the schooner *Adelaide* was to work independently, surveying in more detail the western coast north of the Magellan Straits. The *Beagle* was given a considerable task: FitzRoy had to cover the whole coast of Tierra del Fuego, the bottom two sides of the inverted triangle, that is to say, which constitutes the much serrated tip of South America below the Magellan Straits. Were there perhaps some east-west passages through this tip, such as would be useful to small vessels wishing to avoid the difficulties of Cape Horn? He must be at Rio de Janiero by June 20th of the next year, preparatory to returning to England: he had nine months for the job.

FitzRoy, searching his area of operation, found himself amongst a multiplicity of inlets and islands, as of course he knew he would be, though the complexity and dangers were greater than he had anticipated: the chart of one part, he complains, lapsing uncharacteristically into something approaching whimsicality, 'with all its stars to mark the rocks, looks like a map of

[2] FitzRoy was a competent artist and two of his sketches are reproduced in Volume II of the *Narrative*: both feature Fuegian natives prominently. Of one of his efforts, to sketch an old woman, he wrote: 'She took out her red paint, and put some on her own cheeks as drawn on the paper, and then was quite satisfied, sitting as still as a mouse, while I made another sketch. In return for the compliment paid to her countenance, she daubed my face, as well as my coxswain's, with the same red mixture.'

part of the heavens, rather than part of the earth.' This survey was, more than ever, a job for boats and not ships, and he continued the practice of finding a decent anchorage for the *Beagle* and then of sending out his boats. He usually employed two, one in either direction, the ship's master and himself in charge.

A new factor was a slow but definite deterioration in relationship with the natives. Their importunity and propensity to steal had early been realized. But the Fuegians along the western coast seemed more sullen and suspicious than those of the Strait, and even dangerous and quite undependable. During the days of Christmas the master and mate were overdue from an expedition and great anxiety was felt. On the 27th the mate and coxswain turned up, having walked overland to report that their companions had been prevented by the weather from returning by boat and had completely run out of food. Not only that, but on the way back the pair of them, weak and exhausted, had been set upon by a band of armed Fuegians and the coxswain had been forcibly relieved of some of his clothes. Fortunately the weather at that moment improved and a relief party met the rest of the expedition returning safely in its whaleboat. No trace of the natives could be found—they had wisely decamped. That was the end of that incident.

A month later the *Beagle* had reached nearly to latitude 55°, and found shelter south of the Cockburn Channel and near to a promontory that Captain Cook had called Cape Desolation. The Master, Mr Murray, was again sent out on a whaleboat expedition, to survey around this cape.

Again his return became overdue. News came after he had been away a week; and this time it was more serious. There was now begun the train of events referred to at the beginning of this chapter. They were often dramatic, occasionally ludicrous, and had quite different results from those originally intended.

FitzRoy's description begins under the date, February 5th 1830: 'At three this morning I was called up to hear that the whaleboat was lost—stolen by the natives.' The theft had occurred in a cove under Cape Desolation, 'now doubly deserving of its name', a whole day's boat-journey away; and the master and his crew had been abandoned by the natives, stranded and provisionless and in constant fear of another attack. A boat had been ingeniously improvised out of canvas and withies, and three men had managed to paddle it back to the *Beagle* with the news.

Not a moment was lost in preparing a rescue expedition in the other whaleboat. It comprised ten men and FitzRoy himself, it took a fortnight's provisions, and its purpose, besides rescuing the ship's master, was to catch the thieves and retrieve that essential working tool, the whaleboat.

By eleven in the morning, in spite of rain and squalls, the anxious master was found and the site of the tragedy inspected. FitzRoy was satisfied that no blame accrued to anybody and handsomely admitted that the same thing would have happened to him. It now remained to find the boat.

The first search lasted eighteen days and was followed by a second one after the return to the *Beagle*. FitzRoy in his narrative is at pains to excuse his remarkable pertinacity, explaining that in any case surveying work was going on in his absence and that the greater knowledge of the Fuegians that he was obtaining was a useful thing.

Almost at once, on a small island only two miles away and near to a lately used wigwam, the search party found the boat's mast, cut off and discarded. 'Our next point was then to be considered, for to chase the thieves I was determined.'

FitzRoy's plan was to search all the likely coves, even to some distance, believing that the thieves, whose intention would be to use the boat on their fishing expeditions, would at the start do their best to hide it, and perhaps not too near the scene of the crime.

'In the evening we met a canoe containing two Fuegians, a man and a woman, who made us understand, by signs, that several canoes had gone to the northward. This raised our hopes and we pushed on.'

After two nights, the second with a gale blowing, FitzRoy came upon a native family and, searching their canoes, found the whaleboat's lead line. 'This was a prize indeed; and we immediately took the man who had it in his boat, making him comprehend that he must show us where the people were from whom he got it.'

The man took them to more Fuegians, mostly women and children. A few more traces of the whaleboat were found; and, with a second man as guide, the search continued.

That night the two natives escaped, taking with them the tarpaulin jackets kindly lent them by the ship's master.

FitzRoy returned for more guides, but could not even get near the natives. There followed three days of guideless search, in bad weather. Then back once more went FitzRoy to the camp of the thieves. He was determined this time to surround them and to take some of them away, not as guides in the search for the boat, but as hostages for its return.

Creeping cautiously through the bushes, the armed party had nearly surrounded the Fuegians when a dog barked. 'Further concealment was impossible, so we rushed on as fast as we could through the bushes. At first the Indians began to run away; but hearing us shout on both sides, some tried to hide themselves, by squatting under the banks of a stream of water. The foremost of our party, Elsmore by name, in jumping across this stream, slipped, and fell in just where two men and a woman were concealed: they instantly attacked him, trying to hold him down and beat out his brains with stones; and before any one could assist him, he had received several severe blows, and one eye was almost destroyed, by a dangerous stroke near the temple. Mr Murray, seeing the man's danger, fired at one of the Fuegians, who staggered back and let Elsmore escape; but immediately recovering himself, picked up stones from the bed of the stream, or was supplied with them by those who stood close to him, and threw them from each hand with astonishing force and precision. His first stone struck the master with much force, broke a powder-horn hung round his neck, and nearly knocked him backwards: and two others were thrown so truly at the heads of those nearest him, that they barely saved themselves by dropping down. All this passed in a few seconds, so quick was he with each hand: but, poor fellow, it was his last struggle; unfortunately he was mortally wounded, and, throwing one more stone, he fell against the bank and expired. After some struggling, and a few hard blows, those who tried to secrete themselves were taken, but several who ran away along the beach escaped: so strong and stout were the females, that I, for one, had no idea that it was a woman, whose arms I and my coxswain endeavoured to pinion, until I heard some one say so.'

Saddened by the loss of life, FitzRoy collected his haul of prisoners—which consisted of two men, three women and six children—and made his way back with them to the *Beagle*. There they were clothed in blankets and fed on salt pork and shell-fish, which pleased them.

FitzRoy then started again. Thinking that by this time the thieves might be using the whaleboat on their fishing expeditions, he shifted the *Beagle*'s anchorage, moving to the western point of Stewart Island at the mouth of the as yet undiscovered Beagle Channel. Thence he set out again, with his ship's master and two of his captives as guides. As these two were mothers of children left on board he did not imagine that they would try to escape. But he was wrong. Almost before his eyes, two huddled Fuegians sleeping under piles of blankets by the camp fire became piles of blankets only.

The second search found nothing and met nothing but wind and rain. At the end of a week it was called off. 'We reached the *Beagle* in the evening, but found that all the other prisoners, except three children, had escaped by swimming ashore during the preceding night. Thus, after much trouble and anxiety, much valuable time lost, and as fine a boat of her kind as ever was seen being stolen from us by these savages, I found myself with three young children to take care of, and no prospect whatever of recovering the boat.'

FitzRoy at last decided to make the best of a bad business. He would move the *Beagle* again, into some sheltered cove, and there build a new whaleboat on the spot.

He could not help continuing, nevertheless, to think about the loss, and about the Fuegians. 'I became convinced that so long as we were ignorant of the Fuegian language, and the natives were equally ignorant of ours, we should never know much about them, or the interior of their country: nor would there be the slightest chance of their being raised one step above the low place which they thus held in our estimation.'

The desired cove for the *Beagle* was duly found, Christmas Sound, 'the very spot where the *Adventure* lay when Cook was here'. The carpentry work on the new boat was started, and the surveying work was resumed. Murray, the master, was sent out on a survey in the direction whence the *Beagle* had come, and he was told to take the three remaining Fuegian children back to their tribe. When the time for departure came, however, one of these showed not the least desire to leave the *Beagle*. She had been christened Fuegia Basket, after the makeshift boat built when the trouble had started, and by her smiling cheerfulness had already achieved great popularity. 'She seemed so happy and healthy,' wrote FitzRoy, little knowing what an important decision he was making, 'that I determined to detain her as a hostage for the stolen boat, and try to teach her English.'

The accent of the story now shifts more than ever from whale-boats to Fuegians, though hope of recovering the loss was not yet abandoned and did indeed yet receive some encouragement. The collection of useful natives continued.

The second acquisition came after FitzRoy, in protection of the shore workshop where Mr May had started on his boat-building, had sent out an officer to warn off a flotilla of visiting Fuegian canoes. 'Reflecting that by getting one of these natives on board, there would be a chance of his learning enough English to be an interpreter, and that by his means we might recover our lost boat, I resolved to take the youngest man on board, as he, in all probability, had less strong ties to bind him to his people than others who were older, and might have families. With these ideas I went after them, and hauling their canoe alongside of my boat, told a young man to come into it; he did so, quite unconcernedly, and sat down, apparently contented and at his ease. The others said nothing, either to me or to him, but paddled out of the harbour as fast as they could.'

This, the second Fuegian, was named York Minster, after the promontory that had reminded Captain Cook of that cathedral and which dominated these waters. He was to prove a sullen young man and the least successful of FitzRoy's acquisitions; but on board he was cheered by Fuegia Basket's merriment and by food.

Five days later the boat-building was again disturbed by marauding canoes, and FitzRoy, going out to investigate, found himself involved in a more serious incident and also supplied with tantalizing new hopes. He followed the Fuegians on shore, found them to be threatening, and sent for reinforcements. Then, under a shower of stones, he searched their canoes—and found some of Master Murray's bottled beer, that is to say the bottles. Following up this clue the next day, he discovered in a deserted wigwam a piece of the whale-boat's rope.

Then, looking up, FitzRoy saw two canoes escaping across the water. He gave chase, and finally fished out of the water a young man who had dived overboard. This young man, christened Boat Memory, seemed a little frightened, but on board the *Beagle*, and after a good meal and a sleep, regained his composure. 'The meeting between him and York Minster,' FitzRoy reported, 'was very tame, for, at first, they would not appear to recognize or speak to each other. "Boat" was the best-featured Fuegian I had seen, and being young and well made, was a very favourable specimen of the race. "York" was one of the stoutest men I had observed among them; but little Fuegia was almost as broad as she was high: she seemed to be so merry and happy, that I do not think she would willingly have quitted us. Three natives of Tierra del Fuego, better suited for the purpose of instruction, and for giving, as well as receiving information, could not, I think, have been found.'

So the whaleboat episode was at last ended. But hardly so was the Fuegian, for the three natives were still on board, and continued to be so even when at the end of a month the new whaleboat was built and the *Beagle* moved on in her surveying job to an anchorage over a hundred miles eastwards, in Nasau Bay. New ideas were forming in FitzRoy's mind, for he obviously would not wish to retrace his path in order to restore his three charges to their tribes around Stewart Island.

A fresh discovery intrigued him: the natives they were now meeting were different, with a different dialect, 'Yapoos', whom in fact York and Fuegia and Boat Memory affected to despise. Meeting some on a boat trip, 'without any previous intention, I told one of the boys in a canoe to come into our boat, and gave the man who was with him a large, shining mother-of-pearl button. The boy got into my boat directly, and sat down'. Soon he too was on board the *Beagle*, being laughed at by the others and told to put some clothes on, and being christened, *à propos* of his purchase price, Jemmy Button. Not long afterwards FitzRoy was reaching his final decision, if he had not already done so. Finding that all four were happy and in good health, 'I began to think of the various advantages which might result to them and their countrymen as well as to us, by taking them to England'.

The time for the final rendezvous with Captain King was now approaching, and FitzRoy stepped up his surveying activities. In fact in the last few months he must have performed a phenomenal amount of successful work. It was now that his ship's master, passing northwards through the Murray Narrows, discovered the Beagle Channel, that strange canal-like cut through the tip of Tierra del Fuego. FitzRoy himself made a landing on Cape Horn Island and marched to the tip, where, surveying two oceans and taking his bearings, he built with his men a monumental pile of stones and drank a toast to the British king. Finally, as winter and the last few weeks approached, he was surveying amidst snow and ice the Le Maire Straits and risking but surviving many dangers.

He was only a few days late at the rendezvous, and on August 6th 1830 he was sailing out from Rio harbour, with the *Adventure*, for home.

FitzRoy had undoubtedly established himself as a brilliant and courageous captain of sail, with a flair for surveying. He had also done a very personal and somewhat surprising thing. Many

sailors had brought home natives from their travels to show to
their countrymen. But no one had brought home any quite so
primitive as the Fuegians, or with the philanthropic intention of
educating and returning them.

BOOK 2

The Great Voyage

CHAPTER 5

Strange Cause for a
Second Voyage

Beagle, at sea, Sept. 12 1830

Sir,

I have the honour of reporting to you that there are now on board of his Majesty's sloop, under my command, four natives of Tierra del Fuego.

Their names and estimated ages are,

> York Minster 26
> Boat Memory 20
> James Button 14
> Fuegia Basket (a girl) 9

I have maintained them entirely at my own expense, and hold myself responsible for their comfort while away from, and for their safe return to their own country: and I have now to request that, as senior officer of the Expedition, you will consider of the possibility of some public advantage being derived from this circumstance; and of the propriety of offering them, with that view, to His Majesty's Government...[1]

So wrote FitzRoy to King; and a stranger letter cannot often have been sent from one naval captain to another, nor a stranger

[1] This correspondence is quoted by FitzRoy in Chapter I of Volume II of the *Narrative*.

offer made to a British government. The letter goes on to explain the circumstances of the collection of these natives. It ends with the following two paragraphs stating unequivocally what are the intentions of their captor and would-be benefactor:

> When about to depart from the Fuegian coast, I decided to keep these four natives on board, for they appeared to be quite cheerful and contented with their situation; and I thought that many good effects might be the consequence of their living a short time in England. They have lived, and have been clothed like the seamen, and are now, and have been always, in excellent health and very happy. They understand why they were taken, and look forward with pleasure to seeing our country, as well as returning to their own.
>
> Should not his Majesty's Government direct otherwise, I shall procure for these people a suitable education, and, after two or three years, shall send or take them back to their country, with as large a stock as I can collect of those articles most useful to them, and most likely to improve the condition of their countrymen, who are scarcely superior to the brute creation.

Captain King sent on this letter to the Admiralty when the expedition landed in England a few weeks later. He received the following reply, formally and somewhat negatively worded except for the definite promise with which it ends:

> Admiralty Office, 19th Oct. 1830
>
> Sir,
>
> Having laid before my Lords Commissioners of the Admiralty your letter and its enclosure from Commander Fitz-Roy,[2] of the *Beagle*, relative to the four Indians whom he has brought from Tierra del Fuego under the circumstances therein stated: I am commanded to acquaint you that their Lordships will not interfere with Commander Fitz-Roy's personal superintendence of, or benevolent intentions towards these four people, but will afford him any facilities towards maintaining and educating them in England, and will give them a passage home again.

[2] His then substantive rank; he achieved captain's rank during the second voyage. In the *Narrative* FitzRoy spells his name with a hyphen, but later ceases to do so.

Backed by this encouragement, FitzRoy allowed his benevolent intentions full play. His first efforts led to discouraging results, and also indeed failed to avoid tragedy. The four Fuegians were first taken to lodgings in Plymouth, where the *Beagle* had berthed. They were then as soon as possible moved to more salubrious quarters in a nearby farmhouse. The vicar of Plymstock then wrote to the Church Missionary Society on their behalf, enclosing an explanatory note from FitzRoy. That Society was, however, at the time concerned only with Africa and the East and, in any case, was chronically short of funds. The request therefore for the provision of religious instruction was turned down.[3]

Worse was to follow. In spite of their quick removal from the crowded dockland, and in spite of two vaccinations (following a previous one at Monte Video that had not taken), the most stalwart of the Fuegians, Boat Memory, contracted smallpox. Intense activity obtained the willing help of the local naval doctors and the benevolent permission of the Admiralty in London: all four Fuegians were admitted into the efficient Plymouth Royal Naval Hospital, James Bennett, the *Beagle*'s coxswain, faithfully accompanying them. FitzRoy had hardly reached London, however, whither pressing duties had sent him, before he received news of Boat Memory's death.

The other three Fuegians remained in the hospital for some time and continued healthy. Something had to be done about them however; and now the Church Missionary Society proved helpful. FitzRoy was put in touch by them with the secretary of the National Society for Providing the Education of the Poor in the Principles of the Established Church. This person was a Reverend Joseph Wigram, and he was the son (and fifteenth child) of Sir Robert Wigram of Walthamstow House. He approached the Rector of Walthamstow, a certain William Wilson, who was greatly forthcoming. It was arranged that York and

[3] Copy from the Society's Minutes in Volume II, page 334: 'Read a letter from the Rev. J. L. Harris, dated Plymstock, the 1st Nov. (1830)...*Resolved*. That Mr Harris be informed that the Committee do not conceive it to be in the province of this Society to take charge of the Individuals mentioned in his letter.' Harris was vicar from 1826 to 1833.

Jemmy and Fuegia should be taken in by the master of the local infant school 'as boarders and pupils', while the two clergymen, Messrs Wilson and Wigram, should keep an eye on them.[4] Delighted, FitzRoy made immediate arrangements for the transfer of his three remaining charges.

'The inside of a stage-coach was taken, and under the guidance of Mr Murray (the *Beagle*'s late master), attended by James Bennett, they arrived in Piccadilly, and were immediately carried to Walthamstow, without attracting any notice. Mr Murray told me that they seemed to enjoy their journey in the coach, and were very much struck by the repeated changing of horses.'

FitzRoy himself met them off the coach, to take them the rest of the journey. During the *Beagle*'s voyage home he had, he says, found time to see much of them, and had grown to like the boy and girl and to form a high opinion of their intelligence; York Minster, however, he designated 'a displeasing specimen of uncivilized human nature'. He noticed that when their attention was particularly excited they seemed to relapse into a sort of stupid, glazed wonder, though the passing of a steam ship on their entrance into Falmouth had really aroused their emotions. Now one of them at least was to display an even more unexpected excitement.

'They were glad to see me', FitzRoy continues in his *Narrative*, 'but seemed bewildered by the multitude of objects. Passing Charing Cross, there was a start and exclamation of astonishment from York. "Look!" he said, fixing his eyes on the lion upon Northumberland House which he certainly thought alive, and walking there. I never saw him show such sudden emotion at any other time. They were pleased with the rooms prepared for them at Walthamstow; and the schoolmaster and his wife were equally pleased to find the future inmates of their house very well disposed, quiet and cleanly people; instead of fierce and dirty savages.'

As well they indeed might be pleased! They were, it may be

[4] Joseph Wigram was at this time Assistant Preacher at St James's, Westminster but was apparently still living in his father's Walthamstow House. He later became Bishop of Rochester.

hoped, the sort of people who took things for granted, especially
when ordained by their social superiors. No doubt the school-
children themselves would take the extraordinary situation very
much for granted, as children will; though it must have been disconcerting to have a bulky and full-grown Fuegian sitting next
to one while learning the ABC. During their ten months' stay in
Walthamstow the Fuegians retreated tantalizingly into almost
total oblivion, except for one brilliant, highlighted, episode.

FitzRoy took a considerable interest in them. By agreement
they were taught, 'English, and the plainer truths of Christianity,
as the first object; and the use of common tools, a slight acquaintance with husbandry, gardening, and mechanism, as the second'.
Fuegia and Jemmy Button responded favourably; but York was
'hard to teach, except mechanically', and hated having to try
to read. They had many visitors, out of curiosity, who however
gave them presents or contributed to the stock of useful articles
which FitzRoy was collecting against their return. So too did the
friends of FitzRoy to whom he took them on occasion, their
favourite excursion being to see Fanny Rice-Trevor (later Lady
Dynevor), who was 'Capen sisser' (Captain's sister).

Then in the summer of 1831 came the summons to FitzRoy to
show his Fuegians to the King and Queen. The audience was an
obvious success. The Sailor King asked intelligent and interested
questions. 'I hope I may be permitted,' wrote FitzRoy in the
Narrative, 'to remark that, during an equal space of time, no
person ever asked me so many sensible and thoroughly pertinent
questions respecting the Fuegians and their country also relating
to the survey in which I had myself been engaged, as did his
Majesty.' Queen Adelaide displayed her great good-heartedness—
and a woman who, deprived of any immediate issue, could so
unquestioningly succour her consort's illegitimate children as
had William's long-suffering queen, must indeed have been good-
hearted. Leaving the rooms for a moment, she returned with
one of her own bonnets and placed it on Fuegia's head. She followed this with a ring from her finger and a purse wherewith
to buy an outfit of clothes.

FitzRoy however was already becoming restive. It is true that in his letter to Captain King which had been sent on to the Admiralty he had spoken of a stay by the Fuegians of two or three years. But that had been written before ever he had arrived back in England; and when he came to put his intentions into practice he soon began to change his mind. There is no specific evidence of difficulty. Nevertheless, towards the end of May FitzRoy is again addressing the Lord of the Admiralty, anxiously, but with perhaps a little of imperiousness underlying the conventional humility of language.

Captain King, on submitting his subordinate's completed charts and plans, had sent in a most handsome, magnanimous, informed, and indeed glowing report of FitzRoy's surveying work.[5] He called himself fortunate in that Sir Robert Otway had ordered him to take FitzRoy in Captain Stokes's place; he referred to the necessary privations and difficulties of open-boat surveying and the splendid example of the *Beagle*'s commander; he ended by telling their Lordships that FitzRoy 'merits their distinction and patronage', and by recommending him 'in the strongest manner to their favourable consideration'.

Not only so, but King in a private conversation, had led FitzRoy to suppose that the survey of the South American coast was certainly going to continue; and, as he himself was retiring, FitzRoy was the obvious commander. By March all FitzRoy's duties in connection with the recent voyage were completed. By May however nothing further had happened; and he had discovered, he says, that 'an entire change had taken place in the views of the Lords of the Admiralty and that there was no intention to prosecute the survey'.

Hence his further letter to the Admiralty. It had a very definite plan in view.

FitzRoy enclosed a copy of their Lordships' promise to convey the Fuegians back to their native land, though he was not so impolitic as to refer to this specifically. He contented himself with observing that the natives had been with him for fourteen months in all and that even if plans were put under way to

---

[5] Number 1 in the Appendix volume of the *Narrative*, coming after the meteorological tables.

return them during this season another five months would elapse
before they reached their home. If another year were let go by—
to arrive during the Fuegian winter was tacitly accepted as
inadvisable—then the Fuegians would be disappointed 'and I fear
that discontent and disease may be the consequence'.

The letter continued by setting down what had been the
writer's hopes and intentions in bringing the Fuegians to England,
an elaboration of his previously rather vague reference to his
action's 'good effects'. 'Having been led to suppose', he starts
slyly as a preamble, 'that a vessel would be sent to South America
to continue the survey,' he then continues: 'I hoped to have seen
these people become useful as interpreters, and be the means of
establishing a friendly disposition towards Englishmen on the
part of their countrymen, if not a regular intercourse with them.
By supplying these natives with some animals, seeds, tools etc.,
and placing them, with some of their own tribe, on the fertile
country lying at the east side of Tierra del Fuego, I thought that
in a few years, ships might have been enabled to obtain fresh
provisions, as well as wood and water, during their passage from
the Atlantic to the Pacific Ocean, on a part of the coast which
can always be approached with ease and safety.'

Then comes the specific request. If their Lordships did not
think his ideas worthy of attention and support—then might he
please have twelve months' leave of absence in order to 'keep
faith' with the natives of Tierra del Fuego.

The leave of absence was duly granted.

FitzRoy lost no time in chartering a vessel at his own expense
to take him and the Fuegians. He had determined to go himself,
he explains, because he felt he could not trust anyone alone to
go to the necessary trouble of landing the natives amongst their
own tribes and at the spots from which they had been taken. A
formal agreement was drawn up and signed, and the fee that
FitzRoy agreed to pay out of his own pocket was a thousand
pounds.

Then 'a kind uncle' came to FitzRoy's rescue. This could have
been either the Fourth Duke of Grafton, sporting squire and
once winner of the Derby, or Castlereagh's half-brother Lord

Londonderry; since Lord Londonderry was later to take his nephew under his political wing it was more likely to have been he who made the decisive step. This step was to persuade the Admiralty to send FitzRoy on another South American surveying voyage forthwith. This reversal of decision did not come however until after FitzRoy had signed the agreement with the merchant shipowner; and—*noblesse oblige*—he paid the 'larger part' of the thousand pounds. (He was also left with a number of goats on his hands purchased on his instructions by James Bennett 'for the purpose of stocking some of the islands of Tierra del Fuego'.)

To achieve this second voyage there must have been some wire-pulling. But it would be difficult to contend that it did not prove wire-pulling with very good results.

On June 27th 1831 FitzRoy was re-appointed to his 'well-tried little vessel', the *Beagle*. Naturally, he was at once busy in very many ways, but the Fuegians still had his attention.

In August the somewhat long-suffering Admiralty was receiving another letter. The initiative, however, had come this time not from FitzRoy but from the Rector of Walthamstow: Mr Wilson thought that it would be a good idea if two missionaries should accompany the natives back to Tierra del Fuego. Would the Navy and FitzRoy, the letter continued, be willing to take them; would perhaps the Government allow them to be maintained on board at public expense; would FitzRoy even be so good as to visit them again to see how they were getting on after they had been landed? 'A subscription has been set on foot by gentlemen who are extremely desirous that this opportunity of extending the benefits of civilization should not be lost; and, in consequence of their united wishes, I now take the liberty of asking these questions.'

The answers were all most obligingly in the affirmative. Only one volunteer for the contemplated two missionary posts could, however, be found, a young 'catechist' by the name of Richard Matthews who already had an elder brother a missionary in New Zealand.

The *Beagle*, in process of being extensively refitted, lay at Plymouth. 'In October,' writes FitzRoy, 'the party from Walthamstow arrived, in a steam-vessel at Plymouth, and not a few boats were required to transport to our ship the large cargo of clothes, tools, crockery-ware, books, and various things which the families at Walthamstow and other kind-hearted persons had given. In the small hold of the *Beagle*, it is not easy to find places for the stowage of so many extra stores; and when dividing the contents of large chests, in order to pack them differently, some very fair jokes were enjoyed by the seamen, at the expense of those who had ordered complete sets of crockery-ware, without desiring that any selection of articles should be made. (It is possible to guess what articles were causing the most merriment.) Charles Darwin, however, when later he had watched this miscellany being unpacked onto the southern tip of the Americas, had this to say.

> The choice of articles showed the most culpable folly and negligency. Wine glasses, butter-bolts, tea trays, soup turins, mahogany dressing case, fine white linen, beaver hats and an endless variety of similar things, show how little was thought about the country where they were going to. The means absolutely wasted on such things would have purchased an immense stock of really useful articles. [6]

Darwin in this instance was being less patient than his captain. How he ever came to be present at this unloading will be related in the following chapter.

[6] Page 129 of *Charles Darwin's Diary of the Voyage of H.M.S. Beagle*, edited by Nora Barlow (C.U.P. 1933).

CHAPTER 6

Darwin Enters

My dear Henslow,

Captain FitzRoy is going out to survey the southern coast of Tierra del Fuego, and afterwards to visit many of the South Sea Islands, and to return by the Indian Archipelago. The vessel is fitted out expressly for scientific purposes, combined with the survey; it will furnish, therefore, a rare opportunity for a naturalist, and it would be a great misfortune that it should be lost.

An offer has been made to me to recommend a proper person to go out as a naturalist with this expedition; he will be treated with every consideration. The Captain is a young man of very pleasing manners (a nephew of the Duke of Grafton), of great zeal in his profession, and who is very highly spoken of; if Leonard Jenyns could go, what treasures he might bring home with him, as the ship would be placed at his disposal whenever his inquiries made it necessary or desirable. In the absence of so accomplished a naturalist, is there any person whom you could strongly recommend? he must be such a person as would do credit to our recommendation...[1]

So wrote in August 1831 one Cambridge don to another. The writer was George Peacock, Professor of Astronomy, and the recipient Professor of Botany and friend of the recently

[1] See page 115 of the one-volume edition (1892) of Francis Darwin's *Life* of his father.

graduated Charles Darwin. The offer to Peacock had been
made by the naval hydrographer, Captain Beaufort. But the
initiative had come from FitzRoy himself: 'Anxious that no
opportunity of collecting useful information, during the voyage,
should be lost; I proposed to the Hydrographer that some
well-educated and scientific person should be sought for who
would willingly share such accommodation as I had to offer,
in order to profit by the opportunity of visiting distant countries
yet little known.' Professor Henslow, FitzRoy goes on to re-
late (in Chapter II of Volume II of the *Narrative*) 'named
Mr Charles Darwin, grandson of Dr Darwin the poet,[2] as a young
man of promising ability, extremely fond of geology, and indeed
all branches of natural history.'

There was nothing eccentric in this idea of FitzRoy's: fifteen
years later Thomas Huxley was also to go voyaging with the
Navy; and the *Beagle* on her first voyage found room for a
'botanical collector'. From a purely personal point of view Fitz-
Roy was seeking a congenial companion to relieve the proverbial
loneliness of the Captain, for whoever was chosen would mess
alone with him in his cabin. But he was also seeking to do all in
his power to enhance the importance and ensure the success of
the forthcoming voyage. He might, for instance, have chosen
the ship's artist as a companion. But he did not. He chose, as
most likely to serve both his purposes, a scientist. Later FitzRoy
was to become a Fellow of the Royal Society; and the idea that
he himself was not scientific—or, as it would more likely have
been phrased in those days, 'philosophical'—would never at any
time have entered his head.

Apart altogether from the deeper implications of the choice,
FitzRoy was indeed lucky to light upon somebody so equable and
good-natured, a young man so fundamentally nice, as Charles
Darwin must have been. Even so, however, the appointment was
not finally made without some trouble and hesitation, and that on

[2] Erasmus Darwin, now best known as an early propounder, in his
Zoonomia, of 'Lamarckian' evolutionary theories. He speculated widely
in long poems full of Spenserian imagery and with such titles as *The
Temple of Nature, The Loves of the Plants.*

both sides. The captain and the hydrographer are perhaps guilty of painting too rosy a picture: both knew that the voyage was likely to last more than two years, though neither at that time expected five; and Peacock's phrase about the ship being at the naturalist's disposal reads a little surprisingly. However, such mild bias can hardly be called unfairly dressing the bait, though FitzRoy's subsequent reference to a rival candidate for the honour of sharing his cabin does have something of a specious ring.

The chances and difficulties that had to be met and overcome on Darwin's side were to prove considerable indeed. That all, of whatever origin, were surmounted serves to give an unescapable feeling that Fate herself was taking a hand. Though they will be familiar to anyone well acquainted with the life of Darwin, they deserve to be recounted.

The first hazard was that the proposed Leonard Jenyns (Henslow's brother-in-law), or even Henslow himself, might have accepted the job; both in fact nearly did, Henslow only turning it down because his wife 'looked so miserable' at the prospect. The second hazard was that Darwin, owing to his absence from home, did not read Peacock's letter to Henslow and Henslow's covering letter until five days after the latter was written. The third hazard was more serious, in fact nearly fatal, and since it shows the reactions of a respectable, but by no means unintelligent, citizen of the times, that is to say Darwin's father, to the naval enterprise in question, it may be given in some detail.

The burly and forceful doctor who was Darwin's father had unequivocally advised his son to turn the offer down, rashly but fair-mindedly however providing an escape clause, to the effect that, if Charles could find 'any man of common sense' who advised him to go, he would be willing to consider changing his mind. Several factors made it unlikely that the son would ever go without obtaining his father's consent. Charles, long since mother-less, was a dutiful and a rather overawed son; and the appointment, which attached no salary, would involve the father in considerable expense. Further, having first partially trained as a doctor at Edinburgh and then moved over to Cambridge with the idea of becoming a clergyman, Charles had already put his father to great expense and was in fact beginning to earn in the latter's eyes the reputation of an idle fellow unwilling to settle down. With a sad heart therefore the young man wrote to Henslow definitely refusing the magnificent offer. He then rode across, as he had originally intended, to stay at his uncle's house at Maer for the shooting. His uncle was Josiah Wedgwood, the second of the great potters. He and his family were shown Henslow's letter, and without exception took a much less cautious view of the offer.

The immediate upshot was a letter from Charles Darwin at Maer to his father at home at Shrewsbury. It pleaded for a reconsideration of the parental veto, and it enclosed a revealing document which was Charles's list of his father's objections as he remembered them, and his uncle's comments thereon. These are the objections:[3]

1. Disreputable to my character as a clergyman hereafter.
2. A wild scheme.
3. That they must have offered to many others before me the place of Naturalist.
4. And from its not being accepted there must be some serious objection to the vessel or expedition.
5. That I should never settle down to a steady life hereafter.
6. That my accommodation would be most uncomfortable.
7. That you, that is Dr Darwin, should consider it again as changing my profession.
8. That it would be a useless undertaking.

It is really the old story of the prophet being without honour in his own house that lies behind these objections: Dr Darwin had no idea that his son, while taking a mediocre classics degree, had made a name for himself at Cambridge as a born and enthusiastic naturalist. For the rest it is the sound bourgeois objection to anything so rackety as sailoring. Uncle Jos dealt with the objections circumspectly, cunningly, but also forthrightly. To No 5 he replied that of course the doctor knows his son better than he does, and it might undoubtedly be a weighty objection; but, 'is it

[3] See page 26 of Nora Barlow's *Charles Darwin and the Voyage of the Beagle* (London, 1945).

not the case that sailors are prone to settle in domestic and quiet habits?' For the rest: 'Natural History, though certainly not professional, is very suitable to a clergyman, and Charles might well acquire habits of application; one could not conceive of the Admiralty sending out a bad vessel; and the undertaking afforded 'any man of enlarged curiosity such an opportunity of seeing men and things as happens to few.' The kind uncle then followed up the sending of the letter by riding back with Charles to Shrewsbury and talking to his brother-in-law personally. As a result, parental permission was granted. Young Darwin tried to soften the financial blow by saying that if he managed to spend more than his allowance on board the *Beagle* he would be 'deuced clever'. To which his father answered with a smile, 'But they tell me you are very clever!' Charles hurriedly wrote a letter of acceptance 'if not too late', and followed it to Henslow and Cambridge.

He was not too late. Nevertheless the prize was not yet his. At Cambridge he met a friend by the name of Wood, who, being a nephew of Lord Londonderry, was therefore a relation or connection of FitzRoy. This Mr Wood had nothing but good to report of both the Captain and the impending voyage: the Admiralty, they said, pronounced FitzRoy's charts as 'most perfect' and the Captain himself declared that he had 'a right good set' of officers coming with him. Darwin, pleased, prevailed upon his friend to write to FitzRoy on his behalf.

This proved something of a false move. However much he may have recommended Darwin, Mr Wood, being a Londonderry and therefore an out-and-out Tory, saw fit to warn the Captain that he would probably be taking on a Whig. As a result FitzRoy suddenly blew cold. He replied to Wood. In his letter, which the unhappy Darwin could not in fairness describe as anything but 'most straightforward and gentlemanlike', he discouraged Wood's friend from seeking the post and stated that in any case the writer now had a friend of his own, a Mr Chester, who would probably be taking the vacant place in his mess.[4]

[4] See pages 119 and 42 respectively of Francis Darwin's and Nora Barlow's books already mentioned.

Darwin said he would give up, and Henslow agreed, adding that it was very wrong of Peacock so to have misrepresented things. Perhaps this very agreement spurred Charles on to make one last bid for the job. The next morning he travelled to London, to interview personally the Hydrographer and FitzRoy at the Admiralty.

To have witnessed the first meeting of these two young men could surely have been rather like watching a block of ice begin to melt with unexpected and spectacular rapidity. As he was later to confide to his friend, FitzRoy felt first that anyone with Darwin's nose could only doubtfully possess sufficient energy and determination to be a success on the voyage—the fantastic inaccuracy of the diagnosis ought to have cured FitzRoy forever of a belief in phrenology. He brought up his friend Chester again. But then he was confiding that actually only five minutes ago he had had a letter from Chester and Chester was not coming after all. Soon he was offering to go shares with everything in his cabin and telling Darwin airily that five hundred pounds ought easily to cover all preliminary expenses. Only a few hours later Darwin was writing excitedly to his sister:

Captain FitzRoy is in town and I have seen him; it is no use attempting to praise him as much as I feel inclined to do for you would not believe me. One thing I am certain, nothing could be more open and kind than he was to me... He says nothing would be so miserable for him as having me with him if I was uncomfortable, as in a small vessel we must be thrown together, and thought it his duty to state everything in the worst point of view: I think I shall go on Sunday to Plymouth to see the vessel. There is something most extremely attractive in his manners and way of coming straight to the point. If I live with him, he says I must live poorly—no wine, and the plainest dinners...I like his manner of proceeding. He asked me at once, 'Shall you bear being told that I want the cabin to myself? when I want to be alone. If we treat each other this way, I hope we shall suit; if not probably we should wish each other at the Devil.'...I am writing in a great hurry: I do not know whether you take interest enough to excuse treble postage. I hope I am judging reasonably, and not through prejudice, about Cap. FitzRoy: if so

I am sure we shall suit. I dine with him today. I could write great deal more if I thought you liked it, and I had at present time. There is indeed a tide in the affairs of man, and I have experienced it, and I had *entirely* given it up till 1 to-day.

They duly dined, and the next day Charles was dashing off another excited letter. First came various practical commissions for his sister Susan to execute. Then:

I write all this as if it was settled, but it is not more than it was, excepting that from Capt. Fitzroy wishing me so much to go, and from his kindness, I feel a predestination I shall start. I spent a very pleasant evening with him yesterday: he must be more than 23 years old [he was 26]; he is of a slight figure, and a dark but handsome edition of Mr Kynaston, and, according to my notions, pre-eminently good manners...This is the first really cheerful day I have spent since I received the letter, and it is all owing to the sort of involuntary confidence I place in my beau ideal of a Captain...

All of course *was* settled. The die was cast: though there were details to be discussed and a further interview with the Hydrographer to be arranged, nothing now was going to stop Darwin accepting the job or for that matter FitzRoy accepting Darwin. Beaufort, the Hydrographer, Darwin found 'too deep a fish' for him; but FitzRoy was wholly on Darwin's side and encouraged him to stir the official 'with a long pole and obtain favourable conditions'.

As Darwin had hoped, FitzRoy took him down to Devonport the next week-end, journeying by steam packet around the coast. FitzRoy also brought with him a young midshipman named Musters,[5] and he continued to earn Darwin's golden opinions by his kindness to the boy.

It must be remembered to what a different world Darwin was now being introduced. Here was a young man of a very prosperous but middle class, midland, family, whose knowledge of the sea can have been little more than an occasional holiday view of it. Here was a young and recently promoted captain in a Navy

[5] The son of the Mary Chaworth with whom Byron had been infatuated as a youth.

that was still Nelsonian and that accorded to its ships' commanders an altitude that was unapproachable and an authority that was absolute. With some captains Darwin's inherent niceness and friendliness might have been of little avail and it says much for the characters and humanity of both men that the trying weeks of preparation for the voyage were got through with so little friction.

These were by no means easy weeks. As a start, and inevitably, Darwin was appalled at the smallness and closeness of the quarters. Then, though not appalled, he was a little disconcerted on meeting the rest of the *Beagle*'s officers. He found their conversation, one imagines, a trifle unintellectual. 'Like the freshest of freshmen', he described them to his sister; though later in the voyage he was going on walks and land expeditions with one or another of them, even the youngest, and describing them as the very best of fellows.

One of the things that impressed Darwin at Plymouth had little to do with his relationship with FitzRoy, but does throw a light on the latter's forcefulness at that time, and his capacity, whether through 'interest', or persistency and self-confidence, or all three, to extract all that he wanted out of the Admiralty. The *Beagle* was being refitted in a manner quite remarkable. It came near to being rebuilt. Soon Darwin was writing (to Henslow) with almost proprietary enthusiasm about her: 'She looks most beautiful, even a landsman must admire her. *We* all think her the most perfect vessel ever turned out by the Dockyard. One thing is certain, no vessel has been fitted out so expensively, and with so much care. Everything that can be made so is of mahogany, and nothing can exceed the neatness and beauty of all the accommodations.' And later: 'Everything is on a grand scale... In short, everything is as prosperous as human means can make it.' To quote in a little more technical detail from FitzRoy himself:

I resolved to spare neither expense nor trouble in making our little Expedition as complete, with respect to material and preparation, as my means and exertion would allow, when supported by the considerate and satisfactory arrangements of the Admiralty...

The *Beagle* was commissioned on the 4th of July 1831, and was immediately taken into dock to be thoroughly examined, and prepared for a long period of foreign service. As she required a new deck, a good deal of repair about the upper works, I obtained permission to have the upper-deck raised considerably, which afterwards proved to be of the greatest advantage to her as a sea boat besides adding so materially to the comfort of all on board. While in dock, a sheathing of two-inch fir plank was nailed on the vessel's bottom, over which was a coating of felt, and then new copper. This sheathing added about fifteen tons to her displacement, and nearly seven to her actual measurement. Therefore, instead of 235 tons, she might be considered about 242 tons burthen. The rudder was fitted according to the plan of Captain Lihou: a patent windlass supplied the place of a capstan: one of Frazer's stoves, with an oven attached, was taken instead of a common 'galley' fire-place; and the lightning-conductors, invented by Mr Harris, were fixed in all the masts, the bowsprit, and even in the flying jib-boom. The arrangements made in the fittings, both inside and outside, by the officers of the Dockyard, left nothing to be desired. Our ropes, sails, and spars, were the best that could be procured; and to complete our excellent outfit, six superior boats (two of them private property) were built expressly for us, and so contrived and stowed that they could all be carried in any weather.

Considering the limited disposal space in so very small a ship, we contrived to carry more instruments and books than one would really suppose could be stowed away in dry and secure places; and in a part of my own cabin twenty-two chronometers were carefully placed...

I must not omit to mention that among our provisions were various antiscorbutics—such as pickles, dried apples, and lemon juice—of the best quality, and in as great abundance as we could stow away; we had also on board a very large quantity of Kilner and Moorsom's preserved meat, vegetables, and soup: and from the Medical Department we received an ample supply of antiseptics, and articles useful for preserving specimens of natural history.

The *Beagle* in fact was fitted out with every modern and scientific convenience of the day.

This thorough and lavish preparation naturally consumed time, and FitzRoy did not receive his official sailing orders from the Admiralty until November 15th. Darwin, who had expected to sail in October, became miserably restless. In totally strange surroundings, unable to be useful, in the throes of indecision as to whether he had done the right thing in persuading his father to let him go, he experienced the added worry of suffering from palpitations. He was convinced that he had heart disease, but equally convinced that he was not going near a doctor lest he be prevented from sailing.

Worse was to follow, for the wind would not shift to a propitious quarter—in this matter things had not changed much since the days of Agamemnon and Menelaus—and two abortive attempts were made by the ship to clear her moorings in Barn's Pool under Mount Edgecumbe. Short of a sacrifice, the ship's company did indulge in a sort of Saturnalia on Christmas Day, the crew being allowed to get gloriously drunk. On December 27th of the year 1831 the *Beagle* finally sailed—with many of the crew suffering physical punishment for having allowed themselves to go beyond the permitted limits.[6]

The over-all length of the *Beagle* was about a hundred feet, and her deck measured some ninety feet by twenty-five at its widest. Into this small vessel[7] were stowed no less than seventy-four persons. There were thirty-four seamen, six boys and eight marines. Mr May, ship's carpenter and replacer of lost whaleboats, was there, as were also the three Fuegians whose presence

[6] An anecdote of Sulivan's, while midshipman on the *Thetis*, is relevant. He was in charge of a boat's crew making a call at Monte Video and had been instructed not to keep the men to the boat in harbour: if they could not resist the grog-shops it was their own lookout. In trying to prevent one of the best of the crew from succumbing to temptation, he was told: 'Mr. Sulivan, I'll get away if I can, and I'll get drunk if I can, and I can take my "batty" for it as well as another man.' The 'batty' was three dozen lashes for the first offence and six more for each further offence on the voyage.

[7] The *Beagle*'s 'burthen', of 242 tons, would represent about 24,200 cubic feet of space, at least on the modern arbitrary calculation of 'registered tonnage' at 100 cubic feet per ton. (Naval vessels are now rated in terms of displacement, i.e. total weight of water displaced.) Miss Lois Darling, in America's *Nature Magazine*, has gone into the *Beagle*'s exact measurements in detail.

was a consequence of such loss, together with their new tutor, the young missionary Matthews. There were also the officers.

These Darwin was to remember all his life, and he was soon to be making a reassessment of their characters. Stokes he liked specially, Sulivan 'took the palm for talk', and Wickham was 'a glorious fine fellow'. One midshipman amused him by truculently introducing himself as: 'I'm Arthur Mellersh of Midhurst, I have read Lord Byron and I don't care a damn for anyone!' The other, Captain King's son, he delighted to take with him on botanizing expeditions.

Darwin's most intimate shipmate, the Captain, would deserve, and receive, a more careful assessment.

CHAPTER 7

Success and Efficiency

THIS most important event in the life of
Robert FitzRoy, the 1831–36 voyage of the *Beagle*, may be
looked upon in two ways.

Firstly, the voyage was a great success, a great personal triumph
for its captain, who as a consequence could look forward to a
brilliant subsequent career. Secondly, the voyage brought out
those flaws and excesses of FitzRoy's character that were so to
militate against him all his life, for he was indeed his own
worst enemy. It seemed to be frustration and disappointment
that brought out the damaging and less admirable side of
FitzRoy's character, as they were likely to do in one so forceful,
fervent and autocratic. Chief among these frustrations and disap-
pointments were, on the one hand, the final outcome of his
Fuegian philanthropy and, on the other, his dealings with the
Admiralty with regard to the purchase of supplementary schooners. A third exacerbating factor must have been the slow realiza-
tion that Charles Darwin was not quite the man he had hoped for.
FitzRoy was later to confide to paper that one of his reasons for
asking for a naturalist to accompany him had been the hope that
this expert would discover added evidence to support his own
growing conviction that the Bible's description of creation was
wholly true. This, in the eighteen-thirties, was by no means an

unreasonable hope; indeed it would not easily occur to FitzRoy that a naturalist would do anything else but support such a view, the only unpredictable feature being the extent to which he would do so. That FitzRoy should have chosen of all people Charles Darwin as his naturalist is one of the minor ironies of history.

Naturally the episodes in the long voyage that illustrate the two different viewpoints are intertwined. It should be possible, however, to separate them without sacrificing clarity, and the ensuing chapters will do so, alternating between the successful and efficient on the one hand and the disappointing and frustrating on the other. This chapter covers the first seven or so months of the voyage; and, in spite of the delayed and rather inauspicious start, it is a cheerful story and shows the *Beagle*'s captain in a bright and admirable light.

It will be well first to summarize and quote from the Memorandum by Captain Beaufort, the Hydrographer, which accompanied the Admiralty's orders for the voyage. It shows what considerable achievement was expected of FitzRoy.

'Few vessels,' the Hydrographer first points out, 'will have ever left this country with a better set of chronometers.' Chronometers, however perfect, are liable to be affected by shock and varying heat; and, being an invention of only seventy years ago, they were less perfect then than now. The reason for taking so many was that the discovered mean of the most reliable would give an accurate measurement; and the reason for taking any at all was to 'establish a chain of meridians round the world'. In other words, having procured the accuracy of his timing instrument, the Captain should, by celestial observations, obtain accurate readings of longitude at places right around the earth's surface.

But the real work of the survey, Beaufort points out, will begin south of La Plata estuary. Little is known of this coast except that it contains some large rivers and a few good harbours, and it is most inaccurately mapped. Not an inviting coast, but

FitzRoy must remember that 'the more hopeless and forbidding any long line of coast may be, the more precious becomes the discovery of a port which affords safe anchorage and wholesome refreshment.' The River Negro, amongst other features, might well be explored.

Then come the Magellan Straits and Tierra del Fuego. Captain Beaufort was obviously very well aware of what had been done already by the *Beagle* and *Adventure* and does not ask for any duplication. 'Those two singular inland seas' for instance, Skyring and Otway Waters, scene of FitzRoy's crew-testing adventure on the first voyage, will probably not deserve a much more detailed account. But a long list of necessary surveying work is given, together with such large phrases as 'and any other places which the Commander's local knowledge may point out as being requisite to complete his former survey.' All this, adds Captain Beaufort airily—and having repeated the advice that 'the more inhospitable the region, the more valuable is a known port of refuge'—all this should take, with two trips back to Monte Video for refreshment, the best part of two years.

Next, it would be useful if FitzRoy could help to enlighten the sailors' present ignorance of the Falkland Islands.

After that should come the West coast of South America (where Captain Stokes had committed suicide). Again an uninviting coast; but it was necessary 'to remove a blank from this great survey, which was undertaken by Great Britain from such disinterested motives, and which was executed by Captains King and FitzRoy with so much skill and zeal.' Not only so, but the Spanish charts, on which the world's shipping so far depended, gave only 'a half knowledge' of which 'we have had too much: the present state of science, which affords such ample means, seems to demand that whatever is now done should be finally done; and that coasts, which are constantly visited by English vessels, should no longer have the motley appearance of alternate error and accuracy.' The *Beagle* on this occasion should therefore voyage considerably farther northwards up the coast than the previous limit of Chiloé, as far indeed as its Captain could reasonably manage.

The exact latitude of the ensuing strike westwards across the Pacific would, of course, depend on how far northwards the survey of the American coast had proceeded. But a visit to the Galapagos Islands would be desirable, as also to Tahiti, 'in order to verify the chronometers at Point Venus'. A list of places to be visited if possible around the Torres Strait and the East Indies ended the specific instructions.

But it remained 'to make some general remarks on the conduct of the whole survey'—they in fact take up six further printed pages.

There are fairly detailed instructions on the making of charts and the observation and recording of tides, winds and weather: FitzRoy would have been justified in feeling that he hardly needed these. There is a warning against 'exhausting the catalogue of public characters or private friends' when naming discovered geographical features, though it is allowed that a ship's crew does deserve some immortality in this respect. If FitzRoy felt this piece of advice to be aimed particularly at himself, he may have felt so even more ruefully over another: that patience and restraint should be observed in dealing with natives, lest such a peaceable expedition 'should be stained by a single act of hostility'. One instruction at least, however, must have seemed to him at the moment very unlikely to be needed: that if by some 'accident' command of the ship had to devolve on someone else the survey must be cut short and the *Beagle* return home.

So much for the Memorandum. It is couched in accommodating terms, in places even admiring terms. Nevertheless it is a formidable document and one written by a formidable person, Captain Beaufort having been a great surveyor in his own right (and the inventor incidentally of a scale for measuring wind velocities which is still in use). To anyone less forceful and self-confident than FitzRoy, therefore, it might well have been found intimidating. He seemed to find it in fact nothing more nor less than a stimulating challenge. It seemed to make him expand, to make him a little larger than life-size, an effect that a challenge confidently accepted may have upon a person. It is an effect, incidentally, that can prove a little trying to any subordinates who do not get taken up in the enthusiasm. But none such seemed to exist on the *Beagle*.

FitzRoy had begun with a forthright speech to his officers and men, coupled with some written instructions. Both of these his admiring lieutenant, Sulivan, found worthy of praise. FitzRoy had been kind to Sulivan on the previous voyage, sending him home as a midshipman so that he might take his promotion exam, and Sulivan had responded by once again electing to sign on under FitzRoy. He had followed this up by working indefatigably to help get the ship loaded and seaworthy, so much so that he had, one evening, fallen asleep and missed a ball whereat he had hoped to meet the girl with whom he was in love, a mishap that had however a happy sequel since the girl waited for him and married him at the end of the voyage. Forgetting, no doubt, his own troubles at the call of duty, Sulivan had listened with approval to FitzRoy's warning: 'If a man falls overboard, if we lose a spar or ship at sea, I shall blame the officer of the watch.' He read with approval the unheroic but sensible order that no one was ever to go out of sight of shore except in the company of at least two others, one to go for assistance and one to stay with the victim of any mishap—an order that seems to have been only twice disobeyed, once by the ship's clerk, with fatal result, and once by the Captain himself, who was lucky but admitted his foolishness.

Teneriffe was to have been the ship's first port of call. The officers and crew, looking forward to a chance to stretch their legs, met instead a renewed example of their captain's stern forthrightness. Unexpectedly, a twelve-day quarantine was demanded before anybody could be allowed to land. Would the Captain brook the delay? 'There was,' wrote Darwin to his sister, 'a deathlike stillness in the ship; till the Captain cried "Up Jib", and we left this long wished for place.' The decision had been instant—and nobody had dreamt of questioning it.

Reward came at the Cape Verde Islands, where a stay of three weeks was made and the officers managed some joyful trips into the interior on 'indifferent' horses. Such trips were not for FitzRoy, however, who was busy not only on his official duties but in appraising the commercial value of the islands for subsequent report. Darwin at this time wrote home with appreciation and wonder. 'The Captain continues steadily kind and does everything in his power to assist me. We see very little of each other when in harbour, our pursuits lead us in such different tracks. I never in my life met with a man who could endure nearly so great a share of fatigue. He works incessantly, and when apparently not employed, he is thinking. If he does not kill himself, he will, during this voyage, do a wonderful quantity of work.'

At the wild and isolated St Paul's Rock came a slight relaxation. The place teemed with birds that seemed to invite being collected for the game bag, and FitzRoy at the memory of it in his *Narrative* writes light-heartedly. 'Even the geological hammer became a missile. "Lend me the hammer?" asked one. "No, no," replied the owner, "you'll break the handle"; but hardly had he said so, when, overcome by the novelty of the scene, and the example of those around him, away went the hammer, with all the force of his own right arm.' The Captain is laughing at his new friend.

The next day FitzRoy laughed once more, and again no doubt at Darwin's expense, for the latter was suffering from the horseplay perpetrated upon all those who were crossing the equator for the first time. The Captain's indulgence to his crew was however calculated, and his entry in his *Narrative* is highly serious. 'These sports,' he quotes with approval from an earlier voyager, 'while they serve to keep up the spirits of the men, and make them forget the difficulties they have to go through, produce also the most beneficial influence upon their health; a cheerful man being much more capable of resisting a fit of sickness than a melancholy one.' The *Beagle*, refreshed, continued on her way and on the 28th February 1832 reached the South American coast, anchoring at Bahia (modern San Salvador) in tropical Brazil.

.   .   .

Two things need to be realized before the story of the voyage proceeds. The first is that out of the voyage's total of fifty-seven months no less than forty-two of them were spent in South American waters. The second is that between the outstanding and significant events the routine business of surveying and observation and discovery was going on all the time, either actively or in preparation or completion. Darwin was collecting his marine and land fauna and flora, using his geological hammer for its legitimate purpose, discovering his fossils: though he may have been, unbeknownst to his shipmates or even himself, in the preliminary process of changing scientific history, he was also doing the job that his captain had recruited him to do. The officers, in a miscellany of boats, hired, bought or borrowed or launched from the decks of the *Beagle*, were making, as on the previous voyage, their arduous trips. The Captain, besides going on many of the trips, was organizing and controlling the whole affair.

In the telling the details of maritime surveying become monotonous. The Captain gets over the difficulty by relegating to the Appendix of his *Narrative* a general description of his surveying methods, and by helping towards an appreciation of the continuity of his somewhat discursive story by the insertion of dates at the head of his pages. Here the method will be something both more and less. The description of the methods of surveying is very shortly summarized; but, to protect the reader from a sense of confusion in contemplating the events of the long span of the voyage, a time-table of the main moves in American waters is given in an appendix.

The most effective way to give an idea of the difficulties and methods of FitzRoy's South American surveying is to reproduce one of the specimen charts which he inserts in his *Narrative* to illustrate his Appendix No 39, 'Notes on Surveying a Wild Coast'. What is significant here is not only the number of angles taken but the fact that so many of them are taken from heights on land: FitzRoy explains that, what with the swell, the bad weather and the precipitous shores, the ship could not easily be anchored for the purpose of taking observations. However, anchorages, if often difficult and dangerous of entry and egress, were plentiful. Therefore:

> Our first object was to find a safe harbour in which to secure the ship. There we made observations for latitude, time and true bearing; on the tides and magnetism. We also made a plan of the harbour and its environs; and triangulations, including all the visible heights, and more remarkable features of the coast, so far as it could be clearly distinguished from the summits of the highest hills near the harbour. Upon these summits a good theodolite was used...

Sometimes an anchorage is described in the *Narrative*, but only where there was particular interest or difficulty. For instance, there were occasions when the *Beagle* was suddenly rocked violently by the unexpected and terrifying 'williwaws', gusts of wind from over the cliffs of a deep anchorage that came down almost vertically. But after a while these obviously become almost routine, and an inconvenience rather than a terror. Sometimes a boat landing is mentioned—there was the famous occasion, to be noticed later, when Darwin by his promptitude was instrumental in saving the boats from destruction. Sometimes the climb up a hill is mentioned. But only if the view is magnificent or the long clamber laden with instruments is made particularly difficult, as when the only way to get beyond a thicket of dense stunted beech is to crawl over the top. For the rest, the hard, exacting, day-to-day work is taken for granted.

We return to the *Beagle* at its first South American anchorage. Everyone was pleased with the beauties and social amenities of Bahia, not least Charles Darwin. A British man-of-war lay in the harbour, and Darwin was most impressed when in a competition in furling sail the little *Beagle* won. 'I suppose the Captain is a most excellent officer,' he wrote home.

Nineteen days at Bahia and they were moving on to survey the Abrolhos Islands, 400 miles south along the coast on the way to Rio. The existing charts were hopelessly inaccurate, and the *Beagle*'s job was a sort of *feeling* towards the islands and a hazar-

dous one at that: 'More than once we had four or five fathoms
under one side of the vessel, and from fifteen to twenty under the
other. These sudden and startling changes, called by the French
"*Sauts de sonde*", are very unpleasant and perplexing.' Darwin
must have been again impressed. Soon he was being stung into
quite enthusiastic praise. They had entered Rio harbour, where
lay the flagship of the British South American fleet, and another
piece of bravado and morale-boosting was indulged in. As they
passed the admiral's ship the crew took in every inch of canvas
and then immediately reset it. 'A sounding ship doing such a
perfect manoeuvre with such certainty and rapidity is an event
hitherto unknown in that class. It is a great satisfaction to know
that we are in such beautiful order and discipline.'

The Captain meanwhile had been indulging in nostalgia. For
he was back at Rio, where three and a half years ago he had been
given his great chance in the appointment to the *Beagle*, and
whither over a dozen years ago he had first come as Midshipman
in the *Glendower*. In his *Narrative* he tells how moved and impressed he had then been; and now he delayed the *Beagle*'s
entry until daylight, so that all might see the beautiful harbour
(and the Flagship see them). Alas, however, the charm and
novelty were gone. The Captain turned to the prosaic duty of
getting the *Beagle* repainted and recaulked.

Darwin, ashore, had time not only to botanize and geologize,
but to gather in his impressions and write home again. There
came soon, in a letter to his sister Caroline, this longer and
revealing assessment, couched in unusual superlatives:

And now for the Captain, as I daresay you feel some interest in
him. As far as I can judge, he is a very extraordinary person. I
never before came across a man whom I could fancy being a
Napoleon or Nelson. I should not call him clever, yet I feel convinced nothing is too great or too high for him. His ascendancy
over everybody is quite curious: the extent to which every
officer and man feels the slightest rebuke or praise, would have
been before seeing him, incomprehensible. It is very amusing to
see all hands hauling at a rope, they not supposing him on deck,
and then observe the effect when he utters a syllable; it is like a

string of dray horses, when the waggoner gives one of his awful smacks. His candour and sincerity are to me unparalleled, and using his own words his 'vanity and petulance' are nearly so. I have felt the effects of the latter: but the bringing into play the former ones so forcibly make one hardly regret them. His greatest fault as a companion is his austere silence: produced from excessive thinking: his many good qualities are great and numerous: altogether he is the strongest marked character I ever fell in with.

For a while after this the naturalist was relieved of his captain's austere silence. This was the result of a surprising development. Though FitzRoy could at times echo his Hydrographer's criticism of too great a meticulousness, yet he knew when such meticulousness was warranted; and if it were warranted then obviously there was no question but that it must be exercised. FitzRoy had discovered that his chronometers had unexpectedly shown an apparent error in the difference of longitude between Rio de Janiero and Bahia. All the way back to Bahia therefore did he order his ship—Darwin being allowed to remain on shore at Rio.

Back at Rio in a few weeks' time, FitzRoy found another opportunity to keep up the morale of his crew and to impress his admiral. To the amazement of the local inhabitants he organized a regatta. Darwin, the realist, confided to his diary: 'Racing was rather too long; especially as the *Beagle* did not come off quite so triumphantly as might have been wished for.' FitzRoy however, watching perhaps with both a more technically aware and more fatherly eye, was well satisfied. More light-hearted foot races on shore finished the day, and he was no doubt happy that the health and spirits of his ship's company had been further buttressed for a while.

When, four weeks later, the *Beagle* sailed out of Rio harbour to proceed on her mission, FitzRoy was proud to receive from the sailors he was leaving behind a salute to his ship of three hearty cheers. 'Strict etiquette might have been offended at such a compliment to a little ten-gun brig,' he writes, 'or, indeed, to any vessel unless she were going out to meet an enemy, or were returning into port victorious: but although not about to encounter a foe, our lonely vessel was going to undertake a task laborious, and often dangerous, to the zealous execution of which the encouragement of our brother-seamen was no trifling inducement.' He would be a hard man who would take exception to the sententiousness of that remark.

Eighteen days' sail southwards, and then the *Beagle* was entering the vast and dreary estuary of La Plata. Excitement with a slightly more serious background was in store for her captain and officers and crew.

Even to this present generation South America still seems a continent famed for political insecurity and for revolutions often more picturesque than real. In the times of the *Beagle*'s visits the insecurity was greater, and more new and raw. Escape from the bondage of Spanish rule was quite recent, in some places very recent, and in some instances regretted rather than enjoyed. Further and as a cross-current to this somewhat violent process of change, the bending of the native Indian will to European mastery was still in harsh process of being completed. When, therefore, after moving on from Monte Video and on entering the harbour of Buenos Aires, the *Beagle* was summarily fired upon by an Argentinian guardship, no one can have been intensely surprised. All were intensely affronted, however, and the more so when the empty discharge was followed by a live shot whistling over the *Beagle*'s rigging.

The Captain in his *Narrative* makes comparative light of this incident and of what followed. But not so Darwin, who, now as loyal a member of the crew as any, wrote this in his diary:

Before she could get another gun ready we had passed her range. When we arrived at our anchorage, which is more than three miles distant from the landing place, two boats were lowered, and a large party started in order to stay some days in the city. Wickham went with us, and intended immediately going to Mr Fox, the English minister, to inform him of the insult offered to the British flag. When close to the shore, we were met by a quarantine boat, which said we must all return on board, to have our bill of health inspected, from fears of the Cholera. Nothing which we could say about being a man of war—having left England

7 months, and lying in an open roadstead—had any effect. They said we ought to have waited for a boat from the guard-ship and that we must pull the whole distance back to the vessel, with the wind dead on end against us and a strong tide running in. During our absence, a boat had come with an officer, whom the Captain soon despatched with a message to his Commander to say, 'He was sorry he was not aware he was entering an uncivilized port, or he would have had his broadside ready for answering his shot.' When our boats and health one [quarantine boat] came alongside, the Captain immediately gave orders to get under way and return to M. Video. At the same time, sending to the Governor, through the Spanish officer, the same message which he had sent to the guard-ship, adding that the case should be thoroughly investigated in other quarters. We then loaded and pointed all the guns on one broadside, and ran down close along the guard-ship. Hailed her, and said, that when we again entered the port, we should be prepared as at present and if she dared to fire a shot we should send our whole broadside into her rotten hulk.

The *Beagle* then returned in a dignified manner to Monte Video, where the captain of a resident British frigate, the *Druid*, obligingly promised to sail to Buenos Aires on behalf of the *Beagle*, to perform her commission (which was the collection of some old Spanish charts that FitzRoy wanted) and to demand the necessary apology. 'Oh,' wrote the young and loyal and bloodthirsty Charles Darwin in his diary, 'I hope the Guard-ship will fire a gun at the Frigate; if she does, it will be her last day above water.'

It was not. But trouble now broke out at Monte Video,[1] traditional sort of trouble and where the *Beagle* was more likely to be importuned for help than insulted with warning shots.

That is in fact what happened. The Captain's account is sternly unemotional:

Scarcely had the *Druid* disappeared beneath the horizon, when the chief of the Monte Video police and the captain of the port came

[1] Though both towns are in the La Plata estuary Buenos Aires and Monte Video stand a hundred miles apart and have very different histories behind them, the latter being originally a colony of the former.

on board the *Beagle* to request assistance in preserving order in the town, and in preventing the aggressions of some mutinous Negro soldiers. I was also requested by the Consul-general to afford the British residents any protection in my power; and understanding that our lives, as well as property, were endangered by the turbulent mutineers, who were more than a match for the few well-disposed soldiers left in the town, I landed some fifty well-armed men, and remained on shore, garrisoning the principal fort, and thus holding the mutineers in check, until more troops were brought in from the neighbouring country, by whom they were surrounded and reduced to subordination. The *Beagle*'s crew were on shore more than twenty-four hours, and were not called upon to act in any way; but I was told by the principal persons whose lives and property were threatened, that the presence of those seamen certainly prevented bloodshed.

Darwin's account, since it was not written for the public eye, is somewhat more colourful. It dates July 5th 1832:

This has been an eventful day in the history of the *Beagle*. At 10 o'clock in the morning the Minister from the present military government came on board and begged for assistance against a serious insurrection of some black troops. Captain FitzRoy immediately went ashore to ascertain whether it was a party affair, or that the inhabitants were really in danger of having their houses ransacked. The head of the Police (Dumas) had continued in power through both governments, and is considered as entirely neutral; being applied to, he gave it as his opinion that it would be doing a service to the state to land our force. Whilst this was going on ashore, the [South] Americans landed their boats and occupied the Custom house. Immediately the Captain arrived at the mole, he made the signal to hoist out and man our boats. In a very few minutes the Yawl, Cutter, Whaleboats and Gig were ready with 52 men heavily armed with Muskets, Cutlasses and Pistols. After waiting some time on the pier Signor Dumas arrived and we marched to a central fort, the seat of government. During this time the insurgents had planted artillery to command some of the streets, but otherwise remained quiet. They had previously broken open the prison and armed the prisoners. The chief cause of apprehension was owing to their being in possession of the citadel, which contains all the ammunition. It is suspected that all this

disturbance is owing to the manoeuvring of the former consti-
tutional government. But the politics of the place are quite unin-
telligible: it has always been said that the interest of the soldiers
and the present government are identical; and now it would seem
to be the reverse. Capt. FitzRoy would have nothing to do with
all this: he would only remain to see that private property was
not attacked...Whilst the different parties were trying to ne-
gotiate matters, we remained at our station and amused ourselves
by cooking beefsteaks in the Courtyard.   At sunset the boats
were sent on board and one returned with warm clothing for the
men to bivouac during the night. As I had a bad headache, I also
came and remained on board. The few left in the ship, under the
command of Mr Chaffers [Ship's Master] have been most busily
engaged of the whole crew. They have triced up the Boarding
netting, loaded and pointed the guns and cleared for action. We
are now at night in a high state of preparation so as to make the
best defence possible, if the *Beagle* should be attacked. To obtain
ammunition could be the only possible motive.

On the next day the affair seemed likely to fizzle out, or at least
to develop into something relatively harmless to the British
residents, and FitzRoy, deeming himself in danger of becoming
embroiled and of not being able to retain his neutrality, decided
to pull out. Darwin, who the day before had been cooking steaks
in the courtyard with the rest, ends on the following note:

> There certainly is a great deal of pleasure in the excitement of
> this sort of work; quite sufficient to explain the reckless gaiety
> with which sailors undertake even the most hazardous attacks.
> Yet as time flies, it is an evil to waste so much in empty parade.

This seems a little unfairly critical. Perhaps Darwin felt the
need to assert his unromantic, professional, civilian outlook, if
only to his diary. But not much more than twenty-four hours
had been lost, and the most prudent commander could hardly have
withdrawn much sooner. In any case the Ruritanian episode was
over. Soon, and at the prospect of leaving in a little while for
wilder parts, Darwin is making amends. 'The only thing un-
propitious,' he wrote home, 'is the ferocity of the Indians. But I
would sooner go with the Captain with 10 men, than with any-

body else with 20. He is so very prudent and watchful as long as possible, and so resolutely brave when pushed to it.'

Only one tragedy had so far come to mar and disturb the voyage's confident air of success. In early May, while the ship was receiving its coat of paint in Rio harbour, various land excursions were allowed, one a sporting trip up river where the party stayed out for the night. The result was that a man and two boys died from contracting malaria, one being the midshipman, Musters. Everyone was profoundly affected, and particularly both FitzRoy and Darwin over the death of Musters. Darwin wrote that only two days before his end the unhappy boy had heard of the death of his mother; FitzRoy, that this poor little friend of his was everybody's favourite and had been entrusted to his own particular care. The connection between mosquitoes and the disease was not then known and neither prevention nor cure were efficient. It cannot have helped FitzRoy so very much —remembering happier results from Phillimore's care in *Thetis* days—that the ship's doctor assured him that everything possible had been done.

CHAPTER 8

The Return of the Fuegians

On board the *Beagle* were Jemmy Button, Fuegia Basket, York Minster, and their missionary tutor, Richard Matthews. The exercise which, if by no means the ship's company's main task, was at least the prime cause for their being on board at all, had still to be accomplished. It was to cause the Captain a good deal of anxiety and, though the final scene of the drama of his strange and wilful philanthropy was not yet, a good deal of heart-burning and self-questioning as well.

It is difficult to realize that for a whole twelvemonth from the date of sailing the Fuegians were either on board or with some member of the crew ashore. Until the time comes for them to be taken back to where they belong there is no more than a passing reference to them by Darwin and very little mention indeed by FitzRoy: we learn that Fuegia Basket was housed ashore during the ship's stay at Rio and that Jemmy and York were in the same town taken to see a friend of the Captain's; but that is all. One imagines them still having their practical needs and their discipline looked to by the obviously kindly and patient bo'sun, Bennett; one imagines them at times having the run of the ship and making themselves useful, at times cooped up somewhere with their new mentor, the young Matthews. Matthews had been provided with a long letter of 'suggestions and counsel' from the friends who were sending him out. He was told how much FitzRoy and the Reverend Wilson of Walthamstow had done for the natives, and was recommended to consult freely with the former and cheerfully to conform to his wishes. His paramount duty, the letter continued, was to do for these poor creatures, the Fuegians, all the good in his power and in every practical way; this would not be easy, but he must seek the grace of God. Descending to more practical detail, the letter reminded Matthews that the most urgent necessity for him was to learn the language of his charges. He should seek all the intercourse possible with them, note all new words spoken to him, and in his leisure classify them and reduce them to order, with a view to finally producing a grammar and dictionary. In imparting religious instruction to the natives he should make the Bible the basis of all his teaching. Captain FitzRoy would bring him back to England, 'should circumstances, contrary to our anticipations, turn out to be such that you should deem it unadvisable to remain at Tierra del Fuego.' Matthews, in fact, does not seem to have endeared himself to the Captain or to Darwin. The few references to him show a kind of grudging admiration, coupled with a doubt whether he was up to the job: it rather seems as if he were an insensitive prig, buoyed up by his faith and self-certainty.

When the time comes for the *Beagle* to head for Tierra del Fuego Darwin at last mentions the three natives in his journal and gives a revealing description of them. York Minster is described as a short, thick, powerful man, reserved, taciturn and morose, but intelligent and capable of strong friendships and, when excited, violently passionate. He was, Darwin says, very jealous of any attention paid to Fuegia Basket, whom he had determined to marry as soon as they were settled on shore. Fuegia is described as 'a nice, modest, reserved young girl', with a rather pleasing but sometimes sullen expression, and very quick in learning anything, especially languages. It is Jemmy Button, however, FitzRoy's last and more easterly acquisition, who obviously makes the greatest impression. He too is described as passionate; but his pleasanter disposition was shown in his often merry countenance, and he was the universal favourite on board. When Darwin was seasick Jemmy would express genuine concern and cry in a plaintive voice, 'Poor, poor fellow!' 'But the notion, after his aquatic life, of a man being seasick was too ludicrous and he was generally obliged to turn on one side to hide a smile or laugh.' Jemmy also had become a dandy: 'he used always to wear gloves, his hair was neatly cut, and he was distressed if his well-polished shoes were dirtied.' He liked too to look at himself in the mirror.

Although FitzRoy's determination to keep faith with his Fuegian charges and to bring them home again had been the prime cause of a second surveying trip, their landing with Matthews would after all only be a minor incident in the course of the ship's programme. So must have thought all on board. They knew however that the Fuegian coast was a savage one in every meaning of the word, and they accordingly prepared themselves with some excitement for its rigours. Against a cold climate and a rough time the officers grew their beards.

FitzRoy did more. During the last three months he had been supremely busy, accompanying Darwin on a rather strange inland expedition and buying on his own initiative two small schooners or 'cock boats'—activities which as they represent him at his most successful will be postponed for description until the next chapter. He now caused the *Beagle* to be stuffed with provisions to last for eight months at full allowance together with 'an extra supply of iron and coals for the forge, in case of any serious accident.' On November 27th 1832 the *Beagle* set sail from Monte Video. The ship and her crew had two supremely different experiences in front of them. One was a rounding of the Horn, agonizingly long drawn out and not far from ending in disaster. The other was the landing of the Fuegians. Which experience left the greater mark in the minds of those who suffered them it is impossible to say; but that they were comparable in intensity is obvious, and if we may judge by the comparative amount of space afforded to the two by Darwin and FitzRoy then, in spite of the severity of the storm, it was the Fuegian landing that remained more vividly in the memory.

Darwin began by being in fact remarkably optimistic about the storm that they met in rounding the Horn, not to say off-hand. He ended—besides being exhausted like the rest—a wiser man and with an increased admiration for his Captain's seamanship. The plan was to take York Minster to his home on Christmas Sound, which lay some hundred miles north-westwards past the Horn, then to round the point of Hoste Island and to proceed up the Beagle Channel eastwards until reaching the Murray Narrows and so south to Jemmy Button's home on Ponsonby Sound; the intended further survey of the Beagle Channel could then continue. In practice this plan was never carried out, nor needed to be, for reasons which will become apparent and are significant.

First, however, before the storm, there came a meeting on shore with a crowd of natives, not of any of the three protégés' tribes, but furnishing Matthews and most of the rest of the *Beagle* crew with what was their first sight of Fuegians in the raw. Darwin was profoundly impressed, was indeed shocked. Matthews confided to his Captain afterwards that 'they were no worse than he had supposed them to be.' The Captain himself seems to have stood back and observed with some anxiety what effect on his companions this first meeting would have.

It must have been a very strange meeting, but altogether rather a successful one. The Fuegians were very friendly, highly inquisitive and amusingly imitative, and they proved less inclined than usual to show their propensity to cadge everything they saw and steal if they could not cadge. There is the scene of Darwin walking in friendly intercourse with a hideously painted old man, being invited by signs to show his friendship by patting the fellow's back and chest, and being favoured with the same treatment in return. FitzRoy's boat-crew and the natives danced and sang for each other's benefit; and the Captain only prudently put a stop to the friendly proceedings when wrestling between the two sides was begun. The reactions of both York and Jemmy were not very favourable; they laughed and mocked and would not acknowledge these Fuegians as their countrymen.

Only one person really pleased the Captain by his reaction. This was Lieutenant Hamond, an earlier protégé of his from the *Thetis* days who had transferred to his command from the *Druid*. 'I can never forget', FitzRoy was to write, 'Mr Hamond's earnest expression, "What a pity such fine fellows should be left in such a barbarous state!" It told me that a desire to benefit these ignorant, though by no means contemptible human beings, was a natural emotion, and not the effect of individual caprice or erroneous enthusiasm; and that his feelings were exactly in unison with those I had experienced on former occasions, which had led to my undertaking the heavy charge of those Fuegians whom I brought to England.' Hamond's was obviously a much more satisfactory emotion than that of his friend Darwin, which was going to lead that naturally scientifically-minded person to write objectively in his diary: '…without exception the most curious and interesting spectacle I ever beheld. I would not have believed how entire the difference between savage and civilized man is. It is greater than between a wild and domesticated animal.'

After this episode came the attempt to reach York Minster's home by passage round the Horn. All began well, and it looked as if the passage would be a calm and easy one, as it sometimes could be. Not until they were just past the Horn did the storm hit them. For two days the *Beagle* struggled, not falling to windward, yet gaining nothing. The Captain then decided to make for shelter. While passing Cape Spencer off Hermit Island the ship was met by such a furious hail squall that it was impossible for anyone to see or even look ahead and the Captain could only 'stand on at hazard'. Luck held however and at last the *Beagle* was safely anchored in seventeen fathoms of water and beneath the towering blackness of a great cliff. It was Christmas Eve. The ship and crew had nothing worse than the williwaws and cold damp weather to contend with, and, says FitzRoy, 'we kept our Christmas merrily.' Darwin, Sulivan and Hamond went on a climbing expedition, and let off some of their animal spirits by shouting for echoes and rolling large stones down the mountain side. FitzRoy however was busy observing the weather. The sunset, he noticed, was lurid. At midnight clouds of foam could be seen driven along the sea quite close to them, and hands had to be called out to drop a third anchor. Not until New Year's Eve did FitzRoy dare put to sea again.

The next fourteen days on the little *Beagle* must have been the most unpleasant that its occupants ever spent. The ship battled to make headway, sometimes gaining it, sometimes losing it, constantly changing canvas to take advantage of a safe wind or to avoid disaster from a terrific one. On the third day they were off their course, racing past the islands some fifty miles west-south-west of the Horn called Diego Ramirez. Three days later the same islands were sighted again. When Darwin at breakfast, confident in his captain's ability, expressed a too easy optimism, FitzRoy told him to wait till they shipped a sea. On January the 13th they did so. At three in the morning, says the Captain in his narrative, he reluctantly took in the main-topsail, close-reefed as it was. 'At ten, there was so continued and heavy a rush of wind, that even the diminutive trysails oppressed the vessel too much, and they were still further reduced. Soon after one, the sea had risen to a great height, and I was anxiously watching the successive waves, when three huge rollers approached, whose size and steepness at once told me that our sea-boat, good as she was, would be sorely tried. Having steerage way, the vessel met and rose over the first unharmed, but, of course, her way was checked; the second deadened her way completely, throwing her off the wind; and the third great sea, taking her right a-beam, turned her so far over that all the lee bulwark, from the cat-head to the stern davit, was two or three feet under water. For a moment, our position was critical; but like a cask, she rolled back again, though with some feet of water over the whole deck. Had another sea then struck her, the little ship might have been numbered among the many of her class which have disappeared.'

Later that evening the storm abated and the worst was over. Another whale boat had been lost, damaged beyond repair; some of Darwin's specimens were in the same state, which no doubt helped to make him a sadder and wiser man. With a net gain of only about twenty-five miles north-westwards to his credit, entertaining the conviction that he had survived the worst storm he had ever experienced—a conviction strengthened later by the news that other ships in the vicinity had sunk—Captain FitzRoy doubled back between his previous anchorage and False Cape Horn and made his way north and east to quiet and safety. At the sheltered harbour beyond Nasau Bay called Goree Roads he anchored.

Then occurred the alteration in the Captain's plans. It came from a change of mind on the part of the difficult and unlikable York Minster. FitzRoy was later to impute sinister motives to this change, but at least an added reason may have been York's fear of having to go through such another fourteen days as he had just experienced. He obligingly announced that he and his affianced bride, Fuegia, were quite willing to forego shipment to their home country and to be taken to live with Jemmy's tribe.

FitzRoy at the time was very glad of the concession. It meant that a way could be made round the eastern end of Navarin Island and through the sheltered Beagle Channel to Jemmy's home ground at Ponsonby Sound and thereby a considerable amount of time saved in getting back to the proper duties of surveying. It also meant that Matthews could have all three of his English-speaking Fuegians—such as their English was—on the spot to help him. With the *Beagle* staying at anchor, a boat expedition was at once prepared, for what was hoped would be the successful and culminating act of the Captain's long philanthropic venture.

It was now that Darwin, watching the soup tureens and other impedimenta being unloaded from the hold into the *Beagle*'s yawl, made his strictures on the intelligence of the friends of the missionary venture. This utterly improbable scene enacted at the tip of the American continent does indeed fittingly set the seal of dreamlike quality which both narrators, FitzRoy and Darwin, seem to feel in their description of the next few days.

The dream began almost as beautifully as any pantomime's transformation. In summer weather that for once was fine, through this strange, straight narrow channel, the Beagle Channel, that gave glimpses of great snow-peaked mountains, but whose calm waters were almost touched by overhanging branches, the procession of the laden yawl and its accompanying three whaleboats glided silently along. As the evening approached, FitzRoy chose for camping a beach snugly sheltered by small islands. 'Here,' wrote Darwin, 'we pitched our tents and lighted our fires. Nothing could look more romantic than this scene; the tents supported by the oars, and the smoke curling up the wooded valley formed a picture of quiet and retirement.' The retiring company comprised, besides the four people who were the cause of them all being there, FitzRoy, Darwin, Hamond, Bynoe the surgeon, Bennett the bo'sun, one mate, one midshipman and about twenty sailors and marines.

The first disturbing note was struck when on the next day, passing through more thickly populated country, the boats attracted the excited attention of the natives, who ran yelling beside them. It was the reaction of the three Fuegians in the boats that was surprising. They were, quite simply, horrified. 'Monkeys—dirty—fools—not men!' declared York and Jemmy, both assuring the Captain that these men were vastly inferior in all ways to their own tribes. As for Fuegia (who had not been at the previous meeting) she was so shocked and shamed that she hid herself and would not look on shore a second time. Obviously the three of them, with their tidy hair and in their European clothes, had completely forgotten in the course of three years what their compatriots could be like. It was not a very good omen.

That evening, in an effort to choose a site not likely to be molested, the Captain had to force his tired crew to row farther than he would have liked and to be content with a far less idyllic resting place. His caution was justified when in the morning a party of natives appeared and menaced them with stones. Completely ignorant as they were of the meaning or power of fire-arms, it was difficult to get rid of them without bloodshed. A skirmish was, however, avoided.

The next two days, in continued fine weather and so warm that some of the crew bathed, the party made its way through unin-habited country, a sort of neutral ground, the Captain understood from Jemmy, between the previous 'fools and monkeys' and

Jemmy's own tribe. Then fresh savages began to appear; and they were of Jemmy's tribe and they were, if anything, more abject and more degraded. Two further shocks were now administered, one to the Captain and one to Jemmy. It became apparent that Jemmy experienced considerable difficulty in understanding or making himself understood: he had largely forgotten his own language, a possibility that FitzRoy had never envisaged.

Jemmy's shock was news that his father was dead. His reactions were watched with interest. He looked very grave, reminded Bennett that he had already dreamt of this death, then collected green boughs, set them alight and watched the smoke rise upwards. That done, he rejoined the company and, observing philosophically, 'Me no help it!', proceeded to talk and laugh as usual. Camp had been made, and that night, round the blaze of the great fire which the men as usual built, Jemmy told tales in his pidgin English of fights between his own tribe and the bad men whom they had met on the first day, while the naked men of his own tribe stood around, friendly but uncomprehending, and—so Darwin noticed—sweating profusely. While the crew sang songs and the natives tried rather ridiculously to join in, FitzRoy was keeping as ever, a watchful eye. His party had now turned south out of the Beagle Channel into the Murray Narrows and would soon be in the neighbourhood of Ponsonby Sound and the home ground of Jemmy Button, called Woollya. On the morrow, therefore, a good site of the intended missionary settlement must be found. 'I was much gratified,' FitzRoy wrote, 'by seeing that Matthews still looked at his hazardous undertaking as steadily as ever, betraying no symptom of hesitation.' York Minster, however, was being a little difficult in his absurd jealousy for Fuegia, picking a quarrel with one of the crew who had always been his friend.

Meanwhile and through the night the news of Jemmy's return was being spread amongst his tribe.

The next morning, as everyone was helping to strike camp, a disconcerting sight met their eyes. Natives came running down to them from the hills. Painted black and white and red, they were sweating profusely and flecked with blood; as they chattered excitedly they foamed at the mouth. It was a little difficult to realize that the blood was not the result of battle but of exertion, coming from their noses, and that what was being observed was nothing more sinsister than a lot of natives in a high state of excitement.

Scarcely were the boats stowed and embarked than canoes began to appear over the water in every direction. In each a native stood and shouted at the top of his very powerful voice. From the centre of each rose smoke from the fire that these Fuegians carried.

The morning was fine and beautiful, and more than ever there was a dreamlike quality about the scene. The Englishmen's boats floated on a lake-like expanse of still blue water, across which the nearby cliffs cast deep shadows and beyond which the snow-capped mountains glittered in the early rays of the sun. And on this calm expanse of water came more and more native canoes, while the cliffs echoed with the stentorian shouts of those who were in them. Nobody could have been aware quite how triumphal or how innocent this procession was. FitzRoy wisely urged his men to remain at the head of it. To his relief a slight breeze arose to enable his boats to use their sails and so to keep ahead.

At last they were approaching Woollya, and FitzRoy was looking out for a place for his intended settlement. Again he was fortunate; a likely open space appeared and he ordered a landing. Jemmy Button, desperately anxious that something about his people and his country should give a good impression, was delighted that his Captain appeared pleased. Clear spaces of pasture land, well watered by brooks, were here backed by wooded hills; the presence of flowers, FitzRoy noted approvingly, augured well for the seeds that they intended to sow. At once the men were told to mark out a boundary line; and everyone was relieved to see that the native canoes did not follow them to this shore, but landed at a nearby cove.

There began now five days of hard work, work that went well ahead in spite of a deterioration in the weather. Wood was cut and sawn; three long huts or wigwams began to take shape; the stores and utensils were carried up; two gardens were dug; potatoes and the seed of carrot, turnip, bean, pea, lettuce, onion, leek and cabbage were sown. The Fuegians, leaving their women behind to work, strolled over to watch, and very occasionally to help. FitzRoy watched and supervised. Before the day was out there occurred an incident that should have been pleasing and affecting but was only surprising and disappointing:

> While I was engaged in watching the proceedings at our encampment, and poor Jemmy was getting out of temper at the quizzing he had to endure on account of his countrymen, whom he had extolled so highly until in sight, a deep voice was heard shouting from a canoe more than a mile distant: up started Jemmy from a bag of nails and tools which he was distributing, leaving them to be scrambled for by those nearest, and, upon a repetition of the shout, exclaimed 'My brother!' He then told me that it was his eldest brother's voice, and perched himself on a large stone to watch the canoe, which approached slowly, being loaded with several people. When it arrived, instead of an eager meeting, there was a cautious circumspection which astonished us. Jemmy walked slowly to meet the party, consisting of his mother, two sisters, and four brothers. The old woman hardly looked at him before she hastened away to secure her canoe and hide her property...The girls ran off with her without even looking at Jemmy; and the brothers (a man and three boys) stood still, stared, walked up to Jemmy, and all round him, without uttering a word. Animals when they meet show far more animation and anxiety than was displayed at their meeting. Jemmy was evidently much mortified, and to add to his confusion and disappointment, as well as my own, he was unable to talk to his brothers, except by broken sentences, in which English predominated.

Darwin's comments on this episode, in his diary and journal, are very much in line with FitzRoy's. The meeting was 'not so interesting as that of two horses in a field.' He does add however that they heard afterwards from York (who having been less anxious to learn another language had remembered his own better) that Jemmy's mother was said to have been inconsolable at the time of her loss. As for Jemmy himself, 'it was laughable, but almost pitiable, to hear him speak to his wild brother in English, and then ask him in Spanish (*"no sabe?"*) whether he did not understand him.'

A fresh anxiety assailed FitzRoy on the fifth day. Mostly the relationship between his men and the Fuegians continued excellent, Jemmy's brothers being given nicknames, and the crew being tactful and skilful in keeping those natives who were not helping on the right side of the boundary trench. This business of the boundary line however did prove increasingly difficult to handle. Finally one old man, on being warned off, spat in the sentry's face and then, bending over a sleeping companion, but looking towards the sentry, went through a pantomime which looked like that of skinning and cutting up a man and seemed obviously to mean 'that is the way I would like to treat you!' He and his companions had obviously been very angry.

That evening FitzRoy thought fit to have a little musketry practice, and to put the targets in good view of the watching Fuegians. He had to remember that there were something like three hundred Fuegians in the vicinity, out-numbering his party by about ten to one, and that with their tremendous strength and phenomenal accuracy with spear and stone their lack of firearms was no very great disadvantage.

The target practice, or the sentry episode or both, had a not necessarily bellicose, but certainly disconcerting reaction. When the next morning came not only did no Fuegians turn up, but it could be seen that all of them were striking camp. Soon there were no more than half a dozen natives remaining anywhere. Had they been frightened, or angered, or merely bored? Jemmy, whose family had gone with the rest, could give no clue. Were they planning an attack? In the night a sentry had seen a man skulking round the tents. Was he a spy, or merely a potential thief?

The huts were now ready and all that could be done had been done. FitzRoy had to make his decision. He seems to have thought that in the event of there being an attack on his men Matthews and his charges might be better off if whatever sort of battle ensued did not take place over their compound. In any case both

York and Jemmy had no doubt that all would be well. And Matthews was as steady and as willing as ever. 'So, trusting that Matthews, in his honest intention to do good, would obtain that assistance in which he confided, I decided to leave him for a few days.' Taking the opportunity of landing the most precious of the stores while there were no prying Fuegian eyes to see, the party made their farewells, embarked, and set off. They spent the night in a nearby cove.

During the night FitzRoy changed his intended few days to one. He sailed straight back. On the way he gathered from the conversation of the sailors in his boat that some of them at least did not expect to find Matthews alive.

But all was well. Matthews, first espied carrying a kettle, was cheerful and unconcerned. Jemmy, with one of his brothers already returned, was confident that the rest of his family would arrive during the day and that those of the original crowd who were bad men and not of his tribe had returned to their own country. FitzRoy decided to give the little settlement a rather longer trial period and to carry out some local surveying along the Beagle Channel that would last about ten days.

With the yawl and one whaleboat sent back to the *Beagle*, but with his friends Darwin and Hamond retained amongst the party, FitzRoy sailed up into the channel named after his ship and so westwards, about his proper business. On the eighth day the job was done, and they were returning, their impatience appeased if not their anxiety by the fortune of a favourable wind and tide. FitzRoy had time to notice the phenomenon of a fire eating out the heart of a hollow tree, to speculate whether the slate in another place would be good enough for roofing. But his mind must have been elsewhere. Then they came upon natives; and these were fully painted, as if for raid or battle, and seemed defiant and on the defensive, as if they had already done some harm. Worse, they had upon their persons some linen cloth, lengths of ribbon, and scraps of red cloth: FitzRoy had not much doubt as to where these had come from. He carried on until the last of the light, and broke camp at dawn. Shooting through the Murray Narrows they saw more natives ornamented with strips

of linen and also of tartan cloth. FitzRoy and his party now had
no doubt at all. At noon they arrived at Woollya.

> Our boats touched the shore; the natives came hallooing and
> jumping about us, and then, to my extreme relief, Matthews
> appeared, dressed and looking as usual. After him came Jemmy
> and York, also dressed and looking well: Fuegia, they said, was in a
> wigwam.

But things were nowhere near so well as they looked. With
the Fuegians sitting on their hams along the shore line and
looking, thought FitzRoy, like a pack of hounds waiting for the
fox to be unearthed, the Captain and Darwin sat with Matthews
a few yards out in their boat and listened to his story. It was a
miserable one. He had been degraded and worn down by unre-
lenting petty insults, conduct that rose at times—at least so
Darwin thought—to calculated threats upon his life. Everything
possible was stolen from him, as it was also from Jemmy, though
York managed pretty well to hold his own. Even Jemmy's relations stole, and proudly showed their gains to other Fuegians.
Night and day, large parties of natives surrounded Matthews' hut
and he had to spend his time guarding his property. One old man,
on being ordered to leave the hut, came back brandishing a stone.
On one occasion a whole body of natives advanced with stones and
stakes, while Jemmy's brothers watched, crying. Believing that
they only came to rob, Matthews bought them off with presents.
Matters came to such a state that he was only unmolested if,
hiding his remaining belongings, he went to sit with the women.
The men teased him. They never left him alone. They pushed
him about, made faces at him, plucked the hair from his face
(it being unseemly in their eyes to be other than smooth-skinned).
One man held his head down by force, as if in contempt of his
strength. Very little, except those stores and tools and clothes that
had previously been hidden or that Matthews had managed to
hide, remained.

There was hardly any question as to what must be done, and
Matthews agreed that he had had enough. FitzRoy decided upon
prompt action. Giving the Fuegians as little time as possible to

realize that with their large numbers they could easily impose their will if they wished, he sent his men over the trampled garden to collect all Matthews' remaining belongings.

It remained only to say goodbye. Jemmy at least was very sad. He had even been robbed by his brother—'What fashion do you call that?' He was ashamed that he had not been able to keep his kinfolk from trampling over the gardens—'My people very bad, great fool, know nothing at all, very great fool!' He was quite confident, however, that he was in no danger from them. FitzRoy promised to come back in a few days' time.

Darwin wrote philosophical but not sanguine words in his diary:

> It was quite melancholy leaving our Fuegians amongst their barbarous countrymen. There was one comfort; they appeared to have no personal fears. But, in contradiction of what has often been stated, three years has been sufficient to change savages into, as far as habits go, complete and voluntary Europeans. York, who was a full grown man and with a strong violent mind, will I am certain and in every respect live as far as his means go, like an Englishman. Poor Jemmy looked rather disconsolate and certainly would have liked to have returned with us...I am afraid whatever other ends this excursion to England produces, it will not be conducive to their happiness. They have far too much sense not to see the vast superiority of civilized over uncivilized habits, yet I am afraid to the latter they must return.

Eight days later the anxious captain had come back once more to Woollya, alone except for his boat crew. He returned to the *Beagle* with such a satisfactory report that Darwin was induced to write: 'If the garden succeeds, this little settlement may be yet the means of producing great good and altering the habits of the truly savage inhabitants.' FitzRoy had said that he had found the seeds sprouting, in spite of the trampling. He also found his three charges still clothed, and busy and happy. Even Jemmy's mother was now clothed. Jemmy was happy because he said he had beaten off a foray by strangers, though he admitted he had himself been further robbed. He seemed confident and contented. Fuegia was neat and tidy; and York was busy making a canoe.

FitzRoy left with sanguine hopes of good yet to be done by his returned charges. 'I hoped that through their means our motives in taking them to England would become understood and appreciated among their associates, and that a future visit might find them so favourably disposed towards us, that Matthews might then undertake, with a far better prospect of success, that enterprise which circumstances had obliged him to defer, though not to abandon altogether.'

All in fact was not lost, and FitzRoy could tell himself that his scheme had not necessarily failed. A year was to go by before he was to see Jemmy Button again.

CHAPTER 9

Wish Unconquerable, Hope Deferred

THE highly personal project of the education of the Fuegian natives having met with at least partial failure, nothing must stand in the way of the success of the main venture, the surveying voyage. Within a month of the final departure from Woollya, FitzRoy, moving across on his surveying work to the Falkland Islands, had purchased a schooner of 170 tons burthen.

FitzRoy had long become convinced that he needed a supplementary schooner as much as had King, and he did not intend to suffer the penalty that King had suffered, of having half a season wasted for him while he waited for Admiralty permission. Already he had hired two very small schooners, or 'cock boats' as he called them, of nine and fifteen tons burthen respectively; and while the *Beagle* was engaged at Woollya and across in the Falklands these two tiny ships, one with a cabin only thirty inches high, had been doing great work surveying the Patagonian coast. It says much for what FitzRoy could unquestioningly demand from his subordinates that Lieutenants Wickham and Stokes spent eight months in them, amongst other things experiencing in the open sea the gale that had nearly sunk the *Beagle* off the Horn. FitzRoy had hired the little schooners from a colourful character called Harris, who will be met with in the next chapter when we come to consider the relationships of FitzRoy and Darwin and to describe some of the experiences they shared as companions. FitzRoy had agreed to pay £140 a month for the hire of these boats—this was in September 1832—but he had also agreed to give them up again at the end of eight months. When that time came he would, he realized, be as badly off, and the *Beagle* as unsupported and lonely, as ever.

Now, in the Falklands, FitzRoy met another colourful character. This was Captain Low, a tough and energetic and ruthless sealing ship owner, well known in the southern seas.

Captain Low arrived in the Falklands soon after FitzRoy, in his schooner the *Unicorn*. The phenomenally stormy season had, he said, well nigh ruined him. He was willing to sell his schooner.

'At this time,' wrote FitzRoy in the *Narrative*, 'I had become more fully convinced than ever that the *Beagle* could not execute her allotted task before she, and those in her, would be so much in need of repair and rest, that the most interesting part of her voyage—the carrying a chain of meridian distances around the globe—must eventually be sacrificed to the tedious, although not less useful, details of coast surveying. Our working ground lay so far from ports at which supplies could be obtained, that we were obliged to occupy whole months in making passages merely to get provisions, and then overload our little vessel to a most inconvenient degree, as may be supposed, when I say that eight months' provisions was our usual stock at starting, and that we sailed twice with ten months' supply on board. I had often anxiously longed for a consort.'

He needed for consort a ship that was adapted for carrying cargoes, rigged so as to be easily worked with few hands, and able to keep company with the *Beagle*. Captain Low's *Unicorn* was all of these things. 'When I saw the *Unicorn*, and heard how well she had behaved as a sea-boat my wish to purchase her was unconquerable.' The price was six thousand dollars or nearly £1,300, and she was built of oak from a British yard and reputed to have cost at least £6,000. All she needed was 'a few sheets of copper and an outfit of canvas and rope.' FitzRoy closed the deal— and spent a further £400 in purchasing canvas, cables and stores

from the remains of two local wrecks that had been caught by the
same storm as had nearly destroyed the *Beagle.*

In all other respects the sojourn in the Falkland Islands was
proving a rather anxious and depressing time. The weather was
execrable and the sudden storms a danger to the *Beagle,* even
though at anchor in Berkley Sound. The political situation on the
islands was delicate, as well as confusing.

There occurred now the death of Hellyer, the Captain's clerk
and a favourite. This was the occasion when the standing order
not to proceed on shore alone was fatally disobeyed. The lad,
letting his companion turn back on some good pretext, had swum
to retrieve a duck he had shot and had become entangled in the
kelp: the disinterested motive, FitzRoy believed, had probably
been a desire to get the duck for the Captain's collection. Darwin's
diary for March 5th 1833 reads: 'Mr Hellyer was buried on a
lonely and dreary headland. The procession was a melancholy
one: in front a Union Jack half mast high was carried, and over
the coffin the British ensign was thrown: the funeral from its
simplicity was the more solemn.' Only a few days after this sad
event there arrived Captain Low in his schooner.

And less than a month later, FitzRoy having signed the agreement and paid the stipulated price, the ship, renamed nostalgically the *Adventure,* was setting out under Mr Chaffers, the
master, to start her refit in the La Plata estuary. The unconquerable wish had been made to come true.

For the rest of his stay in the Falklands the Captain was in
good form again. At this juncture the island was going through
a somewhat difficult and unsatisfactory stage of her history, a
colonizing effort from Buenos Aires having petered out in failure
and Great Britain having announced her sovereignty over the
island, while doing remarkably little to establish it. FitzRoy
busied himself supporting the sole British resident, helping to
act as policeman, succouring and arranging transport for the
recently shipwrecked mariners, and—an act that on his next visit
he was to regret—persuading the gauchos who had been sent as
colonizers from Buenos Aires to remain usefully on the island.
Then at the end of April, hearing from Wickham and Stokes in

the cock boats, and sending off before him the newly christened *Adventure* to begin her refitting, he set out once more for a rendezvous off the Patagonian coast. All were glad to leave the dreary Falklands and hopeful at the prospect of having such a fine ship as the new schooner to help them get through the rest of their South American work and so at last into the Pacific and beyond. 'I can plainly see,' wrote Darwin to his sister, 'that there will not be much pleasure or contentment till we get out of these detestable latitudes, and are carrying on all sail to the land where bananas grow.' Wherever it was exactly that Darwin expected to see bananas, it was going to be a long while yet, and a good deal more was to happen, not all satisfactory, before he or any of his shipmates would be in a latitude where the existence of such fruit was even remotely possible.

Another visit to Tierra del Fuego had yet to be made. There was more surveying work waiting in that area; and there was the hope that Matthews might still be installed at Woollya. Meanwhile, through the winter months, there was the summer's work to be sifted, reported upon, charted; there was the *Adventure* to be brought into condition.

That condition had to be as near perfection as possible; and one thing has a habit of leading to another. Captain FitzRoy decided that his new ship would not be fit to work with the *Beagle* in the Pacific unless the whole of her bottom were coppered. Accordingly at Maldanado in the La Plata Estuary the job was undertaken. It meant that the *Beagle* had to be floated beside the *Adventure* and warped to her while the smaller vessel was heaved 'keel out'; and as the *Beagle* was of only seventy more tons burthen than the *Adventure* the job was impossible unless the sea was calm. FitzRoy spent many mornings exercizing his powers of weather forecasting and choosing for work only those dawns that promised an absence of swell on the waters.

Finally, on December 6th 1833, well stocked for another long summer cruise, companioned by her sister ship (Wickham in command) as FitzRoy had wished, the *Beagle* departed Monte

Video. Both vessels spent Christmas day off Port Desire, the crews dining off guanaco shot by Darwin and landing in the afternoon for wrestling and racing and games. Soon after, the new *Adventure* left for the Falkland Islands and the *Beagle* proceeded slowly down the coast, surveying as she went. For the purpose of chronometric readings FitzRoy proceeded up the Magellan Strait as far as Port Famine, this being the *Beagle*'s first visit to these parts on the second voyage. By the beginning of February they were out of the Straits again and surveying the eastern ocean coast of Tierra del Fuego, experiencing less storm weather than in the previous year. By the end of the month they were approaching Woollya and Jemmy Button's country once more, and the weather had deteriorated. Darwin in his diary allowed himself a little gentle sarcasm: 'Dear Tierra del has recollected her old winning ways. The ship is now starting and surging with her gentle breath. Oh the charming country!' On March 1st they had entered the Beagle Channel and were bartering with the natives: how much pleasanter, Darwin reflected, to do so from the commanding height and safety of the ship than to be on equal terms in a boat and at the mercy of their everlasting clamour. He had come to hate the Fuegians and their ever repeated shout, which he interpreted as 'Yammerschooner!' and said meant 'Give me!' On March 5th they were approaching the pleasant and fertile cove where the huts had been built and the gardens planted. What would they find?

They found the huts empty and deserted, the gardens neglected and downtrodden, and all a dead silence. In the silence they dug up a few potatoes and turnips—the Captain and Darwin had them later for dinner, and they were, reflected FitzRoy, optimistically, 'of a fair size'.

They returned on board, but still kept a good look out. Suddenly three canoes were seen racing towards them, not from the shore or Wollya but from nearby Button Island. The occupants were hailing them. FitzRoy wrote:

> Looking through a glass I saw that two of the natives in them were washing their faces, while the rest were paddling with might and main: I was then sure that some of our acquaintances

were there, and in a few minutes recognized Tommy Button, Jemmy's brother. In the other canoe was a face which I knew but could not name. 'It must be some one I have seen before,' said I,—when his sharp eye detected me, and a sudden movement of the hand to his head (as a sailor touches his hat) at once told me it was indeed Jemmy Button.

Darwin in his description said that after the salute Jemmy turned away his face in shame; FitzRoy wrote that he could hardly restrain his own feelings. For how different a Jemmy Button it was. His once smoothed hair was long and matted like his companions'; his body was wretchedly thin and as naked as theirs.

It was the same Jemmy nevertheless, and he had not forgotten his English. He was hurried below, combed and dressed, and taken to dine with Darwin and the Captain.

Jemmy used his knife and fork as well as ever, and he was very cheerful. In spite of his emaciated appearance he assured his listeners that he was very well—'hearty, sir, never better!'—that he managed to get 'plenty fruit and birdies, then guanoco in snow time, and too much fish.' He was very happy, and did not wish to be taken away again.

After dinner Jemmy met some of his old friends and was particularly glad to see the ship's doctor and Bo'sun Bennett. Then something of the reason for his contentment became apparent. A canoe arrived with a good-looking girl—good-looking for a Fuegian as FitzRoy put it—who proved to be his wife. She was loaded with presents, but did not seem very happy until her husband was restored to her.

Jemmy went ashore for the night but came back the next morning for breakfast and a long talk with the Captain.

That must have been a strange interview and the ensuing farewell a poignant experience for all concerned, not least the Captain. Jemmy had told a story that at any rate showed his nakedness not to have been merely in the way of relapse. York Minster, having built his canoe, and after a somewhat disastrous raid by the 'bad' men, persuaded Jemmy and his mother to come with him to have a look at his own country. But on nearing his home, he and Fuegia had crept off into the night, taking all

Jemmy's belongings with them in their big canoe and leaving Jemmy literally as naked and propertyless as when FitzRoy had first found him. All this, FitzRoy believed, York Minster had planned from the day he had obliged the Captain in the matter of his landing. Jemmy had returned home with his mother, and then had decided to move across to Button Island, as being safer from his raiding enemies—in any case the huts had proved too cold to live in through the winter.[1]

So that was the end of an affair. There had been no improvement, only the reverse; there could be no question of leaving Matthews behind a second time. It remained only to say goodbye.

There was a great giving and taking of presents. Jemmy and his wife were loaded. Jemmy for his part had prepared two precious otter skins for 'Cap'n' and one for Bennett; for Darwin were two spear-heads, and a quiver full of arrows to be taken back to Mr Wilson of Walthamstow. Then Jemmy left the deck of the *Beagle* for the last time and paddled away in his canoe. As the *Beagle* stood on her course for the open sea a column of smoke rose up from the land.

As FitzRoy watched that long and last signal of farewell from Jemmy Button his thoughts must have been many and mixed and not very happy. He committed to paper only the more hopeful ones.[2] Jemmy, he observed, did after all have some influence among his family, who were even now using many English words. Everyone had been remarking that they were more humanized than any other Fuegians they had met, more trustful, more amenable. Surely the first step towards the civilization of these natives, that of obtaining their confidence, had been made. One individual, with limited means, could do no more. But even so, perhaps some day some shipwrecked seaman would receive help and kindness from Jemmy Button's children, 'prompted as they cannot fail to be, by the traditions they will have heard of

[1] No more was ever heard of York. But Sulivan, according to a footnote in Darwin's *Journal* (Ch. X), heard, about 1842, from a sealer of a Fuegian woman who came aboard and who spoke some English. 'She lived (I fear the term probably bears a double interpretation) some days on board.'

[2] Pages 326 and 327 of Volume II of the *Narrative*.

men of other lands; and by an idea, however faint, of their duty to God as well as to their neighbour.'

Darwin too put down optimistic words in his diary, and a tribute to his friend in the *Journal*. 'I hope and have little doubt that he (Jemmy) will be as happy as if he had never left his country; which is much more than I formerly thought.' And: 'Everyone must sincerely hope that Captain FitzRoy's noble hope may be fulfilled, of being rewarded for the many generous sacrifices which he made for the Fuegians, by some ship-wrecked sailor being protected by the descendants of Jemmy Button and his tribe.'

All these were not high hopes, only hopes pious and deferred. The strange, optimistic, high-handed venture had in truth failed—as any twentieth century person could have foretold that it would fail. But Captain FitzRoy was not living in the twentieth century.

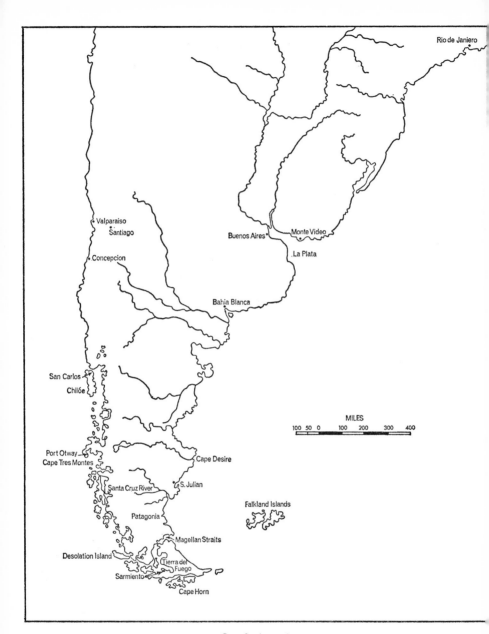

Rio de Janiero

Valparaiso
Santiago

Concepcion

Buenos Aires   Monte Video

.La Plata

Bahia Blanca

San Carlos
Chilóe

MILES
100 50 0   100   200   300   400

Port Otway
Cape Tres Montes

Cape Desire

Santa Cruz River   .S. Julian

Patagonia   Falkland Islands

Magellan Straits

Desolation Island

Tierra del
Fuego

Sarmiento

Cape Horn

South America

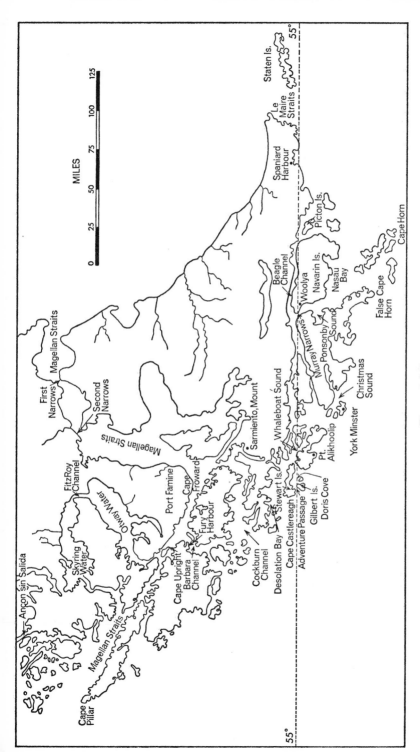

Tierra del Fuego

CHAPTER 10

Mutual Irritation and Mutual Aid

'FitzRoy's character was a singular one...
FitzRoy's temper was a most unfortunate one.' So wrote Charles
Darwin when forty-odd years later he compiled a short autobiography for the benefit of his children. As a half-term assessment between this and the first naïve, enthusiastic 'beau ideal
of a captain' there comes the letter to his sister already quoted,
in which FitzRoy is called the strongest marked character ever
yet met and one perhaps capable of being a Napoleon or a Nelson,
though suffering from the faults, self-confessed, of vanity and
petulance. The mature judgement is far from being so adulatory.
It is very, very far from being a condemnation, however. It is
rather a sort of retrospective sigh of irritated admiration, or of
admiring irritation, coupled with a pity which is nevertheless
not patronizing. Darwin writes more about FitzRoy in his *Autobiography* than any other person, and it will be well to quote
from what he says.

First the 'singularness' of character is qualified by the addition,
'with many noble features'. And these are enumerated. FitzRoy
was 'devoted to his duty, generous to a fault, bold, determined,
indomitably energetic, and an ardent friend to all under his
sway.' As to the possession of an unfortunate temper, this re-
ceives greater elaboration:

This was shown not only by passion but by fits of long-continued moroseness against those who had offended him. His temper was usually worst in the early morning, and with his eagle eye he could generally detect something amiss about the ship, and was then unsparing in his blame. The junior officers when they relieved each other in the forenoon used to ask 'whether much hot coffee had been served out this morning',—which meant how was the Captain's temper? He was also somewhat suspicious and occasionally in very low spirits, on one occasion bordering on insanity. He seemed to me often to fail in sound judgement or common sense. He was extremely kind to me, but was a man very difficult to live with on the intimate terms which necessarily followed our messing by ourselves in the same cabin. We had several quarrels; for when out of temper he was utterly un-reasonable...The difficulty of living on good terms with a Captain of a Man-of-War is much increased by its being almost mutinous to answer him as one would answer anyone else.

A couple of instances of quarrels that verge on the serious are mentioned by Darwin. These will shortly be cited. What will be attempted in the rest of this chapter is a consideration of the reaction of these two strong characters, FitzRoy and Darwin, upon one another, and a description of some of their more outstanding adventures together while cruising around the southern shores of South America, so that the reader may himself be the better able to consider that reaction.

Reference has already been made to the irony of the fact that FitzRoy, increasingly 'fundamentalist' in his religion, should have taken of all people on his voyage Charles Darwin and, by the very fact of that voyage, should have helped to shape the great evolutionary ideas. So far as the voyage itself goes however, that aspect may easily be exaggerated. It is Darwin and not FitzRoy who is laughed at by the other officers on one occasion for quoting the Bible as clinching an argument—and it is, after all, not until 1859 that there appeared *The Origin of Species*. Nora Barlow, who has done so much to edit and expound the diaries and note-books of Darwin, her grandfather, thinks she detects in these notebooks greater trace of evolutionary ways of thinking than was allowed to appear in the published journal and suggests that this holding back might be in deference to FitzRoy and from a desire not to offend him. By substituting evolutionary theory for a Biblical literal interpretation of our world, Darwin destroyed a view already tottering; but in the *Beagle* days, beyond finding FitzRoy's literal acceptance of Biblical creation untenable, he was more or less outwardly orthodox. Charles Darwin was a nice, enthusiastic, hardworking, open-hearted, even-tempered, very kindly-disposed young man—by nature scientifically rather than emotionally minded no doubt, but no more. If young Darwin had been lucky to get the job, young FitzRoy had been lucky to get Darwin: mutual irritation there was bound to be, but mutual aid and support and respect there was also.

FitzRoy was quick to appreciate Darwin's qualities. Early in the voyage he is writing to Beaufort the Hydrographer, 'Darwin is a very sensible hard-working man, and a very pleasant messmate. I never saw a "shore-going fellow" come into the ways of a ship so soon and so thoroughly as Darwin.' In a later letter Darwin is 'a regular Trump'. It must be remembered that Darwin had only so far been an amateur naturalist and geologist, having recently come down from Cambridge where he had taken an ordinary classical degree with a view to becoming a clergyman. He was very much on trial, therefore, but also very much aware that he had been given a miraculous chance to do what he really wanted to do. He was one vast enthusiasm, therefore, ready to meet and foster his Captain's enthusiasm when his Captain was in such a mood.

There were of course differences of background between the two, other than that Darwin was a shore-going fellow. It cannot have been often that FitzRoy seemed to flaunt his aristocracy under the nose of this scion of a Midland doctor and a manufacturer's daughter, he was too much of a gentleman for that. But there are at the beginning amusing traces of this; and more seriously, the two violent quarrels that Darwin cites have perhaps the difference in background as their fundamental cause. On reaching South America Darwin very much appreciated the fact that when in port he found himself being taken with the Captain to visit and dine with the aristocrats of the English colonies and the important Spaniards. There is, nevertheless, one irritated aside in a letter to his sister Caroline at this time: 'I must tell you for your instruction that the Captain says Miss Austen's novels are on everybody's table, which solely means the Jerseys, Londonderrys, etc.'—i.e. FitzRoy's family or connections.

Perhap aristocrats in particular do not like having their veracity questioned, and FitzRoy seems to have been particularly touchy on this count. There occurred a minor incident to illustrate this sensitivity a few days before the *Beagle* sailed from Plymouth, and a more serious incident at about the time of the Jane Austen complaint. At Plymouth FitzRoy had rather thrown his weight about in rebuking a dealer in crockery who had annoyed him. 'The Captain asked the man the price of a very expensive set of china and said, "I should have purchased this if you had not been so disobliging." As I knew that the cabin was amply stocked with crockery, I doubted whether he had any such intention; and I must have shown my doubts in my face, for I said not a word. After leaving the shop he looked at me, saying, You do not believe what I have said, and I was forced to own that it was so. He was silent for a few minutes and then said, You are right, and I acted wrongly in my anger at the blackguard.'

FitzRoy was always magnanimous, and the second quarrel over veracity ended similarly in an apology. But it was so serious that Darwin thought he might have to leave the ship.

It was ostensibly about slavery, which was still being practised by the Spanish South Americans. FitzRoy appeared to Darwin to be condoning it when on returning from the *estanza* of a large slave owner he had expatiated on how the man had called up many of his slaves, had asked them whether they wished to be free, and had received the answer, No! 'I then asked him', wrote Darwin in his *Autobiography*, 'perhaps with a sneer, whether he thought that the answers of slaves in the presence of their master was worth anything. This made him excessively angry, and he said that if I doubted his word, we could not live any longer together.' After the gun-room officers had invited the expelled Darwin to mess with them, however, and after his anger had

had time to cool, the Captain made a handsome apology. This quarrel really shows a naughtiness on the part of both the young men. FitzRoy, by his writing and indeed by his actions, showed himself always to have been highly sympathetic to all natives, under-dogs and slaves, though not perhaps in an evangelical, Wilberforcian sort of way. On the other hand, Darwin was obviously not impugning FitzRoy's veracity, but criticizing his gullibility.

Darwin was chosen to accompany the Captain on many of his expeditions by boat or on land, and often there was shown a particular closeness between them. The first three expeditions to be mentioned occurred before the point in time reached in the previous chapter, that is to say before the early March of 1834, when the final farewell was made to Jemmy Button. The fourth, that of the expedition up the Santa Cruz River, a major effort on FitzRoy's part, occurred after the farewell and after the *Beagle*'s second visit to the Falkland Islands which followed immediately. In order to resume continuity in the narrative, this visit to the Falklands will be shortly described before turning to the fourth expedition of the two friends together: it affected the spirits of both men and is likely, by reaction, to have shaped FitzRoy's ensuing conduct.

One point before we proceed. It is generally known that Charles Darwin on his return from the voyage settled down to a life not only of domestic uneventfulness, but of frequent invalidism. It must not be supposed from this however that the Darwin of the voyage was anything but a highly active, hardy, brave and courageous person, with great powers of endurance—as indeed modern health experts have recognized. Apart from his trips with his captain he went for many on his own, most of which entailed both danger and rough going. On one occasion, as will be seen, he was physically fitter than FitzRoy and put him in his debt by reason of the fact.

The first expedition together, a short one, was in the September of 1832, just a year after the two men's first meeting. They had been sailing down the flat, half-drowned Patagonian coast south of the La Plata Estuary, and had found it an uncomfortable, dreary, difficult and at times dangerous operation. They were glad to arrive at the estuary of Bahia Blanca and very willing no doubt to welcome a change.

They also welcomed the sight of a certain Mr Harris who came sailing down the estuary in one of his little schooners. The *Beagle* was finding it difficult to make her way up to the anchorage at Port Belgrano and Mr Harris was hailed. It transpired that Harris had another of his little schooners at a settlement called Argentina beyond Port Belgrano, and if he could be taken by boat from Belgrano to Argentina so as to fetch this other schooner he would be very willing to pilot the *Beagle* to the anchorage. This offer was promptly and thankfully accepted, and by dusk the *Beagle* was being safely berthed. Preparations were at once put in hand for the boat expedition. This settlement of Argentina was some twenty miles up the estuary—its name had not necessarily any connection with the later name of the country in which it was situated, except that always in this area the Spaniards had expected to find silver. It had only been established some six years ago and was still no more than an outpost in wild country set up in the war against the native Indians, a war that was as yet by no means ended. The trip therefore was likely to prove interesting. Besides the boat crew and Mr Harris, the Captain proposed to take the purser and Darwin.

The next morning, with the prospect of a pleasant breeze to help them, they set out. For many hours the going was only dull and difficult. They were in an area of mud and water and rushes, a strange environment where, says Darwin, 'the only thing within our view which was not level was the horizon; rushes looked like bushes supported in the air by nothing, and water like mud banks and mud banks like water.' Difficulty increased and in spite of Mr Harris's pilotage they several times got stuck. After waiting for the tide to rise they at last reached the creek, some four miles from the Argentina fort and settlement, where lay Mr Harris's boat. Here the whole atmosphere changed, and the dully incredible became the romantically so. They were met by a contingent from the fort.

FitzRoy and Darwin are to differ later in their descriptions, and rather naïvely so. But here they coincide in a cry of utter amazement at the sight before them. In front was a group of soldiers; but no two men were dressed alike and their only military attributes were their general air of ferocity and the invariable possession of a fine horse. Most wore bright coloured shawls drooping down into a sort of petticoat, beneath which appeared fringed drawers. Darwin wondered whether he had arrived in Turkey. But top boots and gargantuan spurs below the drawers disabused him. So too did those of the party in the background. 'A group of almost naked Indian prisoners,' as FitzRoy describes them, 'sat devouring the remains of a half roasted horse; and as they scowled at us with their rough hair and scanty substitute for clothing blown about in the wind, I thought I had never beheld a more sinsister group.'

What should have been a welcome, if a startling one, was at once marred by a misunderstanding. The officer in charge, and his second-in-command, a somewhat aged major, had come to meet an expected supply train from Buenos Aires—hence the prisoners, to help carry the stuff. When disabused of this misapprehension the only thought entering the officers' heads, was that they were confronted with spies. The aged major proved particularly hard to convince.

It is here that the accounts of FitzRoy and Darwin differ, each, perhaps a little complacently, seeing in the other the cause for a continued suspicion. According to FitzRoy it was Harris's explanation of Darwin's profession and reason for being there that was the trouble. '*Un naturalista* was a term unheard of by any person in the settlement, and being unluckily explained by Harris as meaning "a man that knows everything" any further attempt to quiet anxiety was useless.' But in Darwin's estimation it was FitzRoy who put his foot in it. Praising the bay to the old major, he 'assured him he could bring up even a line of battle ships into it. The old gentleman was appalled and in his mind's eye saw the British Marines taking his fort.' However, if a little unwillingly, FitzRoy's party was promised a night's lodging at the fort. For the four mile journey the Captain was offered a horse and took the Purser up behind him, while Darwin and Mr Harris mounted behind two of the gaucho-soldiers. They set off at a hard gallop. They had not eaten for twelve hours, and Darwin at the other end of the journey was exhausted.

They were really very hospitably treated at the fort, though suspicion never quite deserted their hosts and a good eye continued to be kept on them. When they returned to the *Beagle* they even found that a posse of the wild gaucho cavalry had been detailed to keep a watch on the ship from the shore. FitzRoy and Darwin went over to them, and all was friendliness again: a trade was done in ostrich eggs and a demonstration given of the use from the horse's back of that ancient form of lasso called the bolas (Darwin later was to have a try himself, and to amuse the gauchos immoderately by tripping up his own horse). So with good fellowship all round the energetic and highly-coloured episode came to an end.

During the trip to settle Matthews and the Fuegians the two friends were obviously pretty close together—the use of the same simile to describe Jemmy's reunion with his family shows them as likely to have discussed together the day's happenings. The ten days of surveying work carried out while Matthews was left for his trial run brought FitzRoy and Darwin even closer together. At the end of it the Captain was to make a handsome gesture, later to be equally handsomely described:

> The following day we passed into a large expanse of water, which I named Darwin Sound—after my messmate, who so willingly encountered the discomfort and risk of a long cruise in a small loaded boat.

The ten days proved in fact adventurous ones. A difficulty already referred to recurred in more serious guise. This was the blind boldness of the natives, who made nuisances of themselves and could not easily be frightened off without the spilling of blood. Since Hamond soon afterwards sailed home to resign from the service—he could not cure a stammer—it must have been now that occurred an episode which that young officer later retold to friends. At the head of a large body of Fuegians a powerful man had come brandishing a hatchet. 'FitzRoy walked up to the leader, took the hatchet out of his hand, and patted him on the back; this completely subdued his followers.'[1]

An episode during this trip where Darwin and not FitzRoy is the hero is with corresponding modesty not mentioned by the principal protagonist, at least not his personal share in it. They had landed to cook and eat a meal amidst scenery that was both beautiful and grand, in fact near to a great cliff of ice which was nothing less than the end of a glacier. Sitting round the fire and admiring the translucent blue of this wonderful ice-cliff and with the boats drawn up at the water's edge some two hundred yards away, they were startled to see and hear a great mass of the ice topple over into the water. A huge wave was formed and it was suddenly realized that the boats were in very imminent danger. Darwin and two or three of the seamen rushed to the rescue, and, not without great danger to themselves, and a wetting, saved the boats. It needed no great imagination to realize that had the boats been smashed the chances of the party's survival and return to the *Beagle* were not very large. It was on the day following this episode that Darwin had the expanse of water they were traversing named after him.

It was the best part of a year later, when the two of them were on their way down the eastern coast for their last visit to Woollya and Jemmy Button, that FitzRoy was to find his naturalist even physically tougher than himself, as well as a friend in need. While his captain had been busy making his charts and coppering the *Adventure*, Darwin had taken the opportunity to go, as FitzRoy put it, 'shore roving'. He had been on four extensive expeditions on horseback, and was probably therefore in the better physical condition of the two. While the little port of San Julian was being surveyed from the *Beagle*, FitzRoy and Darwin and a small party set out on a trek in search of fresh water. The reading on an old

[1] From *Memoirs of Old Friends* by Caroline Fox.

Spanish map, '*pozos de aqua dulce*', lured them on by false hopes. At last FitzRoy was too utterly exhasted to go any further, and he and the rest of the party lay down on the top of a hill while Darwin volunteered to go on about a couple of miles to investigate what appeared to be two lakes shining in the sun. They watched anxiously, and could eventually see him stoop down to the first lake's edge. But he moved on hurriedly, and as quickly left the second one: they were not lakes but salt-pans, salinas. There was nothing to do but to join Darwin as he returned to them and trudge on. Eventually, FitzRoy, who had burdened himself with a double-barrelled gun as well as instruments, could go no further. With the next most exhausted man he lay down. 'A glass of water would have made me quite fresh, but it was not to be had. After some hours two of my boat's crew returned with water, and we were soon revived. Towards morning we got on board, and no one suffered afterwards from the over-fatigue, except Mr Darwin, who had had no rest during the whole of that thirsty day—now a matter of amusement, but at the time a very serious affair.'

Darwin mentions that two men had to be left behind but does not say that one was the Captain. He observes that the 'lakes' seen from the hill were no more than solid fields of snow-white salt—and he adds uncomplainingly that he spent the next two days feverish in bed. In a letter home a few weeks later he is calling Patagonia a miserable country, but exulting nevertheless in having found some perfect fossil bones, probably of mastadon. 'There is nothing,' he adds, now the experienced and completely dedicated expert, 'like Geology!'

There had followed, as has been recounted in the previous chapter, the short trip up the Magellan Strait and the final visit to the sadly deteriorated Jemmy Button. Our narrative, in recounting the earlier of the two men's expeditions together, has caught up with itself. The next move of the *Beagle* was a second visit to the Falkland Islands.

This visit obviously depressed everybody extremely. Darwin

in a letter home speaks of 'this wretched place, this scene of iniquity.' FitzRoy in his account in his *Narrative* is more restrained but more poignant, for he is the more intimately affected.

After an absence of the best part of a year, the *Beagle* had returned to the aftermath of strange and brutal happenings in the islands. In Darwin's bitter words, the British had seized an island and left to protect it a Union Jack. Taking their opportunity, the discontented gauchos—whom FitzRoy, it will be remembered, had helped to persuade to stay in the place—had turned the settlement at Port Louis into a scene of robbery, anarchy and murder. There had followed an abortive and ill-considered effort on the part of the captain of a visiting ship, *H.M.S. Challenger*, to capture the murderers, in which he had nearly lost his search party from sheer exhaustion. At length the murderers had been rounded up—and then the *Beagle* arrived. FitzRoy took over. He marched three of the prisoners on board, and clapped the ring leader in irons.

Then he turned to the aftermath of his prisoners' activities. One of the men murdered was the sole Englishman at Port Louis, a man whom on the *Beagle*'s previous visit FitzRoy had both helped and liked. The man, by name Brisbane, was a tough old sailor who had led, uncomplainingly, a life of almost unbelievable adventure and hardship: perhaps FitzRoy was particularly attracted because the man had twice been wrecked on the Fuegian coast, and in consequence he saw in him the sort of person that his philanthropic and missionary efforts had been designed to help. But now, in seeking to defend the property of his absent employer this man had been savagely done to death. FitzRoy was affected by the discovery he made:

> At two hundred yards distance from the house in which he had lived, I found to my horror the feet of poor Brisbane protruding from the ground. So shallow was his grave that dogs had disturbed his mortal remains, and had fed upon the corpse. This was the fate of an honest, industrious and most faithful man: of a man who feared no danger, and despised hardships. He was murdered by villains, because he defended the property of his friend; he was

mangled by them to satisfy their hellish spite; dragged by a lasso at a horse's heels, away from the houses, and left to be eaten by dogs.

One more unhappy find was made before the *Beagle* departed, the body of a lieutenant drowned from the *Challenger* on her visit. Burial was made next to the grave of Hellyer.[2] 'After noon, on the same day, we sailed from the Falklands, depressed more than ever by the numerous sad associations connected with their name.'

One bright spot was that Lieutenant Wickham, with whom they had made a rendezvous, could report that the schooner *Adventure* had been doing very useful work indeed.

Irrespective of good news, however, it is only human to try, after experiencing unhappy occasions, to create happy and satisfying ones. Back on the Patagonian coast FitzRoy now determined to put into effect an expedition long contemplated. Some weeks earlier the *Beagle* had hit a submerged rock and ripped a jagged hole in her false copper bottom. It had been an anxious moment. Sulivan, volunteering to dive down to inspect the damage, had emerged scratched and bleeding from the jagged edges, and FitzRoy, never ordering his subordinates to do what he would not do himself, had gone down after him. No damage that could not wait for a convenient time of repair had however been discovered. Now seemed the convenient time. And, while the repairs were being effected on the shores of the mouth of the river Santa Cruz, an expedition could conveniently be mounted to explore that river. It was a river never explored, though believed to rise in the Cordillera of the Andes and to reach almost to the further

[2] By a strange coincidence yet one more seaman's grave was to be added to this sad little row. Another captain took another *H.M.S. Challenger* surveying in the 1870s and also lost a seaman: 'Poor Bush... who was buried in a little enclosure on an exposed swampy moorland, is not alone, for two or three headboards indicate that other wanderers have found rest here.' The account (from *The Cruise of H.M.S. Challenger*, by W. J. J. Spry R.N., London, 1877) then goes on to describe Brisbane's murder by the gauchos.

coast; to trace its course, and if possible its source, would be a work of major discovery. Darwin, becoming increasingly tired of the somewhat featureless plains and hills of Patagonia and the Falklands, and increasingly anxious to reach the Cordillera, the great jagged backbone of the continent, was highly pleased at this chance to do so. He of course was numbered with those who were to go on the expedition.

On April 18th 1834 the party of twenty-five set out in three whaleboats, well armed and with provisions for three weeks. On a flood tide and in fine weather they made a good first day's run. But until they turned back it was the only good day's run they had. The river, three or four hundred yards broad, milky blue and running over a bed of pebbles, took a winding course through a straight valley that was from five to ten miles wide. It had a steady current of from four to six knots at least; and against this current it was impossible to sail or row. There was nothing for it in fact but to pull or 'track' from the shore. The party was divided by the captain into two, and with no exception all took their turn at the rope for shifts of an hour and a half. They continued until sunset; and then, by an efficient drill, wherein the cook of each party immediately started a fire while the rest collected wood, everything in half an hour was ready for the night's stay. A watch of two men and an officer was always kept.

In truth the expedition was a dull one as well as difficult. The windings of the river made progress up the wide valley slow, only a few miles being gained each day. The whole valley was really a bed of shingle, a desolate brown-and-yellow landscape, where the chief vegetation was thorn bushes which impeded their way, whilst animal life of any sort was scarce. 'The curse of sterility is on the land,' wrote Darwin, and FitzRoy echoed him. Even signs of the presence of Indian hunters led to nothing, and Darwin was disappointed. 'They would have been out and out wild gentlemen,' he told his sister. He did shoot a condor however, with a wing span of eight feet; and fishing met with some success. But it was very cold at night and at the fifth camp somebody left behind not only the salt but the spade used to earth up the shingle round the tents to keep out the wind.

Progressing slowly, the party reached even more desolate country, where black basalt cliffs of volcanic origin flanked them and sometimes great fallen boulders made their way more difficult. In a wild glen that they explored were found the carcasses of guanaco and the tracks of pumas or, as the gauchos called them, lions—'*leonum arida nutrix*' quoted FitzRoy. In front was a stationary cloud which some thought was a mountain of the Cordillera, and some just a cloud. On the tenth day a boat was damaged and nearly lost; it was beached and patched up sufficiently to proceed. Darwin, as a good shot, was mostly exempted from hauling, in order to help act as scout and forager; FitzRoy, directing the difficult progress, watched him and Lieutenant Stokes having fun chasing and herding guanacos, of which they might have won more for meat had there been on hand more guns and fewer condors. Sometimes by the time the carcass was reached the condors had made of it a skeleton.

On the fifteenth day they found the valley opening out and for the first time they saw the peaks of the Andes, the jagged, white-edged outline of the Cordillera. But all that day they seemed to come no nearer, and the river, hardly decreasing in width, seemed yet to increase in speed and power against them. They were already on short rations—it was no doubt good for the digestion, says Darwin, but not pleasant; and curious how towards evening everyone began to talk of food. FitzRoy decided on one more day's progress westward before returning, but on foot and overland as being more direct. He and Darwin were of course on this expedition.

They made observations with their instruments, speculated on the probable remaining course of the river, calculated that they were only twenty miles from the base of the mountains and sixty from the Pacific—and regretfully turned about. The return down the river was somewhat dangerous and risky, but they covered in three days what it had taken them sixteen on the way out. Back in the ship almost everyone felt discontented with the expedition: 'much hard work and much time lost and scarcely anything gained.'

Nevertheless Darwin, despite that comment, was personally

very content. Just as the *Beagle*'s shuttling between the mainland and the Falklands had after all given him opportunity to puzzle over the distribution of organic species, so this trip had given him the chance to observe and cogitate over strange geological formations. Similarly FitzRoy had observed, and had in fact collected enough material to be able to lecture to the Royal Geographic Society on the expedition when he returned home.

From the wording of the two men's accounts it is obvious that once again they must have discussed their experiences and exchanged ideas. This strange, arid, pebble-bottomed valley, obviously once covered by the sea, had intrigued them both, and their animadversions on it bear some resemblance. 'On how vast a scale,' wrote FitzRoy, 'and of what duration must have been the action of those waters which smoothed the shingle stones now buried in the deserts of Patagonia.' Darwin talks in the same way about erosion 'in the lapse of ages'. There however the resemblance ends. Darwin dismisses with scorn the explanation of the phenomenon which the old-fashioned geologists would have used, that of a world-wide *débâcle* or (to use their favourite word) 'catastrophe', rather than a slow and continuous evolutionary change.[3] FitzRoy on the other hand, not only goes all the way with the 'catastrophists', insisting that the biblical Flood is the cause, but regrets that at the time he was so misinformed and ignorant as to agree with his friend that it would be anything different.

There are not many such traces of differing outlook in the two men's published accounts of the voyage. But then there are not likely to be, since each was, by agreement, covering a different aspect. We are the more entitled, therefore, to make something of what there is. As the two messmates talked—that is to say when the one could persuade the other out of his brooding silences) there must surely, and increasingly, have been unspoken reservations, and not only so but increasing awareness that such reservations existed.

.   .   .

[3] See Chapter IX of the *Journal*.

Charles Darwin as a young man

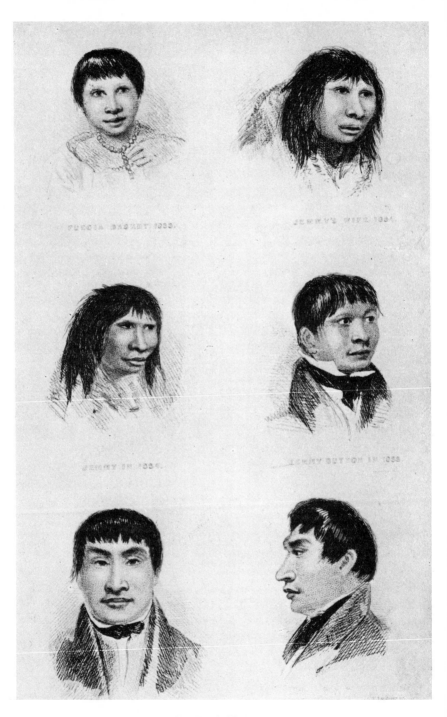

FUEGIA BASKET. 1833.   JEMMY'S WIFE. 1834.

JEMMY IN 1834.   JEMMY BUTTON IN 1833.

FitzRoy's Fuegians

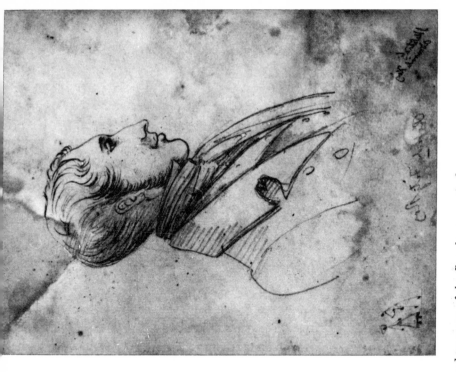

Sketches of FitzRoy on the first and second voyages of the *Beagle*, respectively

FitzRoy's sketch of the construction of the missionary station at Woollya

Wellington Harbour, New Zealand, 1841

FitzRoy's great-great-grandfather, the 2nd Duke of Grafton

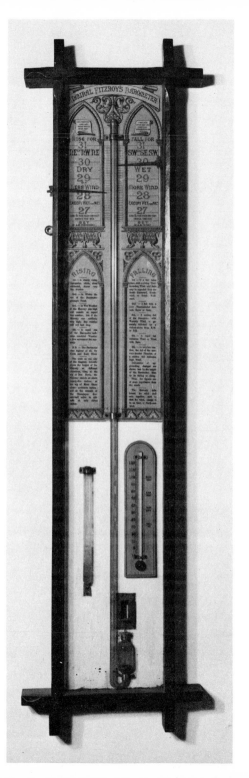

A specimen of the
FitzRoy barometer (c. 1860)

Robert FitzRoy as an older man

As the somewhat depressed expedition came back to the estuary of the Santa Cruz they at least had a cheerful sight to greet them: the *Beagle*, as Darwin put it, 'masts up, fresh painted and as gay as a frigate.' With the supplementary frigate also in service, FitzRoy's plans to complete with efficiency the survey of the whole of the South American coast and then to strike across the Pacific with both ships—plans so dearly worked for and paid for—could go ahead.

CHAPTER 11

'Being Aware of His Hereditary Disposition'

It must have begun to seem to those on the *Beagle* that the Captain's thoroughness would make their cruising of South America's southern waters, on one coast or the other, never-ending. Even in October 1834, four months after they had at last actually transferred to the western coast, Darwin in a letter home is thanking heaven that according to the Captain's promise they will have reached Australia in *two years'* time. He expresses the fear that yet another visit to Tierra del Fuego is in store for them, though this possibility is being kept from the crew lest they should desert—a startling word to find used in connection with the *Beagle*. In practice however they reached Australia in fifteen months from the date of this letter, and there were no more visits to Tierra del Fuego: FitzRoy was to meet with frustrations.

We return to the matter of supplementary schooners. FitzRoy, it will be remembered, had hired two tiny schooners or cock boats from Mr Harris whom he had met at Bahia Blanca in September 1832; and he had bought outright the larger schooner, renamed the *Adventure*, from Mr Low in the Falkland Islands six months later, in March 1833. The story now goes right back to the earlier venture, the hiring of the two cock boats. FitzRoy, as we know, too impatient of success to wait for Admiralty permission, had executed his deal and written afterwards. He wrote as follows:

> Finding Bahia Blanca so excellent a port, and receiving there information respecting the harbour between it and the Rio Negro, which satisfied me of their importance, I engaged two small sealing schooners to assist in their examination.
>
> Lieutenant I. C. Wickham, Senior Lieutenant of the *Beagle*, the Assistant Surveyor [Stokes], two Midshipmen, two marines and two seamen are employed in them, besides the Master, and crew, of each vessel.
>
> A detailed account of this transaction, with the copies of the agreement, and the necessary papers, is forwarded to the Hydrographer. I believe that their Lordships will approve of what I have done; but if I am wrong no inconvenience will result to the public service, since I am alone responsible for the agreement with the owner of the vessel, and am able and willing to pay the stipulated sum.[1]

The response of those at the Admiralty whose duty it was to deal with captains' despatches was to underline with a not very kind blue pencil the phrase 'and am able and willing' and to ask the Hydrographer for a report 'for next Board Day'. Captain Beaufort's report was the fair and noncommittal one of a good public servant:

> There is no expression in the Sailing Orders, or surveying instructions, given to Commander FitzRoy which convey to him any authority for hiring and employing any vessels whatever.
>
> On the other hand, there can be no doubt that by the aid of small craft he will be sooner and better able to accomplish the great length of coast which he has to examine—and which seems to contain so many unknown and valuable harbours;—especially if he finds it necessary to trace the course of a great river, which had been reported to him as being navigable almost to the other side of America.
>
> It may be also stated to their Lordships that the *Beagle* is the only surveying ship to which a smaller vessel or Tender has not been attached.

[1] Captains' Papers from Admiralty archives at the Public Records Office, London: ADM/1/1819.

It might be imagined that the last sentence of this report would have turned the scale in FitzRoy's favour. But not so. Across the corner of the application there is written the Board's ruling: 'Their Lordships do not approve of hiring vessels for the service and therefore desire that they may be discharged as soon as possible.'

FitzRoy did not discharge them as soon as possible, or if he did it was his idea of the possible rather than the Admiralty's. He kept them until August 19th of that year, when he paid out of his own pocket the rent due, which came to the large sum of £1,680.[2]

At what date exactly he received the Admiralty refusal it is impossible to say. But despatches from England usually took about six weeks, and in that case he would receive it in the April of 1833. By that time he had bought the *Adventure*, again paying out from his own pocket a very similar sum. Whether or not he received the refusal before or after buying the *Adventure* and her supplementary stores, it seems probable that he made no attempt to ask the Admiralty to help him financially with *that* particular transaction. There is no trace of any such correspondence; and both his reason and his pride would be likely to have prevented him doing so. He just carried on doggedly using his own money to keep the *Adventure* going.

The position seems to have frightened Darwin. In November of 1833, a little while after the *Adventure* had been re-coppered and fitted out to the Captain's satisfaction, he was writing home about him. Confessing that he himself is worried that he is spending his father's money so freely, he says that he wishes FitzRoy felt the same about his own money. 'He is eating an enormous hole into his capital for the sake of advancing all the objects of the voyage. The schooner (the *Adventure*) which will so very mainly be conducive to our safety he entirely pays for.' Incidentally, Darwin mentions here an added reason for having a sister ship that FitzRoy was perhaps too proud to mention to the Admiralty, the factor of mutual support and added safety: every mariner

[2] For value at the time of writing one should probably multiply by six at least.

from Christopher Columbus to Captain Cook saw to it that if possible his ship did not sail alone.

FitzRoy was obviously so proud of his supplementary schooner, the child of his unconquerable desire. There was the occasion for instance, after the *Beagle* had been keeled down and made to look so new and gay at the mouth of the River Santa Cruz, when the two ships had passed through the Magellan Straits together, at long last leaving the eastern coast and making way to that great sea for which the *Adventure* had been specially prepared. On emerging from the Straits by a new and untried route, FitzRoy had let the smaller ship have the only anchorage, while he sailed the *Beagle* back and forth through a long dark night. And in the morning when at last the daylight broke, 'we saw the *Adventure* coming out to us from the cove where she had passed the night, and then both vessels sailed out of the channel, past Mount Sky-ring and all the Furies as fast as sail could urge them.' And by sunset the ships were standing out into the Pacific, 'with every inch of canvas set which we could carry.' A brave sight which FitzRoy could not forget.

But then there had to be tackled the survey of the coast that had driven FitzRoy's predecessor on the *Beagle* to suicide. It says something for the cumulative effect of the Fuegian coasts that these fresh ones, being on the Pacific side, were welcomed as a relief. 'We all jog along very well together,' Darwin wrote caustically to his sister; 'there is no quarrelling on board, which is something to say. The Captain keeps all smooth by rowing everyone in turn.'

They reached Valparaiso, and things did not seem to go quite so well. The Captain was busy, yet physically inactive, drawing up charts and reports from the work that his two ships had lately done. Someone had to go to the reputedly gay city of Santiago, to pay official respects to the representatives of the Chilean government. FitzRoy denied himself the pleasure, and sent Lieutenant Wickham. That left him with more time to work—and with more time to worry about the expense of the *Adventure*.

There were continual interruptions. There must have occurred now the second of the quarrels on board between FitzRoy and

Darwin, referred to in the latter's autobiography and mentioned at the beginning of the previous chapter. It is a quarrel made by a worried man over-aware of his need to exercise *noblesse oblige* and exacerbated into a determination to fulfil that need, however much it may hurt him to do so. FitzRoy had been receiving much, largely unwanted, hospitality from the Chileans and had complained to his friend bitterly that he must return the hospitality and have a party on board ship. Darwin replied comfortingly that he didn't think there was any need. Whereat FitzRoy observed that Darwin was just the sort of fellow who would think like that, who would receive favours and make no return. This time Darwin walked out of the cabin without being asked. The innocent Wickham had to put up with a solid evening of listening to his Captain's complaints about 'the Professor'; and then FitzRoy, as before, made a handsome apology.

After this Darwin went on one of his overland expeditions and came back ill—he himself put it down to drinking some new-made wine—and the Captain held up the departure of the *Beagle* until his friend's recovery. That left him more time to worry.

At last—it was October 1834, a year and a half since the ship had been purchased—FitzRoy came to the conclusion that he could not bear the expense of the *Adventure* any longer:

> At this time I was made to feel and endure a bitter disappointment; the mortification it caused preyed deeply, and the regret is still vivid. I found that it would be impossible for me to maintain the *Adventure* much longer: my own means had been taxed, even to involving myself in difficulties and as the Lords Commissioners of the Admiralty did not think it proper to give me any assistance, I saw that all my cherished hopes of examining many groups of islands in the Pacific, besides making a complete survey of the Chilean and Peruvian shores, must utterly fail...As soon as my mind was made up, after a most painful struggle, I discharged the *Adventure*'s crew, took the officers back to the *Beagle*, and sold the vessel.

The sale, FitzRoy says, was mismanaged, 'owing to my being dispirited and careless', and he dropped £300 on the net price he had paid, apart from the price of all the stores and gear bought for the *Adventure* at the Falkland Islands.

Nor, as FitzRoy was well aware, was he the only one to suffer from the change. It was a sad come-down for many. 'We are now,' Darwin wrote home, 'in the same state as when we left England, with Wickham for 1st Lieut., which part of the business anyhow is a good job. We shall be very badly off for room; and I shall have trouble enough with stowing my collections. It is in every point of view a grievous affair in our little world.'

Yet things were to be made much worse before they were better. On November 8th, a little less than a month later, Darwin is writing home again:

Capt. FitzRoy has for the last two months been working *extremely* hard, and at the same time constantly annoyed by interruptions from officers of other ships: the selling the Schooner and its consequences were very vexatious; the cold manner the Admiralty (solely I believe because he is a Tory) have treated him, and a thousand other etc. etc., has made him very thin and unwell. This was accompanied by a morbid depression of spirits, and a loss of all decision and resolution. The Captain was afraid that his mind was becoming deranged (being aware of his hereditary disposition), all that Bynoe could say, that it was merely the effect of bodily health and exhaustion after such application, would not do; he invalided and Wickham was appointed to command.

The hereditary disposition referred to is obviously that of his uncle on his mother's side, Lord Castlereagh, who had committed suicide a few years earlier—Darwin, aware of some mental instability in his own family, could be sympathetic. The amount of truth in the allegation of Whig bias against FitzRoy it is not easy to assess; it is true however that FitzRoy must have been well-known to come from traditionally Tory families, and true also that the Whigs had recently come into power after a very long and frustrating period out of office.

The effect upon the ship's company of this dramatic happening was, of course, profound. The unlikely event had occurred, and the instruction to turn for home would have to be obeyed. Darwin for one was appalled at the prospect, though before the event he had been fretting to reach home.

Owing to Wickham's loyalty and common sense however the crisis was shortlived:

> One great source of his [the Captain's] annoyance was the feeling it impossible to fulfill the whole instructions; from his state of mind it never occurred to him that the very instructions order him to do as much of the West coast *as he has time* for, and then proceed across the Pacific. Wickham (very disinterestedly giving up his promotion) urged this most strongly, stating that when he took the command nothing should induce him to go to Tierra del Fuego again; and asked the Captain what would be gained by his resignation? Why not do the more useful part and return as commanded by the Pacific? The Captain at last to everyone's joy, consented, and the resignation was withdrawn...When we are once at sea, I am sure the Captain will be all right again. He has already regained his cool inflexible manner, which he had quite lost.

CHAPTER 12

'Such a Taut Hand'

MATTERS mended, if slowly yet steadily. By the time of the great earthquake of February 1835 FitzRoy had regained all his old ebullient form.

Through the midsummer months the surveying work went on in the area of the island of Chiloé. It was hard, exhausting work, in wet and windy weather. Christmas, FitzRoy describes as 'sombre', though young Sulivan, promoted to the command of boat trips, was having as happy a time overcoming difficulties as young FitzRoy[1] had had in Otway and Skyring waters five and a half years ago. Out of the wreck of his ambitious plans FitzRoy had at least salvaged the services of the *Adventure*'s pilot, who was none other than the sealing captain, the 'ever restless and enterprising' Mr Low, who had sold him the ship. When Mr Low, with a scratch crew of his own choosing, came back from a whaleboat trip with a story of how his men had eaten up all the rations in order to shorten the trip, but that he had carried on as usual, with only shell-fish and seaweed for food, Captain FitzRoy had merely recorded with approval that the man was too inured to hardship to be easily diverted from his plan.

[1] Page 43 and 44 of Sulivan's biography.

FitzRoy at this time was able to perform a small act of philanthropy, at which he was no doubt pleased. Coming in to anchor the *Beagle* in a small bay one evening he was surprised to see five wild men waving frantically from the shore. He took them on board, to find them to be deserters from an American whaler who, unable to reach any place of civilization, had managed to subsist for no less than thirteen months. FitzRoy noted that though thin they were healthy, and saved himself the task of surveying that particular bay by extracting from them their highly detailed knowledge. It was indeed a wild coast and wildly inhabited. The inhabitants were convinced that FitzRoy was engaged in smuggling, a mistake that amused Darwin considerably: 'A person,' he wrote in his diary, 'who could possibly mistake Captain FitzRoy for a smuggler would never perceive any difference between a Lord Chesterfield and his valet.'

When February came the *Beagle*, with no reluctance on the part of those on board, left at last the region of rain and made north for Valdivia, with Concepcion and Valparaiso beyond. In the little but civilized port of Valdivia matters blossomed forth into almost a musical comedy atmosphere. Darwin noted with approval that the ladies could blush. Valdivia's Mayor visited the ship with a boatload of 'charming Senoritas'—whom bad weather constrained to stay the night. Then it is Sulivan's turn to write cheerfully home, of a party on board, when 'all the big children amused themselves seeing the little ones play hide-and-seek and other games about the deck.' What a difference in the Captain!

Then the earthquake struck—and light-heartedness had to give place to efficiency, philanthropy and scientific enquiry.

Experiencing the edges of the earthquake, Darwin who was ashore felt as if he were skating on thin ice, and FitzRoy on board felt as if the ship were driving forward when in reality it was anchored. Valdivia, in any case built of wood, hardly suffered, and the *Beagle* on her duty sailed northward to the dangerous coast around Mocha Island. Anchoring there with difficulty, they felt more shocks, and learnt that the centre of the earthquake was farther north still and that Concepcion was devastated and its port, Talcahuano, swept by a tidal wave. FitzRoy, as soon as duties would allow, hurried north to see whether he could afford any help.

The worst was over, but some practical aid by way of a loan of tents was afforded to the British consul.[2] FitzRoy and Darwin then made themselves busy collecting evidence of this spectacular occurrence. Concepcion was in ruins and its port of Talcahuano a scene of chaos and derelict ships. Both men were appalled yet intensely interested, while at the same time ashamed that their interest should outlast their pity.

The sea had sent in three tidal waves and had seemed to boil, and it was the disturbances at sea that most interested FitzRoy as a sailor. He formed a theory that the levels of the sea bed had altered drastically, and, recruiting an intelligent young German with local knowledge, sailed around the coast and islands taking measurements to prove his theory.

It was this theory, and in particular an extension of it concerning the local currents, that he was very shortly to put to great practical use and human benefit.[3]

At this time *H.M.S. Challenger*, a three-masted brig larger than the *Beagle*, the ship that had made the punitive visit to the Falkland Islands, was cruising on the eastern coast of the continent, its captain quite unaware even that there had been an earthquake. The captain was Michael Seymour, a contemporary and great friend of FitzRoy.

By May the *Challenger* had rounded the Horn onto the western coast and was approaching Mocha Island and Concepcion and the earthquake area. By the same month the *Beagle*, having surveyed as far north as Coquimbo, was on her way back to Valparaiso, to

[2] This fact only comes out incidentally in the *Narrative* page 455, Volume II.

[3] Another observation, and comment, by FitzRoy would have interested Arthur Evans, with whose father incidentally FitzRoy was to cross controversial swords. FitzRoy noticed that shocks were often preceded by an underground rumbling like the roaring of a bull, and also stated that the Araucanian Indians sacrificed bulls to the earthquake spirit. This was just what Arthur Evans found in Crete.

lay in stores for her long delayed and long anticipated strike across the Pacific. The Captain had received news of his promotion to post rank and was in good form.

On the evening of May 19th, sailing before a strong north-west wind, in thick weather with heavy rain, the *Challenger* took a sounding. It showed a depth of 110 fathoms and had been taken largely as a matter of form, for dead reckoning showed her as still at least fifty miles from the coast. A course was set for Concepcion Bay and the ship proceeded. By eight o'clock, when dark, the Captain considered putting his ship's head to the south-west until daylight, but was dissuaded by his confident ship's master. He continued on deck.

About an hour later, just as he had gone below, there came a cry from the officer of the watch to put helm down and about ship. As Seymour rushed on board breakers were seen ahead. In a moment the ship had struck.

She did not break up at once; the waves merely pounded her further onto the rocks. What could be done was done and good discipline was kept. When at last the rising moon gave enough light, attempts were made to get a line ashore. Two men were drowned before this was accomplished. But everyone else reached the shore—and waited for the dawn.

The *Challenger* had wrecked herself on an inhospitable coast. Before morning was out, however, local Indians had come to the rescue of the stranded crew, supplying food and horses to help carry gear and stores up from the ship. Seymour was grateful but wary, because he knew that the west coast Indians could be treacherous and had no good reputation. He felt that the ship would soon break up. He sent off two officers for help and ordered his men to take everything possible off the ship.

The officers had to make a cross-country trek to Concepcion, a distance of about sixty-five miles in a straight line. There they were to enlist the aid of the British Consul, try to hire a rescue boat, and see that a dispatch asking for help was sent on to the naval officer commanding at Valparaiso.

One cannot escape the feeling that these officers and also their captain, while displaying great fortitude and courage, paid undue respect to correct behaviour and the purse of the Admiralty, a fault from which at least FitzRoy seldom suffered. The two emissaries, having set the Consul off on his way to give most practical and efficient aid, having posted their dispatch, duly descended to Concepcion's port and tried to hire a rescue ship. They were offered one, but turned down the offer on the grounds of expense.

Similarly Captain Seymour, back at the scene of the wreck, was insisting that everything possibly movable from the ship, ammunition and some guns included, should be brought up from the ship, however difficult the job might prove. His discipline was good enough for him to be obeyed, so far without grumbling.

Seymour's position was not enviable. He would inevitably face a Court Martial if and when he got home; but that must have been the least of his worries. He was stranded on a coast unprotected from the swell of the Pacific, and it was doubtful whether any ship's commander would dare to try to rescue him. Meanwhile, though the local Indians continued friendly, there were rumours that others, of a fiercer tribe, were approaching. He began to prospect for a better site for his camp, one from which he would have more chance of rescue by sea and less danger from the Indians. He found what he sought some ten miles to the North, on a slope above the mouth of a river called the Leübu.

Again the stores were moved, all but the heaviest, and the crew sat down to wait. Already a fortnight had passed, and idleness was producing disaffection. There was some thieving, followed by two floggings and a harangue by the Captain. There existed those who believed that an attempt should at once be made to travel overland to Concepcion. But such a course, besides obviously not being easy, would have meant abandoning practically everything that at such effort had been salvaged, and Captain Seymour refused to consider it save as a last resource. With the return of wet weather, and with sickness increasing, the days passed.

Up at Valparaiso matters at last began to move.

On June 14th the *Beagle* arrived for her laying in of stores. On the 16th a local merchant received through the Consul a letter giving a laconic account of the total loss of *HMS Challenger*. The news spread in the town but there was no official corroboration.

FitzRoy was aware that recently a Swedish captain had arrived at the port with tales of having seen 'an American brig' wrecked on the shore near the island of Mocha. He went to see the captain and came away convinced that what had been seen was the *Challenger* with one mast struck down. He next went to Commodore Mason of the *Blonde*, the officer in command of the station. Commodore Mason had heard nothing, and did not intend to make any move until he did.

At first light FitzRoy was at the post office. If the merchant had heard privately through the Consul, he felt sure that something official would be arriving at any moment. As he half hoped, half feared, there was a package addressed to the Consulate which he could tell was from the *Challenger*. He took it personally, and found the consul's office not yet open—'Such apathy, on such an occasion!' he recorded. Resisting the temptation to open the package himself, he routed out an official, extracted the letter to Commodore Mason, and took it to the *Blonde*.

It is only Darwin's letter home that gives us some insight into what happened next.[4] 'The old Commodore in the *Blonde*', he wrote, 'was very slack in his motions—in short afraid of getting on that lee-shore in the winter; so that Captain FitzRoy had to bully him and at last offered to go as pilot.' FitzRoy merely says that he made such an offer and that the offer was accepted. The letters that officially cover the transaction—copies of which FitzRoy was careful to despatch to the Admiralty—are equally innocent of any suggestion of strain or bad feeling.[5] From Captain FitzRoy to Commodore Mason of the *Blonde*: 'I could leave her [the *Beagle*] for the next few weeks...I am anxious to place at your disposal what little local knowledge I possess.' From Commodore Mason to Captain FitzRoy: 'I most gladly avail myself of your valuable services.'

[4] Letter to his sister Caroline, dated July 1835 (page 123 of Nora Barlow's *Voyage of the Beagle*).
[5] P.R.O. Papers, ADM/1/1819.

FitzRoy's services comprised the transferring to the *Blonde* not only of himself and his servant but also of his own master's assistant and coxswain and, for good measure, one of the *Beagle*'s whaleboats. At three o'clock on the next morning the *Blonde* set out on its 350 mile sail down the coast to Concepcion's port, Talcahuano.

Arrived there, Mason and FitzRoy were given the news, or rather the opinion, of the port captain, that the spot where the *Challenger* had been wrecked was quite inaccessible to any ship in any weather. Commodore Mason accepted the truth of this. He was told however that boats at least would be able to enter the mouth of the nearby Leübu River. FitzRoy volunteered to reach his friend Seymour and the wrecked crew by a journey overland. His offer was accepted.

It is not known how many days the two officers from the wreck had taken on their journey to Concepcion, though when one considers that it was altogether nearly a month before the despatches they were carrying reached Valparaiso, it does not seem likely to have been few. They may or may not have been able to hire horses. FitzRoy, setting out with horses, took two days and half a night.

There comes through from FitzRoy's account of the journey the fact that he was enjoying himself, as he had obviously enjoyed himself on his first major boat trip from the *Beagle*. The way was at times fantastically difficult, he finally arrived covered from head to foot in mud, he was all the while consumed with impatience and very real anxiety. But he was on a mission of danger, difficulty and philanthropy and what more could he want? There were two added pleasurable facts. One was that he had chosen as his companion the young German who had helped him test his theory about the changing of the sea bed and that this young man was a kindred spirit. The second was that he was travelling through the beautiful country of the Araucanian Indians, a people who had put up a better and more noble resistance to the Spanish Conquistadors than had either the Incas or the Aztecs and for whom FitzRoy had developed a most romantic admiration.

Delayed at the start from the ferrymen's refusal to cross Concepcion's river, the Bio Bio, in the dark—a refusal that he had to admit on experiencing the crossing on the next morning to have been a reasonable one—FitzRoy, with his servant and the young German and a native guide, pushed their horses to the limit and reached a farmstead where they were presented with a poor meal and a poorer response to their request for remounts. Leaving the 'thin-faced dispenser of tough hens and sour apples', and dispensing with their useless native guide, the three men set off again at a gallop. They met a party of Chillians, who gave them the useful news that the *Challenger* party had moved to the mouth of the Leübu River and the disturbing news that the number of hostile Indians was increasing daily.

At the little town of Arauco they were persuaded to stop for the night. The next day it was raining and the difficulties increased. They had come to a land of ravines and rapid rivers, difficult to cross. When night fell FitzRoy pushed on, but was surprised how dark it became. His first intimation that they had come to wooded country was that he was knocked off his horse. Soon he was dismounting again, to feel for the path through mud up to the knees and elbows. Then the young German was coaxing the horses one by one through a stream and FitzRoy was hanging on to his own horse by the tail. At last they had reached the estuary of the Leübu River, and to their immense relief there were seen lights on the farther bank and soon their calls were being answered and the *Challenger*'s only salvaged boat was being sent across. 'Old friends,' wrote FitzRoy, 'meeting under such circumstances, can say but little. Hastening to the encampment, where all had turned out to hear the welcome news of assistance being at hand, we made their hearts rejoice by saying that the *Blonde* was at Talcahuano and coming to their relief...Daylight found Seymour and myself still talking, though he had given me his bed.'

Having ascertained to his own satisfaction that an evacuation by sea was possible from the shores of the Leübu, and leaving behind promises of rapid help, FitzRoy set out at once on his return journey. At one time he lost his way, and if anything the second journey was worse than the first. But the night's lodging at least was a happy affair. At a farm where only the daughters were at home and a little hesitant of hospitality, the young German caught and killed a sheep and FitzRoy liberally paid for it. 'Before long we had such a fire and supper as the old *rancho* had not witnessed since the wedding day of its owner.' FitzRoy departed, covered with flea-bites, but popular, to leave no doubt the memory, which would not leave the daughters of the house for some considerable time, of a mad but handsome English captain.

FitzRoy had now to persuade his senior officer, the Commodore of the *Blonde*, to act.

He found, what cannot have greatly pleased him, that Commodore Mason, in spite of having sent off FitzRoy, had also hired a ship to search the coast and had helped to man it with FitzRoy's assistant master and coxswain from the *Beagle*. This effort was to prove entirely useless since it was such a bad boat that in spite of the *Beagle* men's efforts it was not able to do much more than precariously keep itself afloat: since it was the ship which the *Challenger*'s two officers had turned down, perhaps after all they had been wise as well as cautious, though only the deterrent of cost is mentioned by FitzRoy.

One has to turn to Darwin's letter again to pierce the veil of polite correctness with which FitzRoy himself covers his dealings with Mason of the *Blonde*. Darwin says that speculation about the 'wonderful quarrel' between the two men was the only topic on the *Beagle*, and adds with obvious relish—as militantly loyal to his captain as he had been over the Argentinian guardship episode three years earlier—that FitzRoy had threatened Mason with a court martial for his slowness and that 'such a taut hand as the Captain is has opened the eyes of everyone fore and aft in the *Blonde*.'

When exactly this climax to the quarrel came, now or earlier, is not clear. In any case however, Commodore Mason consented to sail to the rescue.

There occurred an unexpected frustration. In weather of very poor visibility, FitzRoy, this time impatient and angry with himself, could not distinguish the mouth of the Leübu River. Not until the ninth day at sea was the *Challenger*'s camp spotted. With the *Blonde* carefully cruising five miles off shore, FitzRoy took boat and reached his friend again. He found all relatively well, though sickness was increasing. Returning with one of the *Challenger* officers on board, though not until it was dark, FitzRoy climbed aboard again and the *Blonde* 'made sail off shore'.

There follows in FitzRoy's *Narrative* an innocent remark, written with what degree of tongue in cheek it is impossible to tell: 'but a fortunate mistake caused the mainyard to be squared about midnight, and at daybreak next morning we were in a good position off the entrance of the river.' The evacuation then proceeded and without a hitch, all the crew and at least some of the precious stores and equipment being taken on board.

In due course the crowded *Blonde* was making her way north again. Despite the happy issue the atmosphere aboard cannot have been very cheerful. Seymour had a court martial to contemplate; and, as if to stress the seriousness of his crew's sickness during their long encampment, one man died. At Coquimbo the *Challenger* crew and captain were found passage home, and at Callao, port of Lima, FitzRoy found the *Beagle* waiting for him.

If we may be inclined to smile at FitzRoy's high-handed impatience, nothing should prevent us realizing the most signal service that he had rendered to his friend and to the crew of the *Challenger*. There is at this time a letter from FitzRoy to Darwin that the latter quotes and that is poignantly revealing. FitzRoy was in lodgings on shore making arrangements for the completion of the South American survey and Darwin was on board, obviously fretting to be off to the Galapagos Islands. 'Growl not at all,' commanded FitzRoy. 'Lee-way will be made up. Good has been done unaccompanied by evil—*ergo*, I am happier than usual.'

He was even so happy and confident that, having made his arrangements for the completion of the survey under his assistant master and in a loaned ship, he sent a renewed report to the

Admiralty of his activities and expenses in regard to supplementary schooners and a renewed appeal for financial aid.

Nor was FitzRoy's help to Seymour ended, as became clear at the court martial, held at Portsmouth on board the *Victory* three months later.[6]

FitzRoy supplied his friend with a document setting out his findings on the changes in ocean currents due to the earthquake, and expressing his opinion that it was the change in the currents was had caused the *Challenger's* otherwise incomprehensible error in the dead reckoning of her distance from the coast.

Captain Seymour made great use of this letter, stressing that he himself, having recently come from the east coast, had not even heard of the earthquake. He was completely exonerated, with no blame attached whatever. Not only so, but the following handsome rider was added: 'The Court could not close its proceedings without expressing the high sense it entertained of the conduct of Captain Michael Seymour, his surveying officers and ship's company when placed in circumstances of the greatest danger as well as afterwards during a period of seven weeks that they remained on a wild and inhospitable coast, strongly marking the advantages of that steady discipline that has raised the British Navy to the confidence of the country and which in this instance as well as in many others has been the cause of the preservation of the crew and of their arrival with two melancholy exceptions in safety to their own country.' Of this sentiment, if slightly inaccurate (three men died, not two) and a little confused at its end, that is to say as to how other instances of steady discipline could have helped to bring the *Challenger's* crew home safely, Captain Seymour was undoubtedly glad. He was given another ship. As for FitzRoy's spectacular dash to the stubborn Captain Seymour's rescue, no mention was made of it at the Court Martial proceedings. But then it lay outside the defined interest of the Court.

.   .   .

[6] P.R.O. Papers, ADM/I/5481.

When FitzRoy received the Admiralty's reply to his own appeal, he may not have been overduly surprised at its contents:

Inform Capt. FitzRoy that Lords highly disapprove of this proceeding, especially after the orders which he previously received on the subject.[7]

[7] P.R.O. Papers, ADM/I/3848.

CHAPTER 13

Where Your Treasure Is

THERE is about the remainder of the voyage of the *Beagle* a different feeling. At last she had sailed out into the vast and romantic Pacific Ocean, and this was something to which everybody on board had obviously been looking forward. For the rest of the voyage there seemed more time in which, if not to stand and stare, at least to stand back, a little more relaxed than heretofore, and observe. The Captain was as busy and involved as ever, but in rather a different way.

Yet after the arrival at Sydney and with the Southern Pacific and its islands soon to be left behind, one overmastering interest only seems to seize those on board: the desire to reach home. Darwin gives dutiful but comparatively scant notice to Tasmania and the Cocos Islands and Mauritius and the Cape of Good Hope and St Helena and the Azores; FitzRoy gives them no notice at all. Of the thirteen months that remained of the voyage after leaving America it is only the first three, to the Captain at least, that have paramount interest.

Whereas for Darwin the supreme interest was probably the Galapagos Islands, for FitzRoy it was undoubtedly Tahiti and New Zealand. The *Beagle*'s visits to these two places lasted in each instance only ten days. But they were crowded days, partly by reason of the duties that FitzRoy had to perform, partly by reason of the activities in which his increasingly aroused interest involved him.

To FitzRoy the Galapagos Islands were primarily coasts to survey; and the navigation entailed was not always easy. 'We had two narrow escapes this day; while weighing from Chatham Island baffling winds sent us a great deal too close to the cliffs before our anchor was up, or the ship under command.' But the Captain was not above making his own observations, though possibly directed by his Naturalist: 'All the small birds that live on these lava-covered islands have short beaks, very thick at the base, like that of a bullfinch. This appears to be one of those admirable provisions of Infinite Wisdom by which each created thing is adapted to the place for which it was intended.' Put the last sentence from the passive to the active, or rather the reflexive, voice, and one has an unexceptionable tenet of organic evolution.

It took the *Beagle* the best part of four weeks to reach Tahiti from the Galapagos Islands; and it seems likely, from what FitzRoy wrote later in his *Narrative* and what Darwin wrote at the time in his diary and notebook, that the officers spent some of this time in improving their knowledge of the famed South Sea Islands and in discussing what they read. It was just two thirds of a century since Captain Cook had last been in these parts; and the interval was short enough for his memory still to be green, in the mind of any sailor at the least, but long enough for the local situation to have much altered. Here in the Society Islands, and in New Zealand too, were the arenas for Europe's and in particular England's early missionary efforts, the scene for the classic contest between the word of God and the trader's bottle of whisky, the scene too, for there was undoubtedly much cannibalism hereabouts, for what still remains as a stale joke, the missionary in the cooking pot. But there also were islands that had been described as paradise and natives said to be as innocently admirable as Rousseau's noble savage.

Which picture would those on the *Beagle* discover, or what combination of the two pictures? In particular what effect had the missionaries produced by their activities of the last thirty or forty years? FitzRoy, with his own Fuegian effort behind him, would be likely to argue in favour of those who came to witness for the word of God. Darwin would be likely to have an open mind. Both had been reading the *Travels* of Kotzebue.

Kotzebue deserves a little attention. He was a German who travelled round the world in a ship of the Russian Navy and who wrote of his experiences with an independent judgement and a somewhat caustic wit. He had last visited Tahiti[1] in 1824, eleven years before the arrival of the *Beagle*. In his book *A New Voyage Round the World* he comes down heavily against the missionaries. He accuses them of narrowness of outlook, of having killed the natural innocent gaiety of the Tahitians, of an unscrupulous thirst for power, and even of having been the direct cause of bloody strife in the islands. Noting that the most active missionary at the time of his visit had once been a common sailor, and that native pastors were already being employed, he writes: 'In Russia, a careful education and diligent study at schools and universities is necessary to qualify anyone to be a teacher of religion. The London Missionary Society is more easily satisfied; a half savage, confused by the dogmas of an uneducated sailor, is, according to them, perfectly fitted for the sacred office.'

These, and more virulent remarks, had, one cannot help feeling, resulted at least partially from the reception that Kotzebue received on the island when in search of stores for his captain's ship. After an enthusiastic not to say hilarious welcome on the first evening, he found on landing on the following morning, an unaccountable change:

> The warm friendships formed but yesterday seemed already to have cooled; we were quite forgotten. At length we obtained from

[1] Tahiti, largest island of the Society Group, is called by him O Tahaiti, the 'O' being apparently (and with a no doubt entirely fortuitous similarity to the Greek) the definite article. FitzRoy, following Captain Cook more closely, writes it Otaheite, while acknowledging that Tahiti is probably a more correct rendering of the native name. Here, for simplicity 'Tahiti' will be used, even in quotations.

the boat, sent off to us at break of day with provisions, an explanation of this enigma. The inhabitants of Tahiti were celebrating the Sunday, on which account they did not leave their houses, where they lay on their bellies reading the Bible and howling aloud; laying aside every species of occupation, they devoted, as they said, the whole day to prayer.

With his annoyance in no way assuaged, Kotzebue attended divine service. He noted that the natives, discarding their own graceful costume, craved after European clothes, however old, however incongruous, however ill-fitting:

> Many of their wearers can scarcely move their arms, and are forced to stretch them out like the sails of a windmill, while their elbows, curious to see the world, peep through slits in the seams. Let any one imagine such an assembly, perfectly satisfied of the propriety of their costume, and wearing, to complete the comic effect, a most ultra-serious expression of countenance, and he will easily believe that it was impossible for me to be very devout in their presence.

Finally, Kotzebue says, he lost all inclination to laugh: the situation was too tragic. Whether one felt inclined to agree or disagree, any reader of this uninhibited and opinionated account would want to see for himself.

Darwin after a week in Tahiti was writing in his pocket notebook, 'good missionaries—never can believe what is heard', and is expanding this in his diary by a reference to Kotzebue and some other authorities, and by the remark: 'One of my impressions... was decidedly incorrect: viz. that the Tahitians had become a gloomy race and lived in fear of the Missionaries.'

FitzRoy was forming his opinion perhaps more slowly. He was very busy. He had been commissioned with an unlikely but interesting job, though it was one that did bring him into close contact with at least one of the missionaries.

The job had been given him, on the face of it surprisingly, by none other than Commodore Mason of the *Blonde*. It seems as if the Commodore had in the end formed a good opinion of his importunate junior, sufficiently at any rate to give him an unenviable task. In 1831, on the Low or Dangerous Islands (lying east of Tahiti and now called the Tuamotu) the master and mate of a British ship, the *Truro*, had been treacherously murdered. These islands were held to come under the jurisdiction of the ruler of the Society Islands, at that time a young queen who had taken the name of an illustrious predecessor, Pomare. An agreement was accordingly extracted from this inexperienced ruler—it was actually obtained by Captain Seymour visiting in the *Challenger*—wherein she was to pay over the sum of 2,853 dollars, or the equivalent, by September 1st 1835. When FitzRoy and Mason finally parted the time limit had very nearly expired, and FitzRoy was armed with a letter to the Tahitian queen and an instruction to do his best to extract the fine.

Not until the eighth day of his visit to Tahiti did FitzRoy achieve an audience. It was arranged to take place at the 'royal cottage' at Papiete, the chief port of the island, and a curious meeting it proved to be, followed by another even more curious.

FitzRoy was at the meeting place first and was able to witness the arrival of the Queen by boat, a sadly unimpressive affair. The Queen, he wrote, was 'sitting on the gunwale of a whaleboat, loosely dressed in a dark kind of gown, without anything upon her head, hands, or feet, and without any kind of girdle or sash to confine her gown, which was fastened only at the throat. There was no reception at landing: no attendance, no kind of outward ceremony showed that the "Queen of the Isles" had arrived at her home.'

Finding her waiting for him alone in a small room of her cottage, FitzRoy's indignation at the treatment accorded the Queen turned to something more intimate and kindly. 'I could not help pitying her, for it was evident she was expecting a lecture on the subject of the *Truro*, and felt her utter helplessness.' The Commodore's letter was duly delivered; and a meeting or parliament of the chieftains, to which FitzRoy was asked to attend, was arranged for the following day.

That meeting, though strange in setting and though beginning unpropitiously, proved one of the most successful that FitzRoy, or indeed any other representative of British imperialism set to face a primitive people, can have attended. It was held in the missionary chapel, a large bare place of benches and unpainted wood, and again there was no sign of ceremony, or even in fact of any likelihood of order. FitzRoy had brought with him all the officers from the *Beagle* he could spare, and the Queen was supported by several chiefs and an assorted audience of natives of lesser degree. Squeezing himself awkwardly between the benches, FitzRoy shook hands. He asked Queen Pomare to choose an interpreter, and when she chose Mr Pritchard, one of the missionaries, FitzRoy demurred that perhaps his sacred office should raise him above such unpleasant disputes. This sentiment was received with lack of comprehension. But then Mr Pritchard expressed his willingness to function, and all was well.

Nor did the promise of lack of order materialize. The chiefs soon showed themselves to be highly intelligent, reasonable, responsible and honourable persons. FitzRoy's obvious aristocratic dignity and equally obvious spirit of philanthropy must have been apparent, and they reacted favourably towards him.

FitzRoy first referred to the explicit bond that had been entered into and the fact that it had not been honoured. 'I then reminded Pomare of the solemn nature of her agreement; of the loss which her character, and that of her chiefs, would sustain; and of the means England eventually might adopt to recover the property so nefariously taken away from British subjects. I said that I was on my way to England, where her conduct would become known; and if harsh measures should, in consequence, be adopted, she must herself expect to bear the blame.'

There resulted from this uncompromising statement much argument, but orderly argument, amongst the chiefs. Finally came the simple answer: they would pay.

Not only so, but the balance of dollars, above the price of a store of oyster shells which the Queen was willing to sell and representing about half the total sum, would be found by public subscription from the people of Tahiti. The native audience were in fact at once harangued by the principal chief in an appeal for funds.

FitzRoy immediately found himself arguing on the other side. It was hardly fair, he said, that the Tahitians should make themselves responsible for the moral debt of another set of islands. To this the principal chief replied, with dignity: 'The honour of the Queen is our honour. We will share her difficulties. Her friends prefer assisting her in clearing off this debt, to leaving her conduct exposed to censure. We have determined to unite in her cause, and endeavour to pay all before the departure of the man-of-war.'

It was a noble and forthright answer that must have appealed to the heart of FitzRoy: before the meeting had broken up he was inviting the Queen and chiefs to a party on board the *Beagle*. This was not, however, before an opportunity had been taken by FitzRoy to improve the occasion. The Queen, who had pardoned the Low Island murderers, was frightened lest the next visiting man-of-war should demand their extradition. FitzRoy answered conciliatorily that though Britain could certainly not approve of her action he thought that his country would respect Pomare's right as Queen to make her own decisions. He did however accord himself the right to lecture her in a friendly manner against taking the advice of her younger and less responsible subjects or of questionable foreigners, and to express the hope that she would continue to co-operate with the 'highly deserving and devoted' missionaries. The Queen humbly accepted the lecture in good part.

The chiefs then took their chance to turn the occasion to profit. They asked FitzRoy for advice and posed questions concerning international law and custom. FitzRoy did not demur from giving forthright answers. Should a foreigner for instance be allowed to enlist Tahitians as soldiers? FitzRoy, knowing whom they had in mind, answered: impolitic and highly improper. He found—says Darwin in his diary, and surely to his own surprise—that some of his replies were interpreted by the chiefs into laws given verbally on the spot. The Queen's secretary then asked a somewhat delicate question. Recently a British merchant had threatened his government's reprisals if the Tahitians, in their recent prohibitionist campaign, had carried out their threat of forcibly pouring his stock of spirits down the drain; what ought the Tahitians to have done, and what would FitzRoy have done if the merchant had asked him to effect reprisals? FitzRoy, his sense of fairness easily overcoming any patriotic feeling, answered with undiminished forthrightness: 'Had the Tahitians enforced their law, I could in no way have objected.'

Then came something of a surprise, a counter-claim by the Tahitians, and one as long outstanding as that which FitzRoy had come to enforce. It was, they admitted, for a comparatively trifling amount, 390 dollars. But the British Government had not even acknowledged it. It was a claim for indemnity and damages arising out of the arbitrary dumping on their shores by a British whaling captain of thirteen mutineers and of his subsequent refusal to take them back again. FitzRoy could only assure the Queen and her chiefs that an oversight had occurred and that he would do his best to see matters put right. He was so impressed however by the reasonableness of the claim that he later quoted it in full in the *Narrative*.

Finally FitzRoy gave the assembly an assurance couched in Christian terms. He was faced by the chiefs with the expressed fear that the next British warship to call would be less pacific than his own, would in fact come to conquer and enslave them. 'Rest assured,' answered FitzRoy, 'that the ships of Great Britain never will molest Tahitians so long as they conduct themselves towards British subjects as they wish to be treated by Britains.'

On that note the meeting ended. Though few of his naval colleagues could have taken exception to its noble sentiments a more cautious officer—Commodore Mason for instance—might well have been shocked at the unequivocal answers that FitzRoy had given; and a harsher man might have considered that FitzRoy had leant over backwards to take the natives' point of view. The fact remained however that FitzRoy had put the Tahitians thoroughly in the mood to co-operate, had created in the chiefs something of his own feeling of *noblesse oblige* and in all his native audience a self-righteous glow. Nor, in fact, did the glow die down too soon. Collection of the debt began the very next morning; the richer put their names down in a book, and the officers of the *Beagle* even found themselves being asked by the poorer for small change for their precious and exiguous dollars. By the time the *Beagle* sailed all but 515 of the dollars had been collected.

The *Beagle*'s hospitality to the Tahitians on the following evening passed off very well, though FitzRoy wished it could have been more lavish. He did his best, and so did his crew:

> Mr Pritchard undertook the troublesome office of interpreter and master of the ceremonies, and by his assistance we saw the whole party collected on the *Beagle*'s upper deck, while the seamen manned yards, and we all gave the queen three cheers. [Only fear of damaging the chronometers had prevented a gun salute.]
>
> A bad dinner, accepted after the four miles walk, in a manner it did not deserve, was succeeded by a few rockets, blue lights, and false fires.

Luckily the fireworks were good, and they were received with rapture, not only by the guests but by all the Tahitians lining the bay. When making visits to natives, FitzRoy advised, always take fireworks.

> Some presents to each of our guests helped to amuse them and keep up their cheerfulness. After tea I proposed hearing a few of the seamen's songs,—as some of our crew were very good singers— not at the time thinking of their prejudices against any singing except hymns. Mr Pritchard had no word to interpret 'song' but 'hymene': and 'Rule Britannia', with one or two other grave performances, passed off well, but to the perplexing of Mr Pritchard and surprise of the Tahitians, a merry comic song was struck up, which obliged Mr Pritchard to answer the queen's enquiries plainly, by saying, 'No, that was not a hymn,' it was 'sea singing'. 'God save the King' sounded more gravely, and suited better.
>
> We landed the party almost at their doors, and if they were half as well pleased as we were, our little preparations had not been a waste of time and trouble. Their behaviour on board was extremely correct.

Darwin's report of the comic song episode is that the Queen remarked that 'that certainly could not be "hymeni".' He agrees with the Captain that the Tahitians behaved with great propriety on board and seemed to enjoy their visit; the party, he says, did not break up until after midnight.

Mr Pritchard seems to have been of some dissenting denomination, and it was with Mr Wilson of the London (later the Church) Missionary Society that FitzRoy and Darwin had first and greater contact. This Mr Wilson was in fact the 'uneducated sailor' of Kotzebue's strictures, and naturally both men were anxious to discover how much their own impressions would tally with what they had read. Darwin, not tremendously impressed, was quite willing to believe that Mr Wilson's exterior hid 'a great deal of unpretending excellent merit.' FitzRoy was impressed, rather, by the ease and familiarity with which the natives treated Mr Wilson. Here at any rate was none of the 'fear' of the missionaries that had been suggested.

In truth Darwin's description of the missionaries is sometimes more favourable and less critical than FitzRoy's; perhaps the disparity between his own observations and Kotzebue's descriptions particularly affronted his sense of fair-mindedness and need for scientific objectivity. In any case, Darwin's reaction shows that FitzRoy, though his religious outlook was growing ever more dominant, was in no way behaving like a willfuly prejudiced religious crank.

One thing that greatly impressed FitzRoy in Tahiti was his meeting, a few days before the Queen Pomare episode, with the most senior missionary on the island, the aged Mr Nott, who at the time was completing his translation of the Bible into the Tahitian language. 'I paid my respects to the author of this immense undertaking, and asked his advice and opinion respecting the affairs in which I was instructed to take a part while on the island.' Later FitzRoy saw a native reading the New Testament at the door of his hut. 'The superior expression of that man's countenance, and his unaffected employment (for I came upon him suddenly), made an impression upon my mind which, I hope, will not be forgotten.'

Darwin by now had gone on an expedition into the precipitous interior. It was his turn to be impressed—not only by the scenery but also by the unaffected piety of one of his guides at his nightly prayers. 'Those travellers who hint that a Tahitian prays only when the eyes of the missionary are fixed on him, should have slept with us that night on the mountain side.' He also gives thanks to the missionaries for relegating the Ava plant, from which native spirit had used to be made, to growth only in a wild state in inaccessible places. He adds that he was afraid he made his guides to sin, in pressing upon them the contents of his flask. 'As often as they drank a little, they put their fingers before their mouths and uttered the word "Missionary".' Then, more seriously: 'When one reflects on the effect of intemperance on the aboriginals of the two Americas, I think it will be acknowledged that every well wisher of Tahiti owes no common debt of gratitude to the Missionaries.'

Sunday came, and both men went to a well attended divine service. FitzRoy admits there was some inattendance and whispering, particularly amongst the younger natives, who needed an occasional touch from the white wand of a most stern looking old beadle. (But they did have the gold braid of the naval uniforms to thrill them, and what English congregation would have done better?) As for Kotzebue's epithets of ludicrous and grotesque, he saw nothing to justify them.

Later FitzRoy and some of the officers visited the mission school, purposely arriving before the teacher to test whether the accusation of compulsion was justified. It was not—the children were waiting for the teacher. Then the children, with the teacher's encouragement, gleefully showed off before their spectacular visitor. 'The Captain wishes you happiness!' they were told, and were instructed to write this down. They did it very well; and some, of their own accord, added, 'And we wish happiness to the Captain.' Apter pupils, these, than the villainous York Minster had ever been.

FitzRoy had two criticisms to make. One, somewhat in line

with Kotzebue, was that an encouragement to return to some sort of native costume, in preference to the use of dirty scraps of European clothing, might be a good idea. The other was that 'some kind of innocent recreation was much wanted by these light-hearted islanders.' Darwin wrote unequivocably in a letter home: 'The Captain and all on board (whose opinions are worth anything) have come to a very decided conclusion on the high merits of the Missionaries.' And in his diary he wrote: 'There are many who attack even more acrimoniously than Kotzebue, both the Missionaries, their system, and the effect produced. Such reasoners never compare the present to the former state only twenty years before; nor even to that of Europe in this day, but to the high standard of Gospel perfection.' Again a reasonable man's angry indictment of unfairness. And then comes a sentence that must have surely been written with FitzRoy and his Fuegians in mind. After listing some of the horrible and cruel practices from which aboriginals in all parts of the world had been weaned, he adds: 'It is base ingratitude in a voyager to forget these things; at the point of shipwreck on some unknown coast he will most devoutly pray that the lesson of the Missionary may have extended thus far.'

FitzRoy experienced one more encounter before the *Beagle* sailed for New Zealand, in fact with the man whom the native chiefs had had in mind when asking leading questions on international law. It illustrates his violent dislike of the adventurer type, which had already come to abound in this part of the world, the type that possessed no true philanthropy but only a desire for personal gain or personal aggrandizement.

Aggrandizement is the more apt word to use in connection with the highly coloured, not to say well nigh incredible figure of Charles Philippe Hippolytus de Thierry. This is FitzRoy's description of their first meeting:

I went to see a person who styled himself Baron de Thierry, King of Nuhahiva [one of the Marquesas Islands] and sovereign chief of New Zealand. About the house in which resides this self-

called philanthropist—said to be maturing arrangements for civil-
izing Nuhahiva and New Zealand, as well as for cutting a canal
across the Isthmus of Darien—were a motley group of tattooed
New Zealanders, half-clothed natives of Tahiti, and some ill-
looking American seamen. I was received in affected state by
this grandee, who abruptly began to question me with—'Well,
Captain! what news from Panama? Have the Congress settled the
manner in which they are to carry my ideas into effect?' I tried to
be decently civil to him, as well as to the 'baroness'; but could not
diminish my suspicions, and soon cut short our conference.

Baron de Thierry is the sort of person who has made so many
claims for himself in his lifetime that afterwards truth and fiction
about him are a little difficult to disentangle. His career might be
considered no more than a rather sad joke were it not that, in the
eighteen-thirties and -forties and in the Southern Pacific, such
impossibly flamboyant adventures could have a significance.
Born in England in 1793, of French *émigré* parents, and becoming
a music teacher, his first escapade was to elope with one of his
pupils, the daughter of an archdeacon. He then managed to
become a student at Cambridge, though he failed there to get
himself ordained.

He did, however, meet his fate in the shape of Chief Hongi,
a Maori who had been brought from New Zealand for the purpose of helping to compile a dictionary and grammar of his
native language. De Thierry suddenly acquired a passion for all
things New Zealand, a desire to see the country colonized and
to settle there himself. To this end he entrusted Hongi and his
English sponsor with a considerable sum of money with which to
buy land in the home of his choice. When he discovered that he
had become owner of an estate, admittedly of ill-defined boundaries but comprising some 40,000 acres, he was delighted. After
failing to persuade either the English or the French to sponsor a
colonizing scheme, he crossed with his family to America, the
Panama scheme having a bearing on his New Zealand fixation
since his prime intention was to shorten the sailing distance to
that country. Eight years later he was sailing towards his meeting
with FitzRoy and his claim to be considered one of the chief, if

not the chief, landowner in New Zealand. Having considered whether he should call himself King of that country, he settled more modestly for the title of Sovereign Chief; at the Marquesas Islands, or Nuhahiva, however, where he stopped, he was so pleased with the situation and the natives, that he drew up in the presence of the latter a solemn deed declaring himself their monarch.

When FitzRoy met him he had been in Tahiti a few months and had busied himself writing to the Governor of New South Wales and the British Resident in New Zealand, telling them that he was on his way to take up his inheritance. By now he had conceived the idea of, if necessary, arriving in force; and the 'motley group' that FitzRoy discovered around him was his embryo army: FitzRoy adds to his description of their first meeting, 'In his house was a pile of muskets, whose fixed and very long bayonets had not a philanthropic aspect.' The next day, says FitzRoy, 'I again met the titular king of Nuhahiva, and told him my suspicions, so plainly, that he said he should appeal to the governor of New South Wales, to the Admiralty, and to the King of England himself, against the unjust and improper conduct of the captain of the *Beagle*!'

Whether de Thierry did write to all these people is not known, but at least on the very same evening of the second visit he penned a long and angry letter to FitzRoy personally, and this has come down to us, being in the archives of the Dixson Library of New South Wales.[2] It is an interesting document.

Most of the first page is taken up with a recital of the writer's claim to importance. He is godson to the King of France and known personally to the King of England: he has French rights and he has British rights. Then come details of his own claims to sovereignty. 'As King of Nuhahiva I also hoist my flag and declare that I stand free and Independent. I am no Pirate, no obscure adventurer; I am a philanthropist and go forward, strong in my faith in the Protection of God, to save the people of New Zealand and of Nuhahiva from the miseries that have hitherto been accumulated on the devoted heads of aboriginal people.' Next

[2] File of New Zealand material, ref. Add. 207.

comes a statement of his intention to sail to New Zealand to claim his own.

De Thierry then proceeds to turn his attention from himself to FitzRoy. First, he is afraid he does not know the Captain's true rank. Is he Lord, the Honourable, or plain Mister? In any case his insults deserve a court martial. By what right did he say the things he did say, by what right did he throw doubt on all de Thierry's claims, even suggesting that the Nuhahiva document might be a forgery and 'a got up thing'? By what right did he threaten to warn the New Zealand authorities against him as a dangerous personage? And, unkindest cut of all, 'By what right did you presume to insult me by telling me that you could see that I had never been accustomed to good society because I called you "Captain here and Captain there" and that I must have lived in the company of whalers.' Who indeed was FitzRoy to say all this, he who had called 'wearing your undress uniform and coming to my door in your ship's boat'? 'I repeat what I told you in person, that the day will come when your better thoughts will cause you to bitterly regret the above and insults which you lavished upon me in your visits of yesterday and today.' The letter ends with protestations of the writer's importance and noble connections—the English 'Royal hand has more than once been extended to me'—and ends: 'Leaving you to your meditations, I am, Sir, Yours etc.'

De Thierry claimed that FitzRoy wrote him an apology; and this may well be true for poor FitzRoy was always regretting his anger. It would, however, be an apology more dignified than humble: he was not the sort of person ever sincerely to regret that he had not suffered gladly either fools or knaves.

A week later Pritchard the missionary was coming on board the *Beagle* to say goodbye to his friends as they left Tahiti. 'He wished us,' says FitzRoy, 'a great deal more happiness than most of us will probably enjoy.' There followed the uneventful three weeks' journey over what Darwin calls 'the same blue, profoundly deep, ocean', to sight the northern tip of New Zealand just six days before Christmas 1835.

The *Beagle*'s visit to New Zealand was important to Robert FitzRoy. It is no doubt dangerous to isolate an incident in a man's life, an incident which he records yet with no greater emphasis than much else, and to pin-point it as crucial. But such crucial incidents, comparatively trivial in themselves, do happen to everyone; and to omit to make intelligent guesses at them on the part of a biographer would be like depicting on a canvas a hilly landscape as a flat one. Such an incident, therefore, may be considered now to have come FitzRoy's way.

He was with his friends the missionaries again, the missionaries of New Zealand, amongst whom incidentally was the elder brother of Richard Matthews and with whom that possibly priggish but certainly courageous 'catechist' was now to be left. What now touched FitzRoy's heart was a reference to the Fuegian episode:

> It was also gratifying to me to mark the lively interest taken by Mr Williams, Mr Davis, and Mr Baker in every detail connected with the Fuegians, and our attempt to establish Richard Matthews in Tierra del Fuego. Again and again they recurred to the subject, and asked for more information; they would not hear of my calling the attempt 'a failure'. 'It was the first step,' said they, 'and similar in its results to our first step in New Zealand. We failed at first; but by God's blessing upon human exertions, we have at last succeeded far beyond our anticipations.'

'Where your treasure is, there will your heart be also.' FitzRoy's treasure, that gave balm and satisfaction to his soul, was the practice of philanthropy, at times it would seem a somewhat high-handed philanthropy, but no less passionately well meant. The Fuegian adventure was a typical, almost a compulsive, action on FitzRoy's part, and he had often felt the need to defend it. That the missionaries of New Zealand, to whom in any case he was naturally attracted, should have gone out of their way to commend that action, to try to persuade him, with percipient friendliness, that there had been no failure, must have touched him deeply. From now until the end of his stay, therefore, FitzRoy was the close friend and admirer of the New Zealand missionaries; and, even more than in Tahiti, he spent his time with them, viewing their achievements and learning of their difficulties. He was in the position of one who is storing up impressions and forming strong opinions without knowing how significant the occupation was for his own future.

In truth neither FitzRoy nor Darwin received such a favourable impression of New Zealand and its inhabitants as they had of Tahiti. There were reasons for this. The first was a purely fortuitous one. Contrary winds delayed their landing and robbed them of the sort of spontaneously boisterous welcome they were afforded at Tahiti, added to which there was a rumour going round on shore that here was not a peaceful British frigate but none other than the fabulous Baron de Thierry come with his army to claim his kingdom. When FitzRoy heard of this he was highly amused.

The other reason for an unfavourable impression was the simple one that at this time the small part of New Zealand most affected by white penetration and influence did not present a very beautiful face. The little settlement of Kororareka, part white, part Maori, grown up to provide the needs of the visiting sailors and whalers and traders, had earned the expressive name of 'the Pacific Hell'.

The day after their arrival FitzRoy and Darwin visited the place. Neither of them was much edified. FitzRoy marvelled that men could live in such degraded conditions as did some of the Maoris here: 'In a fine climate, surrounded by beautiful trees and luxuriant herbage, can one account for human nature degrading itself so much as to live in such a den? Is it not that the genuine, simple beauties of Creation are understood, and enjoyed, only in proportion as man becomes more refined, and as he differs more from his own species in what is falsely called a state of nature.'

A visit to the nearby little island of Paihia, where the missionaries lived, naturally produced a more favourable reaction. FitzRoy was saddened to find that a fine stone building was not the Anglican church, which was in fact a miserable building. He thought a leaf might be taken out of the Roman Catholic book here: 'Would a little outward show do any harm amongst such ignorant human beings as the savages of New Zealand?' A visit to Mr Busby, the British Resident, produced a great surprise. The admirable fellow possessed practically now powers at all; he had not even the authority of a magistrate.

It was at Paihia that FitzRoy met the Mr Williams and Mr Baker already referred to as pleasing him over their reaction to his Fuegian venture. There were two Williamses, brothers, and FitzRoy was sorry to miss the elder, the Reverend Henry, who was away on a trip, for he had been a lieutenant in the Royal Navy, and a surveyor. It was arranged that Mr Baker should take FitzRoy with him on some of his rounds of duty.

The first meeting, for the purpose of eliciting support for the control of the liquor trade, was with two ex-masters of whaling ships who had purchased an island and settled down there. FitzRoy reacted violently against them. 'Such men as these, strongly prejudiced, deaf to reason, and too often habitually vicious; run-away convicts whose characters may be imagined; and democratic seceders from regular government, cause the principal difficulties against which honest, upright settlers, and the whole missionary body, have to contend.'

Mr Baker then took FitzRoy on another visit in his anti-liquor campaign, this time to a native village. FitzRoy was much more favourably impressed. At Kororareka both he and Darwin had formed a very unfavourable impression of the natives, dirty and in rags, often with vicious countenances. But here things were different, more near to the high self-respect and natural cheerfulness of the Tahitians. As Baker talked, FitzRoy observed, and sketched: 'such heads...such a group for a painter!' Here Baker found himself called upon for advice in connection with a tribal dispute over land; and FitzRoy listened attentively afterwards to his friend's explanation of the difficulty. 'The precise manner in which territory is divided among the savages surprised me not a little: I thought land was but slightly valued by them. Though sold to Europeans for what we consider trifles, the sale is, to them, a matter of high importance, in which every free man of the tribe ought to be consulted.'

There followed Christmas Day and a church service: too long, thought FitzRoy; and the fact that Mr Baker seemed more fluent in Maori than English strengthened him in the feeling that the missionaries tended to pay too little attention to their fellow whites, who were often destroying much good Christian work by setting such a bad example to the Maoris. There followed afterwards a visit to a missionary farming settlement and institute. The scene might have been in England; and FitzRoy was happy as well as impressed. He was also impressed by an old native who 'made a shrewd remark about certain seven-barrelled guns sent among them by some of our countrymen, even while others were preaching the gospel of peace.'

Finally, during his stay, FitzRoy was to become more closely and personally involved in the affairs of New Zealand. The utter lack of any real government or authority in the islands, coupled with the respect that the people had learnt to feel towards the presence of any visiting British warship, resulted in FitzRoy being called in to act as adviser, judge and arbitrator, rather as he had been at Tahiti but more urgently. Realizing that it was of little use to refer disputants to Mr Busby the Resident, since his powers were virtually non-existent, FitzRoy in most instances passed on the final responsibility to the missionaries as being the only *de facto* authority in the land. One case however he did tackle himself, since it involved matters of maritime law, a bitter dispute between the master of a sealing vessel and his ill-treated and mutinous crew. FitzRoy himself boarded the vessel and, holding an informal court of enquiry, managed to achieve a compromise. 'But I felt that the calm was unlikely to last, and two days afterwards fresh appeals were made, to which I could not attend, being in the act of leaving the port.'

FitzRoy left New Zealand with obviously much to occupy his mind. He found the position there in many ways quite anarchical, with the missionaries frustrated and prevented from doing half the good they might have done. It worried and saddened him; and in the *Narrative* he devotes several pages to suggestions for a remedy. These were in essence that the British government should supply for the South Seas a sort of travelling government or source of advice and authority, in the shape of a naval vessel that would be stationed in the area for a term of years and then be replaced by another.

One particular suggestion is interesting. 'And if a sensible man,' wrote FitzRoy humbly, 'whose natural ability had been improved by an education unattainable by sailors, could be tempted to bear the trials and losses of a long sea voyage, in a busily employed ship, how much might science profit by the labours of three or four such years.'

Another job for Darwin in these parts in fact. FitzRoy had no idea that the job would come not to Darwin but to himself.

BOOK 3

The Impassioned
Philanthropist

CHAPTER 14

The Writing of a Book

THE great voyage was over. On October 2nd 1836 the *Beagle* touched at Falmouth, and Darwin had disembarked and rushed home to his family.[1] On October 28th the anchor was let go at Greenwich, where the chronometer rates were ascertained and a loss of only thirty-three seconds in five years was discovered.

Older by those five years of unforgettable experience, the two young men, FitzRoy and Darwin, had to fit themselves back into a landsman's way of living, and to give thought to their future careers. Both men married, Darwin to a Wedgwood cousin a couple of years later, but FitzRoy within a couple of months.

[1] FitzRoy took the opportunity to visit Robert Were Fox, the Quaker scientist of Falmouth, whose daughter wrote the *Memoirs of Old Friends* referred to in note 1 of Chapter 10. Caroline Fox's entry runs: 'October 3.—Captain FitzRoy came to tea. He returned yesterday from a five years' voyage, in *H.M.S. Beagle*, of scientific research round the world, and is going to write a book. He came to see papa's dipping needle deflector, with which he was highly delighted...He stayed till after eleven, and is a most agreeable, gentlemanlike young man. He has had a delightful voyage, and made many discoveries, as there were several scientific men on board. Darwin, the "fly-catcher" and "stone-pounder", had decided that the coral insects do not work up from the bottom of the sea...' There follows a description of Darwin's (correct) theory of the formation of coral islands, which says much for Caroline's acumen as well as for FitzRoy's enthusiastic loyalty to his friend.

The girl, Maria Henrietta O'Brien, daughter of a country gentle-man and major general, must have been waiting for him.

For a little while the *Beagle* was famous. While Darwin, with a mass of material and specimens at his disposal, was being wel-comed into the scientific world, FitzRoy was busy showing visitors over his ship. There is a little story of this, told by the biographer of Lieutenant Sulivan (who also, it will be remembered, had a girl waiting for him):

> On the return of the vessel after such an interesting voyage, so many people came to visit her that the captain gave the order that *respectable-looking persons only* were to be admitted by the accommodation-ladder; others were to enter by the gangway (where some projections three inches wide against the ship's side afford foothold, there being two ropes to assist the climber). Sulivan, who was at the time on watch, noticed the sentry wave a boat away from the ladder round to the gangway. Presently the head of a very pretty, stylish woman appeared in it, and Sulivan went forward to assist her. She was followed by a rather plain-looking man, who asked for the captain. After they had been conducted below, FitzRoy came on deck, much put out, and said, 'Do you know it was the Astronomer Royal who has been treated with such scant ceremony?' He was paying what was somewhat of an official visit, with his wife. [2]

Respectable looking or not, the Astronomer Royal was a great man in FitzRoy's world, and he had had every right to be vexed at being so convicted of discourtesy. Equally he had every right to be pleased when a little later the Royal Geographic Society presented him with their gold medal. FitzRoy was also thanked in Parliament and highly praised by Beaufort, the Naval Hydro-grapher; he had proved himself an extremely competent marine surveyor and a producer of charts that are remembered as examples of their kind in the Royal Navy to this day. [3] But he did not get another surveying job. Sulivan was returning a year later

[2] *Biography*, page 45.
[3] Volume IV of *Medicine and the Navy* notes that the *Beagle* returned with a remarkably good health record—the Kilner preserving jars had helped.

to the Falklands in command of a surveying ketch, and at Fitz-Roy's recommendation. The *Beagle* returned to the coast of Australia, but with Wickham and later Stokes in command. FitzRoy stayed at home.

To do so may well have been what he wanted. Darwin speaks of FitzRoy suffering from ill health at this time.[4] There was also the fact that Mary FitzRoy was going to have a baby. After the presentation to the Admiralty of all his official reports and charts, and after the compiling of a *Sailing Direction* for seamen around the South American coasts, there was to be the production of a book for the public on the *Beagle* voyage.

It was soon clear that this book would involve a major effort. The first volume was to be an account of the earlier voyage of the *Adventure* and *Beagle*; but Captain King had retired and gone back to live in Australia, and he left the production entirely to FitzRoy. The second volume would cover FitzRoy's own account of the second voyage of the *Beagle* under his command; and the third volume would be Darwin's account of the same, from a scientific angle. There finally proved to be a fourth volume, an Appendix of 350 pages and containing, besides ships' logs and official orders and the like, FitzRoy's own 'Remarks' on subjects, varying from tides to the Fuegian languages. His Volume Two extends to something like a quarter of a million words.

Darwin and FitzRoy had as a matter of fact already been collaborators in a small way—in an article on the 'moral state' of Tahiti and New Zealand, of which something more anon. FitzRoy had encouraged Darwin in the writing of a diary during the voyage; and he had first suggested that parts of it should be incorporated in his narrative: this was not unjustifiable condescension, for Darwin had been extremely diffident about 'appearing in print'. Only later, when to praise from his Captain was added praise from his friends and relations at home, did Darwin begin to have other ideas, and the plan was changed—as far as is known entirely amicably—to the production of a separate third volume. Darwin incidentally was a little unkind about Volume One. On a

[4] Darwin suffered too, of course, and chronically; though it has never actually been proved that his ill health was caused by the voyage.

visit to FitzRoy he looked over a few pages; and, 'I was absolutely forced against all love of truth to tell the Captain that I supposed it very good, but in honest reality no pudding for little school-boys ever was so heavy.' He must have struck a bad patch, for although Captain King's efforts are the least interesting of the three they are hardly that heavy.

FitzRoy's *Narrative* deserves some attention, and that in spite of the fact that it has already been quoted from extensively and forms the main authority for the preceding chapters. It deserves it particularly by reason of the two very unexpected chapters with which the book ends. They show a trend of thought and character that up to now has only been apparent in minor ways.

But first shall come some other points about the book, that also have some bearing upon FitzRoy as a man as well as an author.

There is of course much description of events experienced; but there is also much description of places visited and, in particular, of people met, their characteristics, their anthropology and their history. FitzRoy, besides always being interested in people, must have got through a lot of reading, both before and during and after the voyage.

There is for instance his fascinated interest in the Araucanian Indians, so that he is continually interrupting that account of his of the spectacular dash to the wrecked *Challenger* crew with dissertations on Araucanian legend and history. He even goes to the trouble of translating into verse excerpts from the cantos of the sixteenth century poet, Ercilla, whose claim to fame is to have composed an epic poem, 'La Araucana.'[5]

[5] Whether these translations should be considered good, bad, or indifferent is not highly significant. However, there cannot have been many naval captains in any age who would have been either capable or anxious to transpose the verse of a sixteenth century Spaniard into corresponding English, and it may be worth while to give one of his two pieces of translation:

> ...the veteran Villegran
> Heedless of any kind of death,
> Hazarded all upon a cast!

Half a chapter goes to the anthropology of Chiloé and the Chonos Islands on the west coast of South America. Two chapters are devoted to the history and geography of the Falkland Islands; and no less than three chapters deal with the aborigines of the southern tip of the continent, Patagonians as well as Fuegians, an effort being made to analyse their tribal divisions, while sections of the Appendix are given to physical anthropology (called phrenology) and to language.

The presence of this last is interesting. It includes seven pages of vocabulary, mostly covering the dialects of Jemmy Button on the one hand and Fuegia and York Minster on the other.[6] Whether Richard Matthews did more we do not know; but certainly FitzRoy, with less time on his hands, did much: he was sufficiently practical, and modern, in his missionary approach always to stress the primary need for the natives' language to be understood, as also the advantage on the missionary's part of some medical skill and knowledge.

We come to the last two chapters of the book. From internal evidence it is clear they were not written until well on into 1838,

He rode a stately powerful horse,
Purest of Spanish blood—
Strength and activity were well combined
In that courageous steed—
Swift and high-spirited, he yet obeyed
The slightest touch of finger on the rein.

The danger reached—instant as thought—
The warrior's spurs excite the noble brute—
He dashes on—and down the barrier goes.
A deafening crash and dire dismay
Followed, as onward tore their way
Those few determined men.
The gallant steed unhurt appeared,
Strove foremost in the fight, and feared
Only to be the last!

[6] The native names of the three Fuegians, according to FitzRoy, are: Jemmy Button, Orundellico; Fuegia Basket, Yokcushlu; York Minster, Ellaparu.

as much as two years after the return of the *Beagle*. FitzRoy had had time to think, and to brood.

The first of the two chapters begins:

> Having ended my narrative of the *Beagle*'s voyage, I might lay down my pen: but there are some reflections, arising out of circumstances witnessed by myself, and enquiries since made respecting them that I feel anxious to lay before those who take interest in such subjects; and who will detect fallacies which I, in a purblind search after truth, may have overlooked.

After this somewhat typical over-protestation the author begs that his remarks 'may be viewed solely as those of a sailor who writes for the younger members of his profession', and defends himself against the possible accusation of hastily formed opinions by stating that 'from boyhood I have always taken interest in observing the various countenances, heads, shapes, sizes, colours and other peculiarities of the human race.' FitzRoy then propounds and elaborates his theme. It is that all men are of one blood, but have been affected by climate, habit and food and have changed in response to their environment. The fact that they have spread themselves from one geographical source, using as they were bound to do the seaways for their purpose, is borne out by the evidence of the early invention of the boat and the many early legends and stories of its use. Since the primitive boat could only sail before the wind, a study of the world's prevailing winds will help to arrive at the probable lines of migration. FitzRoy then proceeds to set down these probable lines. One of his suggestions is that America was populated from Asia by way of the Aleutian Islands.

It can be legitimately deduced from the above that FitzRoy was being remarkably modern and even ahead of his times. But that is only half the picture. He is tied to a theory that, we should now hold, vitiates his argument and makes him sound gullible and unscientific. It is, quite simply, a belief in the literal truth of the Bible. Thus he considers it axiomatic that all human migration has spread from Asia Minor. No one, he says, can read of India, China, Mexico and Peru, as well as Tartary, Japan and Polynesia 'without being struck by the traces of Hebrew ceremonies and rites, by the evidence of the worship of Baal, or by remains of Arkite observances, scattered through the more populous, if not through all the nations upon earth.' He refers back to his earlier description of his favourite Araucanian Indians, wherein he wrote: 'There is a word in common use among them, meaning 'the great ancestor', or 'the renowned', which is hardly to be distinguished from Shem.'

There is if anything even less good reason for including in the *Narrative* the second of these concluding chapters, 'A Very Few Remarks with Reference to the Deluge.' It begins with the rather surprising disclosure that FitzRoy did not always possess a belief in the literal truth of the Bible but came to it through doubt and self-questioning. After saying that 'reflections arising out of facts witnessed during the *Beagle*'s voyage' have occasioned the remarks that follow, he continues:

I suffered much anxiety in former years from a disposition to doubt, if not disbelieve, the inspired History written by Moses. I knew so little of that record, or of the intimate manner in which the Old Testament is connected with the New, that I fancied some events there related might be mythological or fabulous, while I sincerely believed the truth of others; a wavering between opinions, which could only be productive of an unsettled, and therefore unhappy, state of mind...Much of my uneasiness was caused by reading works written by men of Voltaire's school; and by those of geologists who contradicted by implication, if not in plain terms, the authenticity of the Scriptures; before I had any acquaintance with the volume which they so incautiously impugn...For men who, like myself formerly, are willingly ignorant of the Bible, and doubt its divine inspiration, I can only have one feeling—sincere sorrow.

After this somewhat pugnacious confession FitzRoy reiterates that he is writing with the young sailor particularly in mind and then makes one final self-accusation. Once, he says, when crossing a vast bed of rolled stones (obviously, as has already been stated, the Santa Cruz River valley) he remarked to the friend who was with him (Darwin): 'this could never have been effected by a forty days flood.' Thus was he willing to disbelieve the inspired account 'upon the evidence of a hasty glance'. There then follows the argument, of which an effort will be made to give a fair summary.

First, Moses was not wrong, but indeed shows his god-given knowledge by, for instance, stating (in the first chapter of Genesis) that the sun was created on the day after vegetation was created. Since vegetation cannot live long without light, this shows that when the Bible says a day it means a day, and not a thousand years or a thousand ages. This makes an anomaly of the theory of recent geologists, such as Lyell, that there have been successive creations at vast intervals.

The reference in Genesis i, 29 to green herbs as the meat for beasts has a bearing on the story of the Deluge. It may be objected that some beasts are physically adapted to be carnivores. But dogs can thrive on a vegetable diet; and in any case conditions may have been different before the Flood, as may in fact be concluded from the longevity of the early Biblical characters.

The shells and other fossils discovered by Darwin and himself at the Santa Cruz River and elsewhere show by their condition, FitzRoy considers, not that the land had once sunk beneath the waters but that the waters had risen over the land. And if the waters had risen so vastly over Patagonia they must have risen over the whole world. Alternations of lava and shell-bearing strata, such as Darwin found in the Andes, bear testimony to a vast volcanic catastrophe accompanying the Flood. His, FitzRoy's, only experience of land (as opposed to water) rising after such a catastrophe as the earthquake at Concepcion is that eventually it sinks again.

Having been shown some of the evidence gleaned from the *Beagle*'s voyage, the young reader's attention is next directed to some more general considerations.

To the natural question, where did all the water come from for a universal flood, the simple and adequate answer is 'from the place whence the earth and its oceans came': it should be enough to say, 'it was the will of Him who is Almighty', the Supreme Being using secondary causes to work out his will.

Biblical longevity, it is again pointed out, indicates some fundamental difference in the world's make-up in those days—and for that matter the depth of water needed to cover the earth represents no more than a coat of varnish on a sixteen-inch globe.

There comes now the Ark itself and the objection that such a heterogeneous collection of animals as that assembled by Noah could not have lived together. But, apart from the possible exclusion of the very big for lack of room—a suggestion perhaps borne out by the disappearance ever afterwards of some of the giant animals found as fossils—apart from the again simple answer, 'He who made, could surely manage!', there is always to be remembered the effect of a colossal storm. Those who have not experienced a typhoon cannot realize its effect. The animals would have been much too terrified to entertain thoughts of eating each other.

The arguments of this chapter do not quite end there. But to quote further is to risk exhibiting FitzRoy unjustifiably as a laughing stock to the modern reader. The suggestion that there was not room for the large animals in the Ark was so to stick in Darwin's throat that he was to remember it with ridicule over twenty years later. The point has now to be made that FitzRoy was by no means being so ridiculous, nor so egregious, as might at first sight be imagined.

FitzRoy, it must be remembered, had grown up in, and was living in, an outstandingly religious age, an age of reaction against the pagan rationalism of the eighteenth century. Sir George Trevelyan in his *English Social History* puts it succinctly. In the first thirty years of the nineteenth century, he writes, there had been 'a steady infiltration of evangelical religion into all classes of society, finally not excepting the highest.' The whole Victorian period, he points out, was marked by seriousness of thought and self-discipline of character, an outcome of the Puritan tradition, to which the Wesleyan and Evangelical movements had given another lease of life. And the belief in the verbal inspiration of the Bible was a bastion of that religiosity, 'common to the Nonconformist, to the Church Evangelicals and, to a scarcely less degree, to High Churchmen.'

Not only so, but passionate belief in this verbal inspiration did not necessarily go with an unscientific or anti-scientific frame of mind. On the contrary. The young and rapidly growing science of geology abounded with enthusiasts who saw in it nothing so much as a heaven-sent vehicle for reinforcing their biblical claims. This view was held by such genuine advancers of the science as Hugh Miller of 'Red Sandstone' fame, who in 1852 addressed the Royal Physical Society of Edinburgh on the subject of 'Geological Evidence in favour of Revealed Religion', while at the other end of the scale, according to a contemporary but detached observer, 'every curate in England dabbled in geology and hunted for vestiges of Creation.'[7] Henslow warned his protégé Darwin against Charles Lyell's advanced views, while recommending his book. Then, too, all through the 1830's (at the time that FitzRoy was writing), there were appearing the famous Bridgewater Treatises. These were a series of books published under a legacy from the Eighth Earl of Bridgewater, all of which were to illustrate 'the Power, Wisdom and Goodness of God as manifested in the Creation.' The president of the Royal Society had the choosing of the authors, and these included such a brilliant physiologist as Sir Charles Bell, pioneer in neurology. Yet one of this series (on the manifestation as shown in the creation of animals), while stressing the nice adaptation of organs to their functions, could yet base its analysis of creation on the first chapter of Genesis. On the fifth day, it declares lyrically, 'in an instant, in obedience to that quickening word...the boundless ocean with all its tributary streams became prolific and brought forth by myriads its endless and strange diversity.'

Thus FitzRoy was in good company in his attitude to the natural sciences; and, though the narrative of the voyages of the *Adventure* and *Beagle* was hardly the fitting place for it, his defence of the literal interpretation does not in the least make him an unreasonable or unbalanced sort of person. Or if it does, again he is in good company, good but increasingly unhappy and exacerbated company, which was to come to know that it faced a

---

[7] See *The Education of Henry Adams*, the autobiography of the son of America's diplomatic representative in England in the 1860s.

dangerous enemy and so would find itself pushed into extremes. Equally FitzRoy's religiosity was not exceptional in his class or his profession. The Church, even in the lower reaches of its hierarchy, had become respectable again; and the alternatives of Army, Navy, Divinity, Law as careers for sons must have meant that most gentlemen's families had a clergyman in their midst. Not only so, but the Navy at this time seems in particular to have been producing men of Christian and missionary ardour: to go no further than FitzRoy's own experience, there was Henry Williams in New Zealand and Allen Gardiner who, as we shall see, was to follow him in Tierra del Fuego; his friend Seymour of the *Challenger* had a brother in holy orders, and his young Lieutenant, Sulivan, was reading the Psalms every day as his devout mother had told him to do.

However, though there may be good general reasons for FitzRoy writing the surprising two last chapters of his book, it is not very easy to see what were the particular reasons. If we can satisfactorily find these we shall have gained some clues to his true character and some explanation of his future conduct.

There can only have been two particular and immediate causes: the irritant of Darwin, and the example of the missionaries.

Of the first we must guard against the temptation to make too much. Years later FitzRoy was to declare publicly that he had often expostulated with his old shipmate for entertaining ideas contrary to the first chapter of Genesis. But it is quite possible that he had in later years persuaded himself of something that had not very much foundation in fact. There are not many signs from the two men's accounts of the *Beagle* voyage that there was often any active clashing of views. In one instance there is evidence to the opposite: their literary collaboration in an article on Tahiti and New Zealand already mentioned. This article appeared in the South African Christian Recorder, apparently through the good offices of Sir John Herschel, the astronomer, who was at that time living in Cape Colony and who seems to have been very good to the officers of the *Beagle* on their call during the last lap of their voyage.[8] The article is a defence of the missionaries and their work, against uninformed opinion in South Africa. It anticipates much of what was later to appear in the *Narrative* or the *Journal*, and ends: 'We are very much satisfied that they [the missionaries] thoroughly deserve the warmest support, not only of individuals, but of the British Government. Robert FitzRoy; Charles Darwin.'

Nevertheless, that there must have been some mutual reaction is obvious. It seems rather to have taken the shape of a leaven, which hardly began to work before the two men parted, but that then worked, as leaven does, with great and startling effect. Darwin confesses in his *Autobiography* that, though during the voyage he was 'quite orthodox', he was in the two years following the voyage 'led to think much about religion' and gradually came to hold the opinion 'that the Old Testament from its manifestly false history of the world...was no more to be trusted than the sacred books of the Hindoos or the beliefs of any barbarians.'[9] FitzRoy, as we have seen from his introduction to the last chapter of the *Narrative*, also experienced a change of heart after the voyage, ignorance and anxious doubt turning to comfortable and immovable conviction.

No wonder then that when the two men met in 1839 they found that no longer could they abide each other's views. They had as it were suffered not a sea but a post-sea change. Darwin could conceal his poor opinion of King's writing, he could happily sentimentalize—all this in a letter to his Sister—over the sight of young mother and baby, he could cheerfully report that the Captain was 'going on very well'. But he could not deny himself the irritated addition to this last remark 'that is, for a man who has the most consummate skill in looking at everything and everybody in a perverted manner!' The strength of this reaction is augmented by a sentence in the *Autobiography*: 'I saw FitzRoy

[8] This is apparent from a letter of thanks from FitzRoy to Lady Herschel, in the Herschel Correspondence at the offices of the Royal Society.

[9] These confessions, left out of the earlier editions of the *Autobiography* at the widow's request, first appear in Nora Barlow's edition of 1958.

only occasionally after our return home, for I was always afraid of unintentionally offending him, and did so once, almost beyond mutual reconciliation.' Whether the occasion was at this tea party or later is not known; the important thing is that the occasion arose.[10]

As for the second influence on FitzRoy, that of the Tahitian and in particular the New Zealand missionaries, it was likely to have been an unconscious one, though no less strong for that reason. A person always is influenced by those whom he gratefully admires, particularly when he is young. FitzRoy during the *Beagle*'s visit to the South Seas was only thirty years old.

It would thus seem as if the FitzRoy who commanded the *Beagle* and the FitzRoy who wrote the last two chapters of the *Narrative* were different people. But that would be a great exaggeration. Rather it is that under the stress of experience his character was developing fast.

Always FitzRoy wanted to work for the good of his fellow men. And a major aspect of that innate passion for philanthropy would be to help men to see the Truth as he had come to see it. Hence those last two chapters for the benefit of young sailors. Hence much else in the rest of his life.

FitzRoy was a forceful and practical person however, no mere pious revivalist. In order that he might do what he wanted to do, he would now, if it were possible, try to reach a commanding position in the world. Laying down his proselytizing and didactic pen, he turned to more worldly and more ambitious ways.

[10] The seriousness and size of the point of view that FitzRoy represented, scientific yet in religion orthodox, is well brought out in Loren Eiseley's exhaustive study of the atmosphere in which Charles Darwin wrote: *Darwin's Century* (Gollancz, 1959).

CHAPTER 15

The Disgraceful Episode

IN the world of politics, which FitzRoy was now to enter for a little while, to lose one's temper may have much more considerable and unpleasant effects than to do the same on one's own ship, the other party being more likely to answer back. From the episode that now came his way, though he may have been nearly as sinned against as sinning, FitzRoy cannot be said to emerge with any great credit.

In the summer of 1841—to Queen Victoria's great regret and no doubt to that Whig fellow Darwin's also—Lord Melbourne's ministry fell and a general election followed. In spite of the Reform Bill, the passing of which had aroused so much interest on board the *Beagle*, membership of the House of Commons was still very much a gentleman's preserve and considerably dependent on the patronage of great landowners. It also opened the way to power and prestige. Robert FitzRoy therefore, with his *Narrative* finished and no prospect of another voyage in sight, was no doubt pleased when he received an offer from his maternal uncle, Lord Londonderry. The offer was a candidature for one of the County of Durham's parliamentary seats in place of the retiring Tory member. Durham was now a two-seat constituency and the sitting members had been one of each kind, Whig and Tory or, as they were now beginning to call themselves, Liberal and

Conservative. At first it seemed likely that there would only be two candidates at the election, one of each party for the twin seats, in which case FitzRoy's election would have been a certainty.

But then a second Conservative candidate was adopted, a young man of twenty-six by the name of William Sheppard. Lord Londonderry certainly did not approve. But at first FitzRoy does not seem to have been perturbed: it was quite on the cards that both Conservative candidates might be elected and in any case the Londonderry nominee was likely to have the advantage over the other. All that was necessary was that the Conservatives should be seen to be working in amity and that there could be no suggestion of a pro and anti Londonderry split. A coalition was therefore publicly announced. The two men rode about the country doing their canvassing together and, in Mr Sheppard's words, living together 'in unreserved intimacy'.[1]

The first rift occurred when a Londonderry tenant innocently —or perhaps, for all we know, maliciously—let fall that he had his orders from his landlord to vote for FitzRoy and not for Sheppard. FitzRoy hotly denied that he himself was party to any such arrangement.

But the virus of suspicion had entered in upon Sheppard, and there was plenty of talk to help spread the disease. It occurred to him that he was employing seven agents but FitzRoy only one, FitzRoy thus cashing in on his own much larger expenditure. He then paid a visit to London—and there fed voraciously on an anti-Londonderry diet. His friend Urquhart, candidate for Sheffield, was there; and Mr Urquhart not only could not abide Londonderry's politics, but hinted that the noble and unscrupulous lord was even advising the citizens of Durham to vote Liberal if they would not vote FitzRoy.

[1] From *The Conduct of Captain Robert FitzRoy R.N. in reference to the Electors of Durham and the Laws of Honour, exposed by William Sheppard Esquire* (London, John Ollivier, 1842). The information for this chapter is derived from this pamphlet and from FitzRoy's counterblast, a sixpenny pamphlet published by W. White of London in August 1841 and entitled *Captain FitzRoy's Statement re Collision between William Sheppard and the Author*.

On leaving London, Sheppard made a rapid decision. He withdrew his candidature and moved across to Sheffield to help his friend Urquhart. FitzRoy received a letter announcing the decision and the reason for it: Sheppard felt that he must publicly denounce Lord Londonderry, and if he did so at Durham he would surely spoil FitzRoy's chances of election; he would therefore withdraw. With the letter was a copy of the statement Sheppard was making to the Durham electorate; it gave as his reason for withdrawing 'information [unspecified] that had come to his knowledge.'

FitzRoy did not in the least take this withdrawal as an honourable and friendly act. He saw it as a 'desertion of the conservative cause' and a move that would create such a ferment among his local supporters (who would undoubtedly guess what was the true cause of the rift) that his own chances, far from being safeguarded, would be imperilled. They could of course only be imperilled if another candidate, Conservative or Liberal, were nominated in Sheppard's place, and this we must assume was what FitzRoy feared. But what seems to have shocked and angered FitzRoy, and it is in line with his character that it should be so, was not so much the possible lessening of his own chances, as his partner's desertion of the cause and disloyalty in washing dirty linen in public. He made a speech that evening in Durham, and in it he stressed the second of these two aspects of Sheppard's disaffection. He called it 'a disgraceful desertion' and 'an event unparalleled in the annals of electioneering'. Mr Sheppard in due course read the report of the speech in the local paper.

The trouble now really began. Also began the long series of letters.

Sheppard wrote to FitzRoy, deprecating the blackening of his character in public and asking FitzRoy categorically whether he did use the words he was reported to have used.

FitzRoy replied that he did indeed use the words reported of him, and that he considered his honour had been impunged. It is in fact as difficult to understand why he considered his honour impunged as to understand why, for instance, he had done so when Darwin criticized him for his facile belief in the protestations of slaves. But the fact remains that he did. The trigger of his reaction against any criticism of his integrity as a gentleman was much too lightly sprung.

However Mr Sheppard's trigger was also lightly sprung. Or it may be perhaps no more than that neither man was anything more than typical of his times. At the mention of the word 'honour' the damage was done. Sheppard at once sought out a second, a Lieutenant Colonel Pringle Taylor, who ascertained that his opposite number would be a certain Major Chipchase, and wrote to that gentleman requesting that he would name a time and place where the question between the protagonists could 'be brought to issue'. The days of duelling by the aristocracy were not yet quite over. FitzRoy's other Londonderry uncle, Castlereagh, had indulged in two such affairs before his death nineteen years earlier; in 1829 the Duke of Wellington had fought a duel; and less than a twelvemonth before the present date, Lord Cardigan had not only badly wounded his adversary in a duel, but had been subsequently acquitted of any crime in a trial by his peers.

There followed now a misunderstanding, caused perhaps by a desire on the part of each party, if only a subconscious desire, to treat the matter not too seriously. FitzRoy and his second understood that a meeting to arrange matters was to take place at York, whilst Sheppard and his second understood that the rendezvous was to be in London. However artificial the whole affair may have been, and however much each of the contestants might have wished to deem it so, yet both were, for the moment at least, public figures and both were right to be frightened of being forced into the position of appearing to have funked the issue and consequently to have lost their honour. As the correspondence, therefore, was to grow more virulent and exacerbated, so there was to be a continued reference to this misunderstanding as to the place of meeting and mutual accusations of bad faith.

Yet, in spite of this, the quarrel was now very nearly patched up. There ensued a hurried meeting in London between Sheppard's second, Colonel Pringle Taylor, and FitzRoy himself, followed by an on the whole conciliatory letter from Taylor to FitzRoy, which did, however, accuse the latter of wrongfully laying at the door of his opponent the awful sin of having had truck with the Chartists and generally of 'forcing a young man into a very painful position'.

FitzRoy promptly replied. He admitted that he had done Sheppard an injustice over the matter of the Chartists. But as for the rest, had he on his side no cause for complaint? 'Was I not left in an intensely painful position...was I not exposed to censure on all sides and to *much* suspicion? Was not the loss of *both* Conservative seats risked? And above all what were *my* feelings when I heard and read the attack, so *unjustly* made on the character of a very near and dear relative?' As to the plea of youth: 'I am thirty-six and only about ten years older, and I have wife and child and he not!' However the letter ended, 'Anger does not last with me long'; and a plea was made, not very graciously perhaps, that the whole matter should be dropped.

Dropped it might have been, for Pringle Taylor showed himself to be an eminently reasonable man. But at this point he retired from the position of Sheppard's second to attend to other business, and his place was taken by a younger and less experienced man, a civilian by the name of Mr Stanley.

Negotiations began all over again. The two young men, Sheppard and Stanley, were very conscious one imagines of moral rectitude, yet a little uncertain of themselves and therefore highly suspicious of being manoeuvred into a false position. They called upon Major Chipchase, FitzRoy's second, and demanded an apology. They received a refusal.

But, thought Sheppard, perhaps he had been guilty of a solecism: apparently a principal should not appear at the negotiations between seconds. He accordingly would try again. He sent Mr Stanley, alone, with a note from one second to the other, the gist of which was: Mr Sheppard is sorry—now you get your man to apologize!

Chipchase and FitzRoy were staying at the same hotel in Durham. Chipchase, receiving the letter at Stanley's hands, promptly and robustly committed the gaffe that Sheppard was now being careful to avoid: he called in FitzRoy. All three men sat round a table. Wine was served.

Stanley proved amenable. He even admitted, between friends, that Sheppard had been rather led astray by 'the Urquhartites'. In view of all this, FitzRoy on the spot wrote out a qualified apology. In view of Sheppard's apology, carefully quoted, he acknowledged that 'his own expressions on the 22nd ult with respect to Mr Sheppard were stronger than he should have issued.' With mutual protestations of friendliness, with this letter in his pocket, Mr Stanley departed. All should now have been well.

It was not. Sheppard, highly suspicious, sent Stanley back with a demand for a more strongly worded apology, together with an agreement that all correspondence should forthwith be published. Stanley returned with the stronger apology duly signed but with an insistence that no correspondence should be published whatever.

Sheppard's suspicions flared up high. Forgetting that he had first committed the same breach of the rules, or all the more insistent upon rectitude because he had done so, he accused FitzRoy of being improperly present at the meeting of seconds and the two older men of suborning his young and inexperienced representative. That friendliness, that wine upon the table! It had been 'a carouse'.

From now on, matters rapidly deteriorated. Sheppard's next move was to write saying that, unless there was allowed to appear in the Durham newspapers a jointly signed statement to the effect that FitzRoy's imputations against him had ended in 'satisfactory explanations and apologies', he would publish all correspondence. FitzRoy refused to comply: Mr Stanley, he asserted, had agreed that nothing whatever should be published. Stanley, in return denied this, and made the added good point that a *private* apology for a *public* insult was not good enough. FitzRoy's Major Chipchase replied to this, saying virtually, 'publish and be damned!' But, he warned, if Sheppard published his account of the affair, FitzRoy would do the same. He then added that he also was retiring from his position as second: the matter was at an end.

Sheppard certainly did not consider it at an end. With both original seconds retired, he felt free to write to FitzRoy directly again. He did so in a virulent letter, the letter of a man blazingly angry that he had been forced into a position where there was no satisfactory means of redress. Besides FitzRoy's initial avoidance of a meeting to give satisfaction, besides his befuddling of Mr Stanley over the bottles, there had, he insisted, been intentional delays all along the line. Now, therefore, even if the correspondence were published, few would be interested enough to read it. He had in plain fact been placed before the public as one who lies down to insults. He therefore made a new demand: either a more explicit apology or, once again, 'a meeting'!

FitzRoy replied that the 'winecups' accusation was absurd, that it was not he but Sheppard who had originally avoided a meeting, and that the whole affair must be considered dead.

Sheppard replied hysterically. There was nothing left but for him to denounce FitzRoy as 'a liar and a slanderer'; his conduct showed him to be 'a coward and a knave' and this he would make public.

FitzRoy, deprived of his second, was advised by friends to take no notice.

On August 25th, two months after Sheppard's original retirement from the Durham candidature and with the election over and FitzRoy safely an M.P., there came the startling denouement. The two principals met in the Mall, outside the United Services Club. Sheppard, who had obviously been waiting in a wish to make his demonstration where his enemy's fellow officers and friends could witness it, came up brandishing a whip over his head. He then made the following amazing announcement: 'Captain FitzRoy! I will not strike you. But, consider yourself horsewhipped!'

FitzRoy, who was in no state to see the humour of the situation, instantly struck his tormentor with his umbrella, dropped his umbrella, and collared him. Blows were exchanged and Sheppard fell. A friend of Sheppard ran up and cried, 'Don't strike him, Captain FitzRoy, now he's down!' And FitzRoy desisted.

.   .   .

So the episode is not much to FitzRoy's credit. It cannot have done him much good at the time, except perhaps in the eyes of choleric old generals and admirals, whom one can imagine gobbling, 'Serve the damn feller right!' There followed long letters of self-justification to the press, including one from a returned Colonel Pringle Taylor, which stung FitzRoy into issuing a challenge to *him*. Pringle Taylor replied that he had no intention of accepting a challenge from a man whom he had rightly dubbed 'a liar and slanderer, a coward and a knave', though he would, if he could, lend a hand to FitzRoy to resume his 'lost station as a gentleman'. FitzRoy, again advised to take no notice, could only fume. The episode cannot have been good for his temper.

Both men published their accounts, and both, it must be admitted, were fair and reasonable accounts. FitzRoy, the eternal masochist, left out nothing that might show himself in a bad light.

CHAPTER 16

Mr Gladstone Commends

MEMBERSHIP of Parliament was the gateway either to mildly useful mediocrity, such as had contented FitzRoy's father, or to greater things, much greater things. It is noticeable that when FitzRoy refers to his family it is nearly always to the Londonderry, that is to say the Castlereagh side; and there cannot be much doubt as to the path along which his ambition pointed.

His opportunity lay before him. But his over-spectacular entry into the House might have spoilt his chances from the start, and, speaking more generally, a good quarterdeck manner is not necessarily a good parliamentary manner—one cannot serve out hot coffee with desirable effect to M.P.s.

It does seem as if for a while FitzRoy was skating on thin ice by reason of his notorious quarrel with Sheppard, with below him the freezing waters of Parliament's outraged dignity. A certain Mr Roebuck, member for Bath, accused the twin members for Reading of 'entering into a compromise' during the election; and FitzRoy, taking a possibly dangerous bull by the horns, asked whether he was considered to be involved, to which question Mr Roebuck answered unequivocably, yes! The whole thing fizzled out, however, and in any case to say that FitzRoy and Sheppard had entered into a 'compromise' would have been to stretch language extremely far.

Into the other pitfall, that of taking the quarterdeck manner to the wrong place, FitzRoy certainly does not seem to have fallen. A philanthropist and good Tory, he seems soon to have become an accepted member of this Parliament of Peel's progressive Toryism, speaking informedly on matters near to his heart or to his experience: colonization, the Poor Law, naval armament, breakwaters and the like.[1]

He showed himself, nevertheless and as might have been guessed, no respecter of persons, or, more accurately perhaps, no fearer of personages. At one time he was training his small guns on his own side and asking pertinent questions of the Colonial Secretary, Lord Stanley (later as Lord Derby to be Prime Minister and quite soon to be FitzRoy's employer). Why, he asked, should the naval officer who had been appointed Governor of the Falkland Islands be an *engineer* officer. Lord Stanley replied that he had not made the appointment and did not know.

Then FitzRoy was daring to make fun of the Member for Stockport, who was none other than Richard Cobden: 'The Honourable Member in the course of his travels had no doubt seen many wonderful things—he had told me he had seen cheese on the summits of the Alps—that he had met with negroes at the Antipodes, and that sufficient corn might be brought by steam, amply to supply the wants of the manufacturers.' FitzRoy then went on to make his point, that the one hundred and eighty million acres of wheatland in America (whose produce, Cobden contended, would cure England's present distress if she would only let it in) had not yet been put into cultivation. It was indeed for the *present* distress that everyone sought a remedy—and there was just as deep a feeling for that distress on FitzRoy's side of the House as there was on Cobden's.

It was less than a twelve-months after the election that FitzRoy received two appointments which were the sort of beginnings he might expect and which were very much in his own line of country. He seized upon them to help him make his own considerable contribution to parliamentary and private member

[1] FitzRoy's activities in the House of Commons are covered by Hansard's Parliamentary Debates, 3rd Series, vols. 59 to 65.

legislation. This, it must be made clear, was in no way a careerist's contribution, it was the contribution of, as ever, a would-be philanthropist.

The appointments were to be an Elder of Trinity House and to be Acting Conservator of the River Mersey under a new Mersey Conservancy Act. FitzRoy was soon making a personal inspection of the important river, all the way up as far as Frodsham. Then he issued an eight-page report[2] that set out clearly the problems of tide and current and made practical suggestions for reducing erosion.

What was important to FitzRoy however was the fact that his appointments helped to enhance his status as an expert on marine matters and also no doubt to meet the right people. He sought and obtained permission to bring in a bill 'to require and regulate the examination of all persons who wished to become masters or chief mates of merchant vessels'; and on July 28th 1842, three weeks after his thirty-seventh birthday, he made his speech on the subject.

It is a good speech, the good, practical speech of an expert who is yet also a humanitarian. It may be summarized as follows:—

First FitzRoy reminded the House of the present position. During the Napoleonic wars British ships had gone in convoys, or two or three together, but now they went singly. They went to every quarter of the globe, upwards of 20,000 vessels of over fifty tons. And there was no examination of any kind with respect to the qualifications of the officers in command of those vessels.

What he now proposed had been prepared by a great number of experts in the shipping world, and followed recommendation made in 1813 after an investigation into the cause of wrecks. The House should also be reminded that the *length* of a voyage depended upon a captain's navigational skill, and for all the time a vessel was at sea the passengers' fate was in his hands. He remembered once meeting a ship in the Pacific Ocean whose captain

---

[2] This report is quoted in full in a book in the possession of the City of Liverpool Public Libraries entitled Mersey papers: *The Mersey, its tidal range and tidal column; reports by the Acting Conservators*, by Thomas Webster, 1875.

was some degrees off course but whose only comment was that he was not there to navigate but to fish.

His plan was that there should be, in Britain's principal ports, a number of examining boards powered to give certificates, and that the possession of such a certificate should be a necessity for both captains and first mates. There then follows suggestion as to the qualifications of the examiners, and financial details as to fees to be paid, both by the examinees and to the examiners, though it was considered that the latter would be content to serve for the honour and prestige the office would bequeath.

Finally, FitzRoy asked leave to bring in the bill, not with a view to legislation in the present session, but so that it might be printed and circulated during the recess 'and thus enable the House to collect any objections that might be urged against it.' No doubt by arrangement, the President of the Board of Trade, Mr Gladstone, then rose and, praising the bill for its wisdom, gave it his official blessing.

The result was that in 1845, as a half-way measure, a voluntary system of certificates was inaugurated and in 1850 a Mercantile Marine Act made the possession of certificates compulsory—a state of affairs arrived at none too soon.

By this piece of work FitzRoy can hardly have done anything but increase his reputation. One further job he collected before, in the Spring of 1843, he was given the appointment that was to end his term as an M.P. and set him off in a new career. It was a surprising job and one that may have surprised him. It lay in the gift of the Admiralty; and FitzRoy, as a naval expert as well as an aristocrat with a known charm of manner, may well have seemed the obvious choice. It was the sort of extra job that comes unasked to those who are already being successful. The Archduke Frederick of Austria was coming across to Portsmouth in an Austrian warship, and, while this ship was undergoing experts' repairs, he was to be shown something of Britain's naval might, and military and industrial might as well. FitzRoy was chosen to attend upon him during his tour. *The Times*, whose entries, eight in all, cover a period from October 3rd to December 19th 1842, describes FitzRoy as acting as 'aide-de-camp and interpreter'. That FitzRoy should have known German is surprising. He knew Spanish well enough, there is plenty of evidence for that in his *Narrative of the Beagle*. The Archduke, trailing clouds of Holy Roman Empire, may also have known Spanish; but he did have a German priest to conduct Mass for him in the City. The accuracy of the latter part of *The Times*'s title must therefore remain in question. As aide FitzRoy was undoubtedly kept busy.

The Archduke rushed up to Inverness, and bought fabrics and ancient weapons like any other tourist. He crossed to Glasgow and then by sea down to Liverpool—a 'tempestuous voyage'. A train trip across to Manchester and back. Then a quick look at Chester and the Welsh border. Birmingham. Two days in Oxford. London, Brighton, Portsmouth. He of course entertained or was entertained by the most notable people, including the Prime Minister and the Duke of Wellington. In London he visited the Polytechnic and the Chinese Exhibition and also Mr Beard's Photographic Portrait Rooms, where he and his suite sat and 'were much pleased with the process and gratified with the fidelity of the likeness.' From that to more serious things, inspecting in the company of senior officers Woolwich Dockyard and Arsenal and viewing naval gunnery and military parades. A courtesy visit from Portsmouth to the Queen Dowager on the Isle of Wight, a final round of naval inspection; and on December 21st, the Archduke was off in his repaired warship to the Mediterranean. FitzRoy must have felt that he had earned his Christmas in the bosom of his family.

CHAPTER 17

The Difficult Birth
of a Colony

LORD STANLEY was said never to hurry himself in making the appointments that came to his gift; and when in 1842 Captain Hobson, New Zealand's first Governor, died at his post, the Secretary for the Colonies lived up to his reputation.

Nevertheless, when he did make the necessary move and appointed FitzRoy, it cannot, one would imagine, have been a very difficult decision to make. FitzRoy had shown his interest in colonial affairs in Parliament. On returning from his second *Beagle* voyage he had given evidence upon New Zealand before a House of Lords committee. He was of the class and profession from which governors were appointed; and he had received no adequate reward for his universally acclaimed work as a navigator and surveyor. Finally, the Secretary of the Church Missionary Society both favoured him and had possessed for some time an influence within the Colonial Office.[1]

FitzRoy on the other hand could well have experienced some difficulty in deciding whether to accept the post. There is in fact no sign that he did so, and his own and his wife's letters on the way out show a dedicated seriousness coupled with a cheerful-

[1] Correspondence in possession of the C.M.S. The then secretary's name was Mr Dandeson Coates.

ness quite serene.[2] However, it would scarcely need more than five minutes reading on the then state of New Zealand to make anyone realize that he was not going out to a sinecure of pleasantness and garden parties.

In order that the problems facing FitzRoy may be understood, something of New Zealand's recent history must be given. The twin islands were in 1843 a very young colony indeed, and suffering very much from growing pains: it might be truer to say that New Zealand was a colony only by default and that she was suffering not so much from growing pains as from sheer parental neglect. And while her too distant parents neglected her she was the recipient of a too wide and too varied and too self-interested attention from those nearer at hand.

In their long war canoes the Maoris had proved themselves to be a bold and courageous people, fierce and proud, sometimes friendly but as often unpredictably treacherous. In 1772 an unsuspecting and kindly Frenchman, Marion du Fresne, on a voyage of discovery, had met his death and proved to the world something worse: that the Maoris were confirmed cannibals. In spite of Tasman's and Cook's discoveries, therefore, no white man's government had been anxious to colonize.

Economics, however, finally overcame disinclination on the part of the white men, it being discovered that seals and then that whales abounded in New Zealand waters. Though the reputation of her inhabitants had prevented the country becoming a penal settlement, Port Jackson (near modern Sydney and known popularly as Botany Bay) was not far distant, and from this growing centre of trade and activity came prospectors who were only too anxious to take advantage of this new source of wealth.

The sealing and whaling industries burst into abounding activity, tough and brutal trades engaged in by tough and sometimes brutal men. Contacts between whites and Maoris became closer and more frequent; and, though a few of the former may have come to a violent end, more were to become 'Paheka

<hr />

[2] The private letters from FitzRoy and his wife quoted in this and the following chapters are in the possession of the Mitchell Library, Sydney, N.S.W.

Maoris', married to natives and settled down. In particular at the Bay of Islands, on the northern tip of the more thickly populated North Island, each of the two races found the other useful, and a small white settlement, the Kororareka that by the time of the *Beagle*'s visit had become so vicious, began to grow. 'Making use', as one contemporary observer put it, 'of the power that a civilized man can always exercise over a savage', the early settlers made their influence felt in New Zealand; and the influence, though by no means always good, 'helped in some degree', as another commentator put it, 'to take the rough edge off barbarism, helped to pave the way for something better than they were themselves able to give.'

This something better came from the Anglican missionaries, though these undoubtedly made their early mistakes and for a time it was possible to consider that the country's second state was worse than the first. Samuel Marsden was the pioneer, coming across from the penal settlement at Botany Bay, where he had been the first chaplain. For a while his coming was delayed by the Australian authorities, by reason of another sudden and terrifying upsurge of inexplicable savagery on the part of the Maoris. Bent on revenge or *utu* for a crime of which the unfortunate victims were not even aware, armed natives had suddenly swarmed over the side of a ship at anchor, the *Boyd*, and had murdered crew and passengers, men, women and children. The event in any case did not help to improve the relationship between the Maoris and the settlers on the Bay of Islands, a relationship that was to have deteriorated further by the time that FitzRoy arrived.

When Marsden did eventually sail to New Zealand he took no other ordained priest with him but concentrated rather on an effort to instil the useful arts as a necessary preliminary to Christian teaching. His practical approach, and his undoubted bravery, were rewarded with success. In one aspect, however, he might be said to have been too successful. One of his three teachers, or 'mechanics' as he called them, managed to persuade a certain chieftain with whom he had become friendly to return with him to England, in order to help in the praiseworthy project of compiling a grammar of the Maori language. This chief was a redoubtable person and his name and family cast a significant if lurid light on New Zealand's history during the next few decades. Hongi, or Shongi as he is sometimes called, dazzled not only Baron de Thierry, as already related, but also to some extent the monarch of England, with whom he talked on friendly and equal terms and from whom he extracted considerable gifts. These, with others, he exchanged for firearms directly he reached Sydney on his return journey.

Hongi was not anti-missionary. He was merely guilty of a vast misunderstanding. In the white man's weapons he saw the opportunity to give an entirely new and irresistible direction to the tribal warfare which was a natural part of his and every other Maori chieftain's life. When, rather to his surprise, the missionaries would not help him directly he had used them indirectly to achieve his aim. The result was that for about eight years until his death in 1828 Hongi waged highly successful war; and it came to look to the outside world, or to those of the outside world who bothered to look, as if the main result of missionary interference in New Zealand was to be as much a tragic and unintended increase in bloodshed and the reverse of brotherly love as it was accused of being in Tahiti.

Matters came to a head with the shameful affair of the trading ship *Elizabeth*. The introduction of the Maoris to firearms, and the rise and fall of this petty Napoleon who saw his opportunity to use them, had between them destroyed the ancient harsh but nice balance of power amongst the Maori chiefs and left something like anarchy in its place. Now a white man helped to augment that anarchy in a much more brutal and direct way than ever the missionary 'mechanic' could have been accused of doing. The captain of the *Elizabeth* treacherously lent his ship and his services to one chief in his war upon another. After a successful kidnapping on board, the captain took part in a raid and witnessed a cannibal feast—after which the defeated chief, in Roman fashion, killed his own daughter to save her from a fate which he considered worse than death. Through the missionary Marsden's intervention the captain of the *Elizabeth* was arrested when he reached New South Wales. But from lack of evidence he was acquitted.

The conscience of Britain by this episode was touched. Marsden pressed for a British representative to be appointed to New Zealand; and French rivalry, real or imaginary, at this time strengthened his hand. In 1831 thirteen Maori chiefs wrote to King William IV saying that they had heard that 'the tribe of Marion' (the French) was coming to take over their land and that for preference they would like to have Englishmen for their friends and guardians. At about the same time Edward Gibbon Wakefield, of whom more anon, was beginning to cause a stir in Britain by drawing attention to the evils of the penal settlement system and by suggesting that proper and systematic encouragement of colonization might be a better idea. In 1833, as a rather feeble half-measure, a British Resident was as a consequence appointed, this being the James Busby whom FitzRoy met and found so lacking in powers. Naturally FitzRoy was not the only one to observe this fact and the Maoris had already christened him 'the man-of-war without guns'. A little before the *Beagle*'s visit Busby had tried to form a confederation of the united tribes of New Zealand; and it was FitzRoy's opinion at that time that he had not done much more than still further confuse the native chiefs in their efforts to discover and understand where real power lay. By now the inherent bloodthirstiness of the Maoris seemed to have been at least temporarily allayed by the missionaries. But the emptiness of the real seat of authority in the twin islands had not really been filled, and the time when some foreign government would be forced to establish itself could not be long delayed.

The possibility that this power would not be British unless that country exerted itself became a little greater with the arrival of a French Catholic mission. This mission was by no means so politically minded as a few Frenchmen liked to make out; nevertheless its presence did not add to a feeling of serenity, if any existed, in New Zealand. The Catholic pressure exacerbated in particular the land question, which from the beginning, and increasingly, was the most thorny question that existed: the Catholics priests, possessing no families, had no wish for land; the Protestants, however, possessing the one in abundance, showed a commensurate desire for the other.

Added to the pressure of events in New Zealand was the pressure being put upon the home government by a very active group of political idealists headed by the already mentioned and redoubtable Edward Gibbon Wakefield. Wakefield, the eldest son of a large and forceful family, had gone one better than Baron Thierry in having not only eloped with a young lady in his youth, but also abducted another when he had reached the age of thirty. However, except for a romantic enthusiasm and a propensity to do the spectacular, Wakefield is not comparable with de Thierry, being a much more considerable man. He had by now, 1840, when he was forty-four years old, become a serious and, if not exactly respected, at least considered publicist in the cause of colonial emigration, setting forth with passion the somewhat novel conception that the lands over which Britain 'in a fit of absent-mindedness' was obtaining rule or influence should be purposely peopled by the best that the mother country could provide and not selfishly and sordidly used as a dump for getting rid of the worst. Wakefield's radical idealism, it should be added, however, had its streaks of jingoism and reaction. He envisaged a planned and model economy growing up in the new lands, but it should be an economy patriarchal and capitalistic, and certainly a white man's economy or perhaps more accurately a white gentleman's economy, with white labourers and black sub-labourers. The Maoris were by no means to be forgotten. The chiefs were to have reserved for themselves and their people one tenth of all the land they sold to the whites—'if', that is to say, 'the inferior race of New Zealand can be preserved at all in contact with civilized man.' No wonder that the missionaries from the start looked upon the Wakefieldites with suspicion. The missionaries, anxious for their protégés, did not favour annexation by any power, British or otherwise.

E. G. Wakefield was an impatient man, and the British Government, at least in the matter of colonial expansion, a body of hesitants. That Wakefield should act first and precipitately was almost inevitable. Having changed his New Zealand Association into a joint stock 'New Zealand Company', having raised funds, partly by selling to would-be settlers land that had not yet been purchased, he fitted out a ship called somewhat appropriately the *Tory*. This ship, in May 1839, and in great haste because he thought the Government were going to stop him, he despatched; on board were his only son and his brother, with instructions to prepare the way for the first wave of immigrants. By coincidence the captain of the *Tory* was FitzRoy's ship's master of the second *Beagle* voyage.

Faced with this move, the British Government at last acted. It declared that New South Wales was extended to include as much of New Zealand as might be acquired from the Maoris by agents of the Crown, thus formally recognizing the independence of the Maoris. At the same time it appointed a Lieutenant Governor in the person of William Hobson, a naval captain seeing service in Oceania and, like FitzRoy, having shown great interest in New Zealand.

Hobson, ominously ill on the journey, took over his duties in January 1840. His instructions were to persuade the Maori chiefs to accept British sovereignty, particularly by the argument that they had in their midst settlers 'amenable to no laws or tribunals of their own'—a phrase more realistic than complimentary and showing that there were in these times others besides FitzRoy who took a poor view of the original element amongst the whites. As a significant corollary, Hobson was instructed to have all existing sales of land to white men investigated and all future sales controlled.

As if he knew that he had less than three years to live, Captain Hobson wasted no time. On February 5th, only a week after he had landed, he held a grand meeting in front of Busby's house at Waitangi on the Bay of Islands. A great concourse of chiefs was there, the heads of the two rival sects of missionaries, the Roman Catholic Bishop Pompellier and that ex-naval captain whom Fitz-Roy had regretted to have missed, Henry Williams. The Queen's message was read out, and then there followed a long and impassioned native palaver. Finally—and it was a near thing—the pro-white element won, or rather, it would be fairer to say, those won who favoured white authority to protect them against white lawlessness and shady dealing. The famous Treaty of Waitangi was signed.

It was an initial triumph for Hobson, but it was a triumph that did not help him much. In practice the treaty pleased nobody. It generously gave the Maoris the Queen's protection, 'with all rights and privileges of British subjects'—a phrase that FitzRoy when he came must often have had in mind. That was good. Also good on the face of it was the guarantee to the Maori chiefs, in exchange for accepting British sovereignty, of the undisputed possession of their lands. But then came the rub. The chiefs could sell if they wished; but never again could they sell to private individuals, only to the Government. This displeased the whites, both the speculators and land sharks of Kororareka and also the immigrants and those about to be immigrants, because it put their paper purchases in jeopardy. The natives, always jealous for their land and wary of selling it, were yet highly aware of its value and angry at the disappearance of an open market for it. On wider grounds too they found the treaty unsatisfactory, and under two opposing counts: either that they were not receiving sufficient protection from the rapacious whites, or that they were not being allowed to run their own show. In any case, trade was decreasing and not increasing as expected. Captain Hobson was not in an enviable position.

In fact the situation during Hobson's three years of office became increasingly tragic. To begin with he had little power behind him: he had arrived with the imposing retinue of four mounted constables, and the British troops at his back never numbered more than a hundred. The United States, many of whose nationals were amongst the sealers and whalers, refused to recognize him; and a visiting French naval captain ostentatiously failed to call on him while paying court to the ridiculous and already discredited Baron de Thierry. As for the British in New Zealand, just when increasing Maori dissatisfaction should have made them unite, they were doing the opposite. With the missionaries unhappily and distastefully looking on and inclining to favour the government side as the lesser of two evils, the small Establishment and the growing mass of emigrants, the Hobsonites and the Wakefieldites, were regarding each other with increasing enmity, jealousy and bad feeling.

The Wakefield brother and son, Colonel William Wakefield and Jerningham Wakefield, had made great haste, as well they needed to, in buying the necessary land to meet their paper commitments. They bought an enormous acreage, the boundaries being so vague as for instance to extend to all the heights to be seen from the decks of the *Tory* on which that particular bargaining was taking place. An agreement reached, the trade goods representing the purchase price were brought forth; and young Jerningham watched (and later described) the frenzied scramble that ensued.

Soon the immigrants themselves began to arrive, and in shipload after shipload. They were to be pitied. Their long journey, by sail halfway round the world, had in every case been an ordeal and in some cases a tragedy, with much sickness and death. Seeking to escape from an economic depression at home, they met another in Australian waters. And on top of that they were dumped in a country utterly unready for them.

They landed in and around Cook's Strait, between the two islands; and with great courage, and some initial help from the natives, began to build settlements that were soon to be known as Wellington, Nelson and New Plymouth.

But where was the land that they were expecting? A new problem arose, a new delay. Hobson had, as instructed, created a Land Commissioner and assigned to him the job of reviewing all land purchases already made. This, in theory a good move, added an extra delay at a very delicate time. In another way Hobson annoyed the newly arrived settlers. He created his new administration capital at Auckland, in the North Island where lived most of the Maoris and fairly near to Kororareka where lived most of the original whites. The settlers, already aggrieved, felt slighted.

Hobson died of a stroke on September 10th 1842, leaving his lieutenant, Mr Shortland, to carry on. Nine months later there occurred a much more serious incident. Almost inevitably it was concerned with land.

In Nelson the white land-hunger was chronic. And there another brother of Edward Gibbon Wakefield, a retired Naval

Captain by name Arthur, was doing his best to satisfy it. There was good land some sixty miles north-east of Nelson in the Wairau valley, and Arthur Wakefield genuinely believed that his brother, Colonel William, had already bought it. This land belonged to two chiefs, Te Rauperaha and Te Rangihaeata; and Te Rauperaha, the principal chief, was none other than the villain whom the captain of the ship *Elizabeth* had so notoriously helped in his treacherous attack and cannibal feast. Both chieftains believed with equal conviction that the land had never been sold to the whites.

Arthur Wakefield sent his surveyors to the land in question. The surveyors were interrupted in their work by irate Maoris and finally one of their houses—the Maoris contended that it was only a hut—was burned down. The news reached Nelson; and a magistrate was immediately sent to arrest the two chiefs. He was supported by Arthur Wakefield in person, various other armed 'gentleman volunteers', and a rather rabble-like posse of ill-armed white labourers.

Arthur's brother, the Colonel, later wrote home, describing the scene. On arrival, the magistrate, no military genius, insisted on advancing to make his arrest in spite of finding the natives strongly drawn up in battle formation. The inevitable accidental first shot brought on a volley from the Maoris, and the rabble of white country labourers fled. The magistrate then fluttered a white flag and demanded a truce. The Maori chiefs, surprised at their easy victory, followed their usual practice. They lined up the remaining white men, whom they regarded as their prisoners, and with their tomahawks slaughtered all nineteen of them. 'Consider,' concluded Colonel Wakefield, 'that poor Arthur's life has been sacrificed to a hot-headed inexperienced man... The public papers will give you accounts of this affair with various colouring, but the above is the unvarnished truth.'

The colourings of the papers were lurid with brushes dipped in fierce indignation and horror. Robert FitzRoy was already on the high seas at this time on his way to take up his appointment. When he arrived the indignation was still rampant.

CHAPTER 18

The Governorship

THEY sailed from Tor Bay on July 8th 1843, Robert FitzRoy, just thirty-eight years old, his wife, his father-in-law, and his three very young children. There was no man-of-war to take the governor, as FitzRoy as a middy had helped to carry ambassadors to South America. The *Bangalore* was 'a good sea boat', but the journey to Sydney was to take, nevertheless, five months. On board were other and less exalted immigrants to the new colony; one of them was to record a kindness done him by FitzRoy, while FitzRoy was to record that he and his wife found them 'rather agreeable'. There was also on board a cow, supplied by his brother-in-law for the benefit of the babes, who throve. The voyage was slow because the ship, before rounding the Cape, sailed on a leg westwards to Bahia in Brazil, to replenish her provisions. 'You may suppose,' wrote FitzRoy, in the same letter to his brother-in-law (George Rice-Trevor, married to the Fanny whom Jemmy Button had known as 'Cappen sisser'), 'how much Mrs Robert and I are pleased,' his wife to see a tropical port where the *Beagle* had called, and he to show her it. So much for the cheerful side; but FitzRoy, supplied with documents and copies of New Zealand newspapers by the Colonial Office, could not be unaware of what lay in front of him. 'No one knows,' he wrote later in the voyage, to Captain King, his senior officer on the first *Beagle* voyage, 'no one knows ...what I have before me. My wife and I go willingly, trusting in a superintending Providence—and anxious to raise the New Zealanders. I anticipate no great difficulty with them—but abundant trouble with the whites.'[1]

'Poor FitzRoy!' The phrase is already beginning to become appropriate. Darwin had used it to illustrate his dealings with his old friend during the years that had just passed. Captain King, writing to a mutual friend soon after the end of the New Zealand affair, says, 'Poor fellow, he was sacrificed to principles, a more honest intentioned man does not exist—but he acts too much by rule of three—and does not bend to circumstances.' Perhaps captains of sailing ships do not bend easily to circumstances, nor would be good captains if they did; Hobson before his death had not been over-pliable. As for rule of three, King presumably means to suggest a stubbornly over-simplified logic; at least he is not echoing the irritated Darwin and the accusation that FitzRoy was always seeing things in the wrong light.

Historians vary somewhat in their estimate of FitzRoy's governorship. All are agreed however that he was faced with an ugly situation and almost insoluble problems. William Gisborne, respected for his fairness, being neither kind nor optimistic, puts it like this: Captain FitzRoy, as Governor, had he been endowed with very great abilities, would probably, under the circumstances, have failed; but, unhappily, his qualities were such as to make his failures certain and complete.[2]

Contemporary accounts were hardly ever kind to FitzRoy and not so often fair. But then tempers were high before he reached New Zealand, and remained high, and the habit of vituperating the Governor—the good colonial habit of fighting autocracy—had already become well established. The two most informative accounts are by Arthur S. Thomson, Surgeon Major to the 58th Regiment of Foot, which was called in from Sydney in 1845, and

[1] King Papers, The Mitchell Library, Sydney.
[2] From *New Zealand Rulers and Statesmen from 1804 to 1897* (Sampson Low, 1897).

Edward Jerningham Wakefield, the young son of the great Edward Gibbon Wakefield, who had come out with his uncle on the *Tory*. The first of these tries to be fair though perhaps tries not very hard, Major Thomson cultivating a detached, slightly amused, slightly condescending attitude. Jerningham Wakefield makes no attempt to be anything but violently angry. But then he had some reason for this.

There are also the letters of Mrs FitzRoy[3] to her husband's sister Fanny; these naturally are prejudiced in her husband's favour. Mary FitzRoy earned the reputation of being a good governor's wife. She must have had, though in different ways, almost as difficult a time as her husband, but she shows throughout a naïve, pious, quiet optimism.

The first letter from Mary FitzRoy, written a fortnight after arrival, speaks comfortably of 'a respectable show of ladies' to witness their landing on New Zealand soil. The Surgeon-Major gives a very different and a sardonic account:

> In December 1843 Captain FitzRoy arrived at Auckland, and his landing in Commercial Bay was eminently ridiculous. A gentleman connected with the native department carried a pole surmounted with a crown of flax, from which waved the New Zealand flag; and Captain FitzRoy, excited by the occasion, cried aloud when stepping on shore, 'I have come among you to do all the good I can.' The crowd of fifty persons replied to this noble sentiment with a cheer, and the commanding officer of the company of soldiers in attendance shouted, 'quick march'; immediately the two drummer boys and the fifer of the guard of honour struck up 'The king of the Cannibal islands', to which appropriate air His Excellency marched to Government House. [4]

No doubt Captain Hobson's landing could have been equally ridiculed. We will turn back to Mary FitzRoy.

Arrival had been on a Saturday, December 23rd, so that Sunday and Christmas Day at once intervened:

[3] In the possession of the Mitchell Library, Sydney: ref., Af. 75.
[4] *The Story of New Zealand, Past and Present—Savage and Civilized*, published in two volumes by John Murray 1859 (the same year as Murray published *The Origin of Species*).

We went quietly to church on both days, and with fervent hearts offered our prayers and praises to Him whose protecting Hand had guided us safely to these shores...The comfort of an excellent clergyman and of regular services performed far better than it generally is in England I cannot describe.

That was a word of praise for the recently appointed muscular, forceful and orthodox Bishop Selwyn, something that was later to be returned in kind. Mary then—after a complaint about the inconvenience of the ill-conceived Governor's House and the appalling state in which their predecessor had left it ('but *we* have *all* worked hard and now it looks as comfortable as we can make it')—turned with love to describing for her sister-in-law's benefit the activities, problems and state of health of her husband:

Robert likes his new occupations, entering into them with all his heart; he is up by five o'clock, and begins public business at nine —still all this does not worry him, being varied occupation; he looks very well and is as cheerful as possible...

Robert has been extremely busy; the Colonial Secretary resigned soon after our arrival...

Next week Robert will go to Port Nicholson and Nelson in the *North Star* [the naval frigate that had brought them from Sydney] ...his absence I hope will not exceed six weeks...

We are to have two little dinner parties this week, but except in a small way there can be no society when people are so scattered and have no carriages: the nearest family live at a great distance, and except them I hear of nobody to associate with of the better kind, but among subordinates there are some pleasing and good people...The natives are certainly a most intelligent, interesting race—many very well dressed in European clothing have been with us at different meals and behaved *perfectly*...They appear to understand every measure of govt. thoroughly.

What difficulties, what eruptions of the bitter and prejudiced feelings that were already beginning to appear on all sides, these naïve and simple statements hide! Major Thomson and young Jerningham Wakefield were not nearly so loving.

However well had gone the little dinner parties (with the Maoris letting appear something of their viciously acute intelli-

gence as well as their good manners), it was at FitzRoy's early
levées that discordant notes had been struck and his two critics—
amongst many others—further antagonized.

Next day [wrote Thomson] a curious scene occurred at the
levée. The colonial office had given Captain FitzRoy files of a
New Zealand newspaper famous for abusing Acting Governor
Shortland, to read during the voyage; and when the editor of that
paper was presented at Government House the Governor in-
formed him that he highly approved of the principles of the
Southern Cross. This speech, equivalent to announcing in the
Government Gazette that the colonial secretary [the acting
governor's substantive title] was an arrogant fool, caused Mr
Shortland to resign his office.

Why 'arrogant' is not very clear. But for the rest the criticism
had some justification. Lieutenant Shortland was young and
inexperienced, and had been left for fifteen months without the
backing of substantive rank, a lack that had not been helpful to
anybody, except perhaps mischief makers. Lacking, too, financial
support from the home government, and failing to borrow from a
Sydney bank, though fifteen per cent was offered, he had issued
bills on the British Treasury and had had them dishonoured.
FitzRoy, could he have had another year's experience behind
him, might well have offered heartfelt sympathy rather than
indirect stricture; but no man can see into the future. Shortland
was to be given the sop of the governorship of Nevis Island and
was to depart almost immediately on the *Bangalore*, being given,
we learn from Mary, the FitzRoys' cabin.

Jerningham Wakefield was also soon to leave New Zealand, but
with no sop to his feelings, which were violent, and in something
like disgrace. FitzRoy was again to administer a public rebuke,
and a very severe one.

This occurrence was at another levée, at Nelson, whither
FitzRoy had almost immediately travelled, as Mary had written.
FitzRoy had been left in no doubt by the wording of an 'address
of welcome' presented to him on landing, that his most urgent
task was to do something to allay the bitter feeling that still

existed among the settlers over the Wairau massacre. Nelson was of course the centre of that discontent.

Jerningham Wakefield had lost an uncle in the massacre. And Jerningham Wakefield, though earlier he had found the natives pleasing enough, especially the women, had by now written some highly inflammable and utterly irresponsible newspaper articles about them. Here is his description of his meeting with FitzRoy:

> The arrangements for the levée were rather undignified; no aide-de-camp, sentries or constables had been appointed to keep the ingress through the French windows of the large room in the hotel free; and I got jostled in by the eager crowd, along with two or three other settlers, to a spot nearly under his Excellency's nose. He had just done thanking the members of a deputation from a public meeting for their congratulatory address on the safe arrival of himself and his family. He was proceeding to enlarge upon some other topics as I got within hearing; and a general stillness, a sort of chill or damp seemed to creep over the noisy bustle of the crowd as his opinions were gradually made known. He said that all parties might rely on receiving justice, and nothing but justice at his hands. He then deprecated, in the strongest terms, the feelings displayed by the settlers at Wellington against the native population, of which he judged by what appeared in their newspapers. He stated that he considered the opposition to the natives to have emanated from young, indiscreet men; but he trusted that as they had years before them, they would yet learn experience...Having so lately left England, he could not be ignorant of the intention of people there; none would emigrate to New Zealand unless they believed there was a good understanding between the settlers and the natives, and unless the settlers did all in their power to conciliate the natives, to forgive them, and to make allowances for them because they were natives, even if they were in the wrong.

After an assurance that, 'make no mistake', he would do all in his power to protect the natives whilst he had 'the honour of representing the Queen, my Mistress, in this country', and after having had presented to him some of the Maori chiefs, whom, says Jerningham, he treated with marked courtesy, FitzRoy found himself faced by the young Wakefield himself.

I had made my bow and had passed on into the crowd on the other side, when the Governor called me back by name. I returned and stood in front of him; when he used nearly the following words, with a frown on his face, and the tone of the commander of a frigate reprimanding his youngest midshipman: 'When you are twenty years older, you will have a great deal more prudence and discretion. Your conduct has been most indiscreet. In the observations which I made to this assembly just now, I referred almost entirely to you. I strongly disapprove and very much regret everything that you have written and done regarding the missionaries and the natives in New Zealand. I repeat that your conduct has been most indiscreet.'

I was so perfectly astounded, that I gained some credit for forbearance, which I should otherwise not have deserved. I looked steadily in the Governor's face while he spoke; and when he had done, walked away in silence without bowing again, and left the room.[5]

We must in fairness allow Jerningham Wakefield to put the best face on the matter possible. But a young man addressed by Robert FitzRoy in, as his *Beagle* officers would have said, his hot coffee manner, would be likely to have observed a forbearing silence not from astonishment but from sheer fright. Feeling that he must 'always appear to a certain degree a disgraced member of the society' under FitzRoy's rule, Jerningham had left New Zealand before even the Governor had left Wellington.

Jerningham had written wildly of 'the Saxon blood of the settlers' not long forbearing under its grievances and that the outcome might be the extermination of the Maoris (outnumbering the whites by something in the order of a hundred to one) 'crushed like a wasp in the iron gauntlet of armed civilization.' FitzRoy, therefore, had some reason to feel that he needed to crush Jerningham Wakefield. His public method of doing it, however, certainly caused resentment, and it was a long time before he was to hear the last of the episode. He must at least have become well aware of the degree of anger and hatred that the

[5] From pages 704/6 of the 1908 edition of Edward Jerningham Wakefield's *Adventure in New Zealand*, published by Whitcombe and Tombs Ltd., New Zealand.

Wairau massacre had engendered amongst the whites. Race relations, he believed rightly, were the crux of New Zealand politics, as they were likely to be of any new colony, but more so here because of the spirit and high intelligence of the aborigines, their lack of a wide hinterland to retire to, and their overwhelming majority. And now these relations had been radically and most unhappily changed by the Wairau massacre, for not only had the whites for the first time become really angry but the Maoris for the first time had begun to doubt the fighting prowess of the whites. How he settled the Wairau affair, how he comported himself, would influence irrevocably his future position as Governor in the eyes of both races.

FitzRoy's first meeting was with the Nelson magistrates who had signed the warrant for the arrest of Rauperaha and Rangihaeata after they had set fire to the surveyors' hut. He told them, according to Thomson, that the Maoris could not have been guilty of arson, for the simple reason that arson was the burning down of somebody else's property, and they had burned down their own. 'This speech, delivered in an irritating tone, produced a deep sensation among men mourning the death of their fellow colonists.'

FitzRoy then proceeded to visit one of the *pas* or fortified villages of the Maoris for a meeting with the two chiefs. For a description of this we will turn from Thomson to Jerningham Wakefield, for the reason that the latter uses the report of an eye-witness who seems less prejudiced than either of them.

The Governor arrived on a Sunday, and did no more that day than attend church service and hear some of the Maoris their catechism. To Rauperaha—who had recently turned Christian, comparing his belated conversion to that of St Paul—he did not speak.

The next day came the official meeting. There were present some fifteen whites, officials, missionaries and one or two settlers, and close on five hundred Maoris. FitzRoy had prepared his speech carefully with his primitive audience in mind and a translation had already been made.

When, while still at Sydney, he began, he had heard of the Wairau massacre, 'I was exceedingly angry; my heart was very dark, and my mind was filled with gloom. My first thought was to revenge the death of my friends[6] and the other *paheka* who had been killed, and for that purpose to bring many ships of war, sailing vessels, and vessels moved by fire, with many soldiers; and had I done so, you would have been sacrificed and your *pas* destroyed. But when I considered, I saw that the *paheka* had, in the first instance, been very much to blame; and I determined to come down and enquire into all the circumstances, and see who was really in the wrong. I have visited Wellington and Nelson, and have heard the white man's story; now I have come here—tell me your story, the native's story, that I may judge between them.'

Te Rauperaha was then called upon to reply, and did so with some show of reluctance. As he proceeded, FitzRoy on several occasions questioned him more closely. The chief explained why the Maoris considered the land in question not to have been properly purchased. He stressed the Maoris' initial forbearance, that before setting fire to the hut they had been careful to remove all its contents. In describing the arrival of the magistrate, with his little army and his ostentatiously displayed pair of handcuffs, he made it clear that the threat of being 'tied up' was not only a great indignity for a chief but a really terrifying threat—he would rather have died. He asserted that it was the magistrate who had given the first order to fire, and stuck to his point under cross-questioning. He told how some of the Maori women and children had been wounded, and his own daughter reported as killed. He explained finally that it was the time-honoured custom of victorious Maori chiefs to kill defeated chiefs if captured. He sat down again.

FitzRoy for the best part of half an hour considered his reply, making notes and consulting the interpreter. Then he addressed the Maoris as follows:

[6] FitzRoy may well have known personally his fellow naval officer, the murdered Arthur Wakefield. But Jerningham's claim that they had been midshipmen together cannot be substantiated.

Listen, O ye chiefs and elder men here assembled, to my words. I have now heard the Maori statement and the *paheka* statement of the Wairau affair; and I have made my decision. In the first place the white men were in the wrong. They had no right to survey the land which you had not sold until Mr Spain [the Land Commissioner] had finished his enquiry; they had no right to build the houses they did on that land. As they were, then, first in the wrong, *I will not avenge their deaths*.

These last words were repeated, and repeated in translation. FitzRoy then turned accusingly to the two chiefs.

But although I will not avenge the deaths of the *pahekas* who were killed at the Wairau, I have to tell you that you committed a horrible crime in murdering men who had surrendered themselves in *reliance on your honour as chiefs*. White men never kill their prisoners. For the future let us live peaceably and amicably —the *paheka* with the native, and the Maori with the *paheka*; and let there be no more bloodshed.

He finished with a promise of a speedy settlement of the whole difficult land question, and a warning to the Maoris not to disturb any settlers in the meantime. He then invoked God's blessing on them all.

The result? The whites called him 'weak', 'imbecile', 'coward'. Rauperaha laughed and said he would eat the Governor, and the frigate from which he had landed. FitzRoy had pleased nobody, impressed nobody. From now on, he had no friends, bar the missionaries and his own small entourage.

But it is difficult to see what else he could have done. He might perhaps have taken a token revenge or *utu* by now declaring the land in question confiscated, bought in fact by the white man's blood. That might have impressed the Maoris though it would not have satisfied the settlers. Nor was it likely to have appealed to any governor not of a coldly realistic turn of mind.

FitzRoy defended his action in a pamphlet that he published on his return home. His main point was that the arrest and trial of the two chiefs, besides being doubtfully of any useful result at this last date, would have been highly dangerous. 'These leaders would have retreated into their fastnesses, where no regular troops could have followed: thousands would have joined them: hostilities against the settlers would have been commenced, and their ruin must have followed: ruin under the most horrible circumstances of heathen warfare.'[7] FitzRoy was not exaggerating, though he knew the majority of whites did not in the least agree with him. 'No one,' he complained, 'appeared disposed to give the natives credit for courage, or skill in warfare—no one seemed to doubt that they would fly before a very small detachment of artillery. The prevailing feeling appeared to be anxiety for a collision.' And in the colony were seventy-eight men of the 80th Regiment and fifty-six of the 96th, set to defend seven small white settlements scattered along a thousand difficult miles of coastline.

Now the Governor, with no goodwill behind him, had to get down to the settling of the land question, as he had promised to do, and to rescue his exchequer out of the pit of destitution into which it had sunk. The second problem was the more urgent. 'At the beginning of this year [1844]' reports FitzRoy, 'the local government was twenty-four thousand pounds in debt: the [annual] revenue being then estimated at about twenty thousand pounds. All salaries and ordinary current payments were several months in arrear: there was no prospect of the revenue amounting even to two-thirds of the estimated indispensable expenditure.' FitzRoy knew that he could expect little help from the home government. This was, in general, still in the *laissez-faire*, colonies-ought-to-pay-for-themselves mood, and, in particular, hopeful that Edward Gibbon Wakefield's 'system' of colonization would pay for itself as he had promised it would. There was consequently an embargo on drawing on the British Treasury. At the same time no Australian Bank would lend. FitzRoy took the bull of impending bankruptcy by the horns. He acted in contravention of his instructions as governor and issued paper money. 'It was decided to issue notes, or debentures, bearing five per cent

[7] *Remarks on New Zealand*, published by W. & H. White, London, 1846.

interest after the expiration of one year; and as these debentures were at first refused by several speculators, and therefore seemed likely to be much depreciated, they were made a legal tender.' The result was that other money tended to disappear. 'We never see in change,' Mary FitzRoy told her sister-in-law, 'other than *paper* shillings and sixpences.' But at least there was some money with which to meet government expenditure to pay official salaries, though still only at half rate. A real and great hardship was allayed, a hardship increased by the fact that the funds of Wakefield's New Zealand Company, which had been struggling to keep in some sort of employment the 'labourers' they had brought out, were now fast drying up.

FitzRoy now had to produce national revenue wherewith to meet his debenture interest and to create a belief in national solvency. His predecessor Hobson had turned for revenue from a tax on the sale of land (which when private purchase was banned had shrivelled alarmingly) to a tax on imports, that is to say customs duties. These were already unpopular with the Maoris, particularly those most sophisticated Maoris around the original settlement of Kororareka who had largely become the traders of the country. FitzRoy saw nothing for it, however, but to increase the custom duties.

Thus for lack of a few thousand pounds, for lack of some temporary help from the home government, which might surely have been given as a matter of expediency, FitzRoy, it may be said, drove another nail into his own New Zealand coffin. From now onwards he was bedeviled by deteriorating relationships with the Maoris, the people he most wished to help. To a diminution in their belief in the white man's self-pride and courage was now added a lessening in their belief in his beneficence or fairness.

Yet FitzRoy exercised a great sense of fairness, perhaps exercised it too much. His reversal of a decision made by the Land Commissioner was a case in point. Certain extensive tracts of good land around New Plymouth had been found almost empty of Maoris, largely by reason of the wars waged by the gun-purchasing Hongi and his imitator Rauperaha. The Commissioner, contrary to his usual practice and perhaps as a matter of expediency, had found the purchase made by the New Zealand Company from the victorious Maoris a valid one. But now the original owners of the land, turned out by force of arms, were coming back. They claimed the land as theirs, and began to resort to force in evicting those whites who had begun to move in. FitzRoy reviewed the Commissioner's decision, and summarily reversed it. As in most of his decisions, he was courageous to the point of masochism, justified, but impolitic. To the settlers he was, quite simply, mad.

He now decided on a drastic step which he hoped would please everybody. The embargo on the selling of land to anyone except the New Zealand Government, Government pre-emption as it was called, had resulted in the virtual cessation of all land selling, for the simple reason that the Government had no money with which to buy. FitzRoy cancelled the pre-emption. At the same time he put a tax of ten shillings an acre on all purchases: thus would he not only relieve the constipated land position but also fill the ravenous exchequer. Unfortunately, the tax was too high, sometimes more than the price offered for the land. The Maoris were indignant.

And now began the sort of trouble that FitzRoy had all along been trying to avoid, the fear of which had caused him to be pro-Maori rather than pro-White in his policy, though he was by no means unaware how hard a time some of the settlers were experiencing.[8] Kororareka was but a shadow of its former roisterous, prosperous self, and the Maoris very much regretted the change.

There was nearby a certain young chieftain by the name of Heke, related by marriage to the great warrior Hongi, and, in

[8] On page 23 of his *Remark on New Zealand*, after acknowledging the home government's difficulty in meeting all the demands on its military strength, FitzRoy continues: 'Repeated denials given to reiterated applications of successive governors of New Zealand for more effective support to their position, obliged them to have recourse to a system of forbearance and conciliation, which—in the nature of things—could not long continue, and which encouraged encroachments, as well as injurious trials of strength, on the part of both races. In the colony an extreme of forbearance—arising out of utter inability to carry out the law efficiently, rather than from real leniency, bordered on inhumanity towards the settlers...'

reverse of Rauperaha, having given up Christianity after imbibing if not its principles at least a knowledge of its literature. With a quick brain and a clever tongue he began to stir up trouble. He was egged on to action by some of the discontented whites, and in particular by the local American consul, who was not alone among Americans of those decades in not liking the English. There stood on a hill above Kororareka a tall flag-staff from which flew the Union Jack. There, the trouble-makers told young Heke, was flaunting itself the symbol of the Governor's power, a power that everyone on the Bay of Islands knew was for the bad. Heke, of the stuff of which agitators and sea lawyers are made but anxious to be known of the stuff of a warrior, (and perhaps taking a symbol as more symbolic than it really was), conceived the plan of cutting down the flagstaff. On July 8th 1844, he put his plan into action—successfully.

Now, a symbol of power was a symbol of power, and FitzRoy had no illusion that he could laugh this matter off. He had the flagstaff put up again. With other signs of belligerency making themselves apparent nearer to the main sites of the settlers, impressed by a recent Maori feast which he had attended and which had been really a show of strength on their part, FitzRoy at once sent to Sydney for more troops. The ship taking this message was held up for a fortnight by bad weather before even starting on its journey.

FitzRoy therefore thought it expedient to make concessions. He did not do things by halves. He declared Kororareka a free port, closing the Customs House. It was an unauthorized move, he explained in his *Remarks*, but he 'did not shrink from it'. He followed it up by getting his Legislative Council to abolish customs for the time-being altogether—again without the agreement of his home government.

Bishop Selwyn approved these moves; and they in fact paid off. When, on eventually receiving reinforcements of 250 men, FitzRoy began to prepare a punitive expedition against Heke, he was approached by some of the chiefs, in particular a Christian chief by the name of Waka Nene. An understanding was made by them that if FitzRoy would call off his expedition they would guarantee to make Heke behave himself in future. FitzRoy accepted the bargain and called off his expedition. About the same time he made another concession, reducing the ten shilling land tax to the purely nominal figure of one penny.

Unfortunately, at this juncture the British Government unwittingly destroyed the chances of peace: Heke and his rebels got wind of a Colonial Office proposal to tax all unoccupied Maori lands and in default of payment to confiscate them to the Crown. In righteous anger they restarted their guerilla warfare and once more cut down the flagstaff.

FitzRoy set it up again, and put a price on Heke's head. Heke put the same price on FitzRoy's.

The flagstaff was now iron-bound and permanently guarded. This Heke regarded as a challenge. What happened next was something of a surprise to both sides. At sunrise on March 11th 1845 the rebels, two hundred strong, attacked. By a feint they outwitted the flagstaff's guard, and, amidst cheers, down it came again. There followed a set battle on the beach with the guns of *H.M.S. Hazard* supporting the soldiers from the bay, while the women and children of the town were being embarked onto the ships in the harbour, American included. Then by ill chance the soldiers' powder magazine blew up. The decision was made to abandon the settlement.

Confusion now followed, mixed with almost laughable scenes. The Maoris, amazed at their success, looted, but looted, with a gentlemanly restraint, whilst some of the bolder whites returned from the ships to salvage their belongings. 'One strong-minded woman,' reports Thomson, 'was seen pulling a blanket against an armed native.' Children left on shore were chivalrously sent by the Maoris to rejoin their parents. Kororareka, nevertheless, was burned to the ground.

The conflagration might have spread. In fact nothing of the sort happened, for again Waka Nene and the majority of the chiefs rallied to FitzRoy's support. The whites had that to thank their Governor for, though in fact they did not thank him for anything.

On Cook Strait the mood of the settlers was at first near to panic, with the rumour spreading that Heke and his men were coming south. Things were not much better at Auckland, where joy at the sight of three ships approaching, no doubt with the reinforcements, turned to consternation when it was found that aboard were the wounded and the refugees from Kororareka. At that however the little town rose to the occasion and succoured the wounded and cared for the refugees. The Governor's wife would no doubt have been at the head of the ladies' activities had she not been brought low at that time with her fourth child. And actually, as she told her sister-in-law, she had a very bad time indeed and was dangerously ill for some weeks, an added anxiety for the harassed FitzRoy.

FitzRoy however was not allowing himself to be too cast down. His wife reported, 'He looks quite as well as in his very best days.'

The time for conciliation, for appeasement, had obviously gone by—there had in fact arrived the position that FitzRoy had always feared, that he had warned the people against, that the settlers' intransigence had made increasingly probable. He did two things. He reimposed the customs duties, and he set about reorganizing the expedition against Hona Heke.

One fact at least was in FitzRoy's favour, a fact for which his policy could take the credit: the followers of Heke did not noticeably increase after his success, and the Christian chiefs under Waka Nene did not default.

The leadership of the military reinforcements did not in the least favour FitzRoy, nor illumine the annals of the British Army. The combined force of soldiers of the line (which included Surgeon Major Thomson whose highly critical descriptions we have been quoting) and the Christian Maori allies marched into the interior to rout out Heke. An ill-assorted and mutually suspicious force, with inadequate artillery, they found Heke's *pa* quite impregnable and, suffering from a sortie which inflicted forty casualties, retired.

Heke sent insulting and not highly relevant messages to FitzRoy: 'Caesar, Pontius Pilate, Nebuchadnezzar, Pharaoh, Nicodemus, Agrippa, and Herod were kings and governors; did they confer any benefit, or did they not kill Jesus Christ?'

Collecting some less inadequate artillery, the British, with FitzRoy's encouragement, prepared to try again. This time another officer, a Colonel Despard, was in command. The boastful and initially lucky Heke had now retired from the war of weapons, with a wound administered by the Christian Maoris, and his place had been taken by a better general ensconced in an even better *pa*. Despard's expedition against this *pa*, Oheawai, was disastrous. It was very much the same story told again: inexperienced troops and impatient commanders. After another inadequate artillery preparation the British attacked Oheawai; they failed to breach the defences and they at length retreated, leaving behind dead and wounded and having through the rest of the night—says Major Thomson—to listen to the groans of a prisoner being tortured within the *pa*. The campaign then settled down to a stalemate, with Heke sending further insulting and patronizing messages to FitzRoy.

The settlers in their towns on Cook Strait lived on rumours and were despondent. They had already sent a petition to Parliament for the recall of their Governor. On the first day of October 1845 they were rejoiced by the news that their Governor was to go.

At Wellington there were joyful illuminations; and at Nelson there was carried on high, flanked by those of the two unpopular officials responsible for native 'protection', the effigy of Robert FitzRoy. As a fitting finale, and amidst applause, it was burnt.

CHAPTER 19

'I am Deeply and Irreparably Injured'

THE complaints of the settlers against FitzRoy were not, as is often stated, the primary cause of his recall, for the simple reason that they could not have been received in London until after the decision to remove him from office had been made. Two of these—they will be referred to in detail later —by their dates make this impossible; the third, sent by the 'inhabitants of the southern settlements', though not dated, refers to events and quotes from newspapers of a date up to three months after the letter of dismissal had been sent.

The greater and more direct cause of FitzRoy's downfall was the effect of his conduct upon the man to whom he was responsible and also at one remove upon the rest of the British Cabinet. Lord Stanley, Secretary of State for the Colonies, was to make it clear that his governor's major sins were firstly that he acted contrary to or without instructions and secondly that he failed to keep the home government adequately informed of what he was doing. Since FitzRoy could have avoided these errors if he had really wanted to, the conclusion that he was a wanton masochist is hard to avoid.

It would, however, be an exaggeration. What is true is that FitzRoy's determination to do right in his own eyes and before his own conscience, other eyes and consciences not much matter-ing, took precedence over all else. When his one-time commander, Admiral King, wrote in his letter, 'poor fellow, he was sacrificed to principles', he might more truly have written, 'poor fellow, he has sacrificed himself to his principles'—possibly that is what he meant.

FitzRoy, albeit going out to an extraordinarily difficult situation, had at least started with a fund of goodwill behind him. This may not have existed amongst the officials of the New Zealand Company, but it did exist amongst the settlers as a whole, and it did exist in the hearts of his masters at home. The *Nelson Examiner* of February 10th 1844, in reporting on the Governor's arrival and reply to his address of welcome, had written with its store of goodwill only slightly damped by the impression that His Excellency, although carrying a fund of goodwill, differed with many on some questions. Similarly, Lord Stanley's first despatch, commenting on his governor's report of his early measures and activities, is laudatory though with a slightly nervous undertone —rather perhaps as one might apprehensively praise a domesticated tiger for having done the housework.

This despatch of Lord Stanley's, sent two months after a shorter one announcing to FitzRoy that his salary as Governor had been raised to £1,500, is dated November 11th 1844[1] and is the first to comment on FitzRoy's activities as Governor, as reported to Lord Stanley in the middle of the previous April: so slow is the rate of communication between the two men. Lord Stanley does say that he had been hoping to hear from FitzRoy before writing; but FitzRoy's April despatch had taken five months and two days to arrive, and apparently anything very much less could not be expected.

'I am happy,' Lord Stanley wrote in this despatch, 'to be enabled to convey to you my general approval of the course which you appear to have adopted.' There is approved FitzRoy's 'strong sense of justice…earnest desire to reconcile differences' and 'the

[1] Public Record Office, Colonial Office and Parliamentary papers, contains the FitzRoy–Stanley correspondence.

boldness and promptitude with which you have promulgated and enforced your views and met, by decided measures, the emergencies of your embarrassing position': the British Government had indeed been aware that 'the largest discretion would be needed by their representative.' As to FitzRoy's decision over the Wairau massacre, the problem was one of great difficulty, and, all things considered, 'I am of opinion that in declining to make the conflict the subject of criminal proceedings you took a wise, though undoubtedly a bold decision.' FitzRoy's reversal of the regulation forbidding sale of land to individuals is sanctioned with some hesitation. And in the earlier letter (announcing the increase in salary) there comes the unqualified statement—which surely any more cautious and sensitive governor would have taken as an implied censure—that Lord Stanley is hearing of his otherwise unreported doings through another government office, that of the 'Commander in Chief's'. Here, all in all, was a definite if slight hint of trouble to come.

Lord Stanley's first despatches of complaint are written in the February and March of 1845. They show irritation once again at hearing of what is happening only from extraneous sources. (These no doubt would be, besides the other government offices already mentioned, influential M.P.s with friends and interests in New Zealand, and the New Zealand newspapers, of which there was actually one, a fortnightly called *The New Zealand Journal*, published in London.) The despatches then stress the word *embarrassment*. It is a great embarrassment that FitzRoy's silence is causing to a minister. The issue of debentures, Lord Stanley continues, has in fact been sanctioned and supported by the Government. But surely that involved a decision that at least ought to have been reported without delay? Then the withdrawal of custom duties: 'I am at a loss to understand how you could have supposed such a step within the limit of your discretion.' The second despatch ends with the hope that FitzRoy 'will be able to satisfy me'. If not, the Colonial Secretary may have to advise Her Majesty not 'to continue her confidence in so distant a Government'. The use of the word 'distant' is a neat way of saying a good deal. This news must have been a great shock to

FitzRoy, hardly in practice less great in spite of the fact, stated by him later, that he rather expected it.

In his reply FitzRoy includes excuses for slowness in replying that are inadequate and would perhaps have better been left out: the ship carrying his despatches had been delayed owing to the need to return to port after a mishap. In any case, he continues, abandoning this unaccustomed apologetic stance, he gave all his time to public business, and he was badly understaffed. There is then devoted considerable space to a defence against certain Parliamentary criticism, which had come to his ears, of the tone that he had adopted in dealing with a couple of pro-white and anti-Maori New Zealand gentlemen, one of whom was Jerningham Wakefield. This again, since it was by now pretty ancient history, might have better been left out. However, it is only human to defend oneself. FitzRoy might have done better to be even more human; for with agonizing fairness he gives both sides of the argument and details of the gentlemen's complaints, and in the process does not paint a very flattering picture of himself.

The letter ends with a reference to the threat of dismissal and the following thoroughly unappeasing statement:

> Under the circumstances the arrival of an abler and more trust-worthy Governor will be an unspeakable relief to me. I cannot forget that my predecessor here was hounded to a premature grave by the calumnies and opposition of bad men:—But I thank God that my health has not suffered and I look confidently forward to the change which time and correct information will effect.

The relief was promptly granted him. On April 30th 1845 there was sent the terse intimation of his dismissal, stating that further despatches received had failed to remove the bad impression already gained. It was followed a fortnight later by a more detailed explanation.

Lord Stanley was not inhuman, and he does his best to soften the blow; however, as FitzRoy was to point out, no amount of assurances as to the unimpaired regard for his sterling character was going to alter the blow's effect. The failure of FitzRoy is put very succinctly. 'You sustained,' writes Lord Stanley, 'a peculiarly urgent obligation to state your measures circumspectly, to pursue them with firmness, and to report them with punctuality.' None of these things had been done.

There follow specific complaints, one that FitzRoy has asked the home government to make up the colony's deficiency of £10,000, but gives no detail. Another exemplifies only too clearly the danger to which FitzRoy had exposed himself in allowing news of his activities to percolate into England through the mesh of prejudice and misinformation rather than being poured out directly by himself. After troops had been sent to you, says Lord Stanley, some of the Chiefs apparently surrendered up their muskets to you and yet you gave them back! In which case: either the troops were not needed, or you wasted them. The truth here was that the chiefs in question were those loyal to the Christian Waka Nene, that their offer of muskets was a symbol of friendliness, and that FitzRoy's returning of them was a symbol of equal friendliness which successfully bound them to him as allies and in fact very effective allies. It was probably the best thing that he did.

The Colonial Secretary's indictment ends with a repetition of the real kernel of the complaint: he had been putting the Minister and the Government in a continually embarrassing position: 'We are compelled to avow to Parliament the total insufficiency of our information.'

On November 10th 1845, a few days only before the successor arrived and when all possibility of altering the decision was gone, FitzRoy wrote a long and detailed and less truculent answer. Though not free from self-righteousness, it is a dignified letter and a sad letter to read.

It begins with a statement that further despatches and explanations had been on the way: they might not of course have satisfied his Lordship, but at least 'I think that a few days' delay would not have been ill bestowed on an honest and hardworking public servant.' That cry from the penitent-too-late earned the hard but perhaps inevitable comment from his Lordship in the margin, 'but I had waited for months!'

Though FitzRoy tries hard not to be truculent and is in fact eminently reasonable, there does shine through the whole of his long self-defence the one unbreakable conviction that had guided all his conduct: that everything, finance included, was of minor importance compared with the relationship between the whites and the Maoris and that consequently there was a paramount need to avoid a major head-on collision while the white race was 'entirely in the power of the Coloured'. If he had shown apparent variations of purpose, continues FitzRoy, then it was only because of the need to do something quickly to 'keep up an establishment' which could protect the whites. If he had disobeyed instructions, 'I preferred doing what appeared to me best for the country rather than observe mechanically every direction.' If he had been slow in reporting, the difficulties of communication both out of and within the colony were not appreciated—this is probably very true—and in any case 'I preferred acting first and afterwards writing.' As to his appeal for troops, recent events had shown the need for them. And as for his method of conducting his military campaign, with the help of Christian Maori allies, the wisest and most knowledgeable men in the colony, headed by the Bishop and the Chief Justice, commended him.

The despatch nears its end with an informed and compassionate appeal for an understanding treatment of the natives and a reiteration of the fact that it was the Maori situation and Maori threat that had guided his conduct: 'I looked at the totally exposed and defenceless state of all the settlements, without walls, stockades, or any kind of efficient protection, without even a place of refuge for women and children. I remembered the destruction in Chile of seven Spanish towns, in one night, by aboriginal natives far inferior to the New Zealanders in arms and warlike quality— and I reflected on the inutility of fiscal arrangements should our settlements be similarly destroyed.' FitzRoy's 'inutility' is almost as supercharged a word as Stanley's 'distant'.

Then comes the end of the despatch:

> I am bound to acknowledge the expressions of your Lordship's good feeling, and of the opinion entertained by Her Majesty's Government towards myself personally, which terminates your despatch; but such expressions, however I may appreciate them,

cannot diminish the conviction that I am deeply and irreparably injured.

Was Lord Stanley unjust to FitzRoy? The answer must be: only to an excusable degree, excusable that is to say in terms of politics. Stanley, though he may have been an outstanding one, was a politician. He might perhaps have left his erring governor time and the chance to resign rather than be dismissed. But it is clear that Stanley and his party were under pressure; and any politician who has a healthy desire to save his own skin is likely to ease himself of pressure at the earliest possible moment.[2]

It could even be said that Lord Stanley was forbearing. The comments of his permanent official—they are those presumably of the Permanent Secretary of the Colonial Office, but the signature is illegible—are by no means complimentary. His summing up runs:

> This despatch appears to exhibit a painful effort to execute a task to which the writer is unequal. He was surrounded by many difficulties which increased under his system of government, and was pressed by conflicting interest, which he had not decision and firmness to adjust. Under a constant excitement and perpetual hurry he seemed neither to have had the power to adopt judicious and constant measures nor the calmness to keep the Secretary of State informed on the acts of his Government or the motives of his actions.

As to the pressure upon Lord Stanley and the embarrassment caused him, these were in fact, as has been suggested, greatest after the despatch of dismissal had been sent. They must have been building up, however. Complaints about the conduct of

[2] Stanley had not a seat in the Commons to lose, having moved up to the House of Lords 'in the rights of his father's barony' in the previous year, 1844. But that fact would not have made him any more anxious to be the cause of his Cabinet's and party's downfall. Since, as the 14th Earl of Derby, he was to become three times Prime Minister, we may assume that he had ambitions to that post and ambitions that he would not want to jeopardise. Stanley had shown himself a hard man as Secretary of State for Ireland. But it would be impossible to deny that he was —like FitzRoy—a man of principle. On the principle of the country continuing to get the best government possible, FitzRoy had to go.

affairs in New Zealand were being made in and out of Parliament and merely came to a head in a three-day House of Commons debate on the 17th, 18th and 19th of June 1845, of which more in a moment.

One official petition to Parliament was made by the New Zealand Company, one was made by the settlers in New Zealand and one was made by the settlers 'at present sojourning in England',[3] the same no doubt as those who were running the London *New Zealand Journal*. This paper delighted on December 21st 1844 to show that it was not the only one to criticize FitzRoy by quoting[4] from current articles in *The Times* and *Morning Chronicle*. They concern FitzRoy's financial measures and in particular his turning of his debentures into legal tender. What *The Times* said must have made Lord Stanley angry, and probably apprehensive: 'The Colonial Secretary is so obliging as to vouch "the honour of the Home Government" for the repayment of these precious notes! We are much obliged to him! We are trying to pay our debt by reducing extremes, by paying taxes and living within our income. This is the lesson which old England teaches New Zealand.'

The less august *Morning Chronicle* resorts to heavy humour. 'Does anyone,' it questions, 'know anything of Captain FitzRoy, the Governor of New Zealand? Where was he educated? Where has he lived all his days? Of a truth, we do not ask these questions without reason; for, from all we hear of his proceedings, he seems to us to be a phenomenon whose rearing, in these days of ours, must be well worth studying. We know that when a colonial government is vacant, Lord Stanley never fills it up in a hurry but conscientiously takes pains to find out the most incompetent man there is to be got; but we did not conceive it possible for him to have found, and at this time of day, a man who could venture on absurdities so outrageous as those which Captain FitzRoy has been enacting.' On discovering, continues the article, an adverse balance in the colony's exchequer, 'a plain common-sense man, such as governors used to be in the days of good Queen

[3] British Museum and House of Lords libraries.
[4] Copies in P.R.O. Colonial Office papers.

Bess, would have thought it most natural to bring the expenditure down to the income, for after all it would seem as if £20,000 a year was enough to be spent on a colony containing less than 15,000 souls—at least when it has no more to spend. But Captain FitzRoy seems to think that young colonies, like young men of quality, ought to commence their careers running into debt...'

Even a man less dedicated to his subject than FitzRoy could have shown how that article was self condemned: '15,000 souls'? —that left out the Maoris, who numbered probably round about a quarter of a million, but who presumably had no souls. Newspaper articles, however, do not have to measure their effect by their reasonableness.

Both the petition by the ex-settlers now in England and that by the New Zealand Company refer back to times before FitzRoy's term of office and both are in essence pleas for more democratic and less autocratic government in the colony. But naturally both are not backward in citing acts by FitzRoy which are typically autocratic. The Company's petition complains of the undue influence of the missionary bodies over the Colonial Office; and the third petition, that by the 'Inhabitants of the Southern Settlements', complains of the missionary influence over FitzRoy in particular. This last is certainly unfair, since in practice FitzRoy shows less regard for the missionaries' point of view during his governorship than might have been expected, his support for the Christian Waka Nene being the only significant example of it. However, perhaps nobody could reasonably expect the settlers' petition to be fair. For ever since FitzRoy's forgiveness of the Wairau murderers they had hated him, and their hatred had led them to an extreme outlook which shines balefully through their petition. FitzRoy, they say, treated even bad native characters 'with preposterous civility'. FitzRoy, they assert, had based his methods on the opposite of the 'received theory' for the 'good government of savages'. And what was that received theory? It was 'never to tolerate any display of that arrogance which is natural to every race of savages; most assuredly not to instill into them notions of their own importance... by ostentatious professions of regard and manifestations of respect for them.' A governor a good deal less determinedly philanthropic towards aborigines than FitzRoy was not going to please men who felt like that.

Finally, the three-days' debate in the House of Commons: it took place while FitzRoy, already under sentence of dismissal, was sanctioning the ill-executed and disastrous attack by Colonel Despard upon Oheawai. It debated the motion, 'That this House will resolve itself into a Committee to consider the state of the Colony of New Zealand, and the case of the New Zealand Company', a motion which was regarded by both parties as a vote of lack of confidence in the Colonial Secretary.

The debate, like the petitions, covered more than FitzRoy's governorship, and ranged even more widely. It ended with a statement by Peel himself, which made all things clear, including the intentions of a Prime Minister who had greater troubles on his mind and who in matters large or small reserved to himself the right of adapting his conduct 'to the exigencies of the moment'. It was a speech defending not the Prime Minister's Governor of New Zealand but the Prime Minister's government, which was soon to fall:

> Now, what is the course the Government proposes to pursue under circumstances which I admit to be critical? Disapproving of the conduct of a Governor—for whose personal character I avow I entertain the highest respect—for the difficulties of whose position I own I must make great allowances—(Hear, hear)—we have yet signified in the most formal and authoritative manner that his conduct in the administration of affairs we do not approve of; and with reluctance, but in the performance of a necessary duty, we have removed him from a post which he undertook from the highest and most patriotic motives. (Hear, hear.) We have shown, therefore, in the first instance, that we have no desire to consult the feelings and interests of a friend, to the prejudice of a Colony.

If Robert FitzRoy should have observed, 'God protect me from such friends!' he had in his bitterness ever right to do so. But governments do not go down for the sake of colonial governors— and in fact neither did this one, for the motion was defeated by 223 votes to 173.

.   .   .

In the November of 1845 FitzRoy's successor arrived. He was George Grey, later Sir George Grey—he received, it may be said, the knighthood that FitzRoy missed. He was a captain and he had personal charm: those are about the only similarities between the two men; and he was a captain in the Army and not the Navy and he used his charm more often than FitzRoy seems to have done in New Zealand. For the rest, he was genial, astute, sometimes artful, an opportunist and very much a political animal. None of these was FitzRoy, who must have been the despair of his well-wishers in that he seemed not only ignorant of how to come out of the rain but undesirous of doing so.

With the inevitable unfairness of such things, Grey received the help, in the way of money and better equipped military forces, that had been denied FitzRoy. Heke and his supporters were finally defeated, their *pa* being penetrated on a Sunday while some of the defenders were at prayers. Rauperaha, who had the temerity to rebel, was captured and, with questionable legality, held in prison. Grey in a few months earned a respect from the Maoris such as FitzRoy for all his partisanship had never earned.

Again with an inevitable unfairness, opinion in New Zealand somewhat veered round towards FitzRoy's favour after he had gone. He had, they said, been made a scapegoat for the sins of the idealistic, evangelical, impractical, unhelpful Colonial Office. But this was really almost as far from the truth as the opposite, preceding theory, that FitzRoy was either weak or mad or both. FitzRoy had come to a New Zealand financially bankrupt and torn by hatreds. There was virtually no technical knowledge on which he could draw on the spot, and his superiors were four or five months away. Most of his decisions, taken one at a time in their context, were highly reasonable.

But he was the same FitzRoy of *Beagle* days, and writ a little larger. As he could not wait for permission to buy or hire a schooner, so he could not wait for permission to alter a colony's currency or taxes. And who shall say that in either case he was wrong in his action, if the job was to be done or the situation saved? The trouble was that he was bound to appear wrong in the eyes of his superiors. That he did not mind. In the first instance he was hurt only in his pocket. In the second—and here, such was his inherent passion for selflessness, he seemed almost to bare his chest to wounds—it was his reputation that suffered, and badly. If he was lucky to get the *Beagle* command he was not lucky to get the New Zealand.

And a final word about his quarterdeck manner, his inability to suffer fools gladly or knaves at all. Perhaps FitzRoy never realized what effect an intimation of disapproval by him could have: judging by the prompt reaction of Baron de Thierry on an earlier occasion and the extended reaction of his hearers in New Zealand, it must have been considerable. That bitter tirade against Jerningham Wakefield he was never to be allowed to forget while he remained in the country.

There was indeed, and perhaps significantly, one phrase that stuck in the throats of his enemies and was quoted in their complaint to the home government. It was not even an original phrase on FitzRoy's part, but one that he had read and that had taken his fancy: Jerningham was, he told him, acting as one of 'the Devil's missionaries'.

Missionaries had in fact helped to bring FitzRoy into New Zealand; and an unfortunate reference to missionaries helped to push him out again.

CHAPTER 20

Fuegian Aftermath

' 'Ban, 'Ban, Ca-Caliban,
Has a new master: get a new man.'
The Tempest

FITZROY made his way home from New
Zealand on an east-bound ship, thus circumnavigating the globe
a second time, though now as a passenger, and thus also passing
through the Magellan Straits once more. Not far to the south,
though perhaps little thought of—it was, he says, a tedious journey
and must in contrast to the outward voyage have been an unhappy one—were living the natives who had been his English
guests, the merry Fuegia and her surly husband York, and the
one-time immaculate Jemmy Button. On the Straits themselves,
at Port Famine, a certain retired naval captain Allen Gardiner,
had been trying, not for the first time, to set up a Protestant
Mission in South America.

Allen Gardiner was soon to be consciously taking up FitzRoy's
Fuegian missionary mantle, and to wear it and pass it on to less
worthy wearers. FitzRoy took no active part in the aftermath of
his Fuegian venture. He offered, along with Sulivan, his advice.
To the ship's captain who rediscovered Jemmy Button and wrote
about his discovery he gave permission to quote from the *Narrative* and so must have entered into correspondence with him. But
that is all. For the rest FitzRoy must have read about what
happened; and no one as emotionally humane as he could have
read without being profoundly affected.

236

One enters, in following the exploits of Allen Gardiner and his successors, a different, not to say an alien world. It is the world of deep Victorian piety, which has its own particular outlook, its own self-sufficient rectitude and even its own distinctive language. It is a world that FitzRoy, for all his fundamentalist bent, never really entered.

With Gardiner's earlier missionary efforts this narrative is only concerned to the extent of showing his fanatically determined character. Like FitzRoy and Darwin, he had been impressed by the missionary work at Tahiti on visiting those islands in his naval duties. In 1822, at the age of twenty-eight, he was congratulating himself that he had 'ceased to walk in the broad way or to hasten by rapid strides to the brink of eternal ruin'. Four years later he had retired from the Navy, and by 1834 he had behind him three years work in Natal and a wife who had died after presenting him with five children. He married again and turned his attention to South America. Three years after FitzRoy's dash to the wrecked *Challenger* he was working in the same area. The Araucanian Indians, however, while admiring him, did not respond to his teaching.

Gardiner came home. He next made two attempts to set up a missionary settlement near to Port Famine and one further north in the Gran Chaco. These were interspersed with trips to England in order to raise funds and enthusiasm. Gardiner, finding the Church Missionary Society unwilling to help, founded his own society, the Patagonian Mission.

In the Gran Chaco he met Catholic opposition, as he had in fact done in Arauco: he came to the conclusion, therefore, that the place for him was without question FitzRoy's virgin ground of Tierra del Fuego. In England once more, he persuaded his committee, who 'found it impossible to hold him back',[1] to agree to

[1] This and later quotations in this chapter of the missionaries' activities and letters are taken from *The Story of Commander Allen Gardiner R.N.* by John W. Marsh and W. M. Stirling, written in 1874 and published by Jas. Nisbet & Co., London. A second book, by Allen Gardiner's widow, *Records of the S. American Missionary Society*, published by the Society, takes the story further. Allen Gardiner also wrote his autobiography, but this does not cover his last years.

his plans. In 1848 he was again in Tierra del Fuego, supported by a decked boat with a crew of five, a dinghy, a whaleboat, two wigwams and six months' supplies. Failing, by reason of a gale, to land on Staten Island, the party moved on to Picton Island at the eastern end of the Beagle Channel and not so far from Jemmy Button's home. But 'a very little experience in a very short time' taught them something that FitzRoy could have told them in an even shorter time, that their scheme 'was quite inadequate to the requirements of so hazardous an enterprise in so stormy a latitude'. They had also rapidly lost everything stealable to the Fuegians.

Indefatigably back in England again, Gardiner launched a revised plan. It was a reasonable one. A brigantine of some 120 tons would be bought or built, to act as an immediate base and to be moored alongside the scene of missionary effort, while a more permanent base, with larger supplies, would be set up in the Falkland Islands. Again the C.M.S. was approached, then the Foreign Mission of the Church of Scotland; Gardiner even travelled to Silesia to seek help from the Moravian Church—all to no avail. But a Bristol schoolmaster by the name of the Reverend G. Pakenham Despard, a forceful man and a man who will come into the story again, now became secretary of the mission and gained for Gardiner his backing. A Cheltenham lady gave £700 and then another £300. The committee of the Patagonian Mission gave the signal to proceed.

Still the funds were not large enough for a brigantine. Two twenty-six foot launches were substituted, a poor second-best. As companions Gardiner collected a gentleman practising as a surgeon in Burslem, another 'catechist' who was a nominee of the Y.M.C.A., three pious Cornish fishermen, and the carpenter who had been with him on the previous attempt—and who professed that it was like Heaven being with Captain Gardiner, he was such a man of prayer.

The note of too easy irony is difficult to avoid. The ensuing tragedy of Gardiner and his companions is not only harrowing; it is anger-making. The men wait for their doom with a sort of perverse determination, an ecstatic masochism or at least passivity, everlastingly thanking God for the misfortunes that, as they understood it, he saw fit in his wisdom increasingly to pile upon them.

Matters went wrong from the start. The party had been landed again on Picton Island, and it was Gardiner's intention at once to set sail for Jemmy Button's country and to enlist that ever-obliging young man's support. But before Gardiner could start one of the launches was wrecked and the dinghies of the other were lost; Gardiner decided not to make the attempt, though later a sea captain was to express the opinion that he might have succeeded. The natives, after trading with them grudgingly for a while, left them severely alone. The party finally retired to a safe harbour on the northern shores of the Beagle Channel, Spaniard Harbour, and there endeavoured to settle down, in face of approaching winter, to wait for their relief. They were not perturbed as to their ultimate fate. It was believed that a Government ship left the Falkland Islands monthly to collect timber and that this would be bringing supplies; a Monte Video merchant had directed his trading vessels to keep an eye on them, and a letter had been sent to Captain Sulivan who had recently taken a three-year sabatical leave to go farming with his family in the Falklands.

Fish proved unexpectedly scarce. Powder for the shot-guns had by an oversight not been disembarked. Scurvy and sickness began to appear, and then as their meagre supplies ran out, real starvation. Neither the supposed timber-ship visited them nor any of the vessels of the Monte Video merchant—he had given orders, it transpired, but they were not obeyed.

Mr Williams, the surgeon, was in a bad way. But it was delightful, wrote Gardiner in his diary, to see him so heavenly-minded. In his own diary Williams was writing, ecstatically, 'I am happy, day and night, hour by hour.'

When the fishing net was torn to shreds by ice, Gardiner wrote, 'Thus the Lord has seen fit to render another means abortive, and doubtless to make His power more apparent, and show that all our help is to come immediately from Him.' A little later: 'The Lord in His providence has seen fit to bring us very low...but all is in infinite wisdom, mercy, and love.' Later still: 'The Lord is very pitiful and of tender compassion. He knows our frames. He appoints and measures all His afflictive dispensations, and when His set time is fully come, He will either remove us to His eternal and glorious kingdom, or supply our languishing bodies with food convenient for us.'

There was little doubt now that they were all going to die. There was no recrimination, only heroism and joyful resignation and the digging of graves for the dead by the still living.

Six weeks after Gardiner's last diary entry, succour arrived in the shape of one of the merchant's ships, followed by a naval vessel. All of the seven men were dead. The naval lieutenant sent the story home via his admiral at Valparaiso. It appeared in *The Times* of April 29th 1852, backed by a short letter from the admiral and a long and deadly serious leading article. Those who plan and sponsor such expeditions, said the admiral, should first consider the climate to be met. 'Neither reverence for the cause in which they were engaged,' said the leading article, 'nor admiration of the lofty qualities of the leader of the party, can blind our eyes to the unutterable folly of the enterprise as it was conducted or smother the expression of natural indignation against those who could wantonly risk so many valuable lives on so hopeless an expedition.' It continued with the familiar and rather unfair argument that there was plenty of room for philanthropic effort at home, and ended with the demand, 'Let us hear no more of Patagonian missions!'

The new secretary, G. Pakenham Despard, replied promptly with a statement in *The Times*: 'With God's help the mission shall be maintained!' Judging by the funds that began to come in, his reaction was by far the more popular one. Perhaps even the surprising reaction of the practical and sensible Sulivan was not at all untypical. He saw in the fact that by a series of chances the letter asking for his succour had arrived after he had left the Falkland Islands nothing less beneficial than the workings of a benign Providence: 'Is it not another proof that their deaths were the appointed means for carrying on the mission?'

It was now that Robert FitzRoy's advice was sought, no doubt at Sulivan's instigation. The plan put forward for comment was the one for which the martyred fanatic, to give him his due, had been working. It proposed that a missionary base should be established on one of the Falkland Islands and that from there a party should go out 'to hold cautious intercourse with the Fuegians' and to persuade some of them, 'a task of small difficulty', to come to the base, there to be taught English and in due course to impart a knowledge of their own language. Then, when blessed with this knowledge and with the confidence of the Fuegian exiles' hearts, the missionaries would sail back with them to Tierra del Fuego and set up a base there.

FitzRoy's reply, dated December 6th 1852, just two years after Allen Gardiner's fatal landing on Picton Island, ran as follows:

> I have given the subject of your letter my best consideration. It appears to me that your present plan is practicable and comparatively safe, that it offers a fairer prospect of success than most Missionary enterprises at their commencement, and that it would be difficult to suggest one less objectionable.

Their determination thus armed—if it needed any arming— with this cautious and almost aggressively negative approval, the mission built with the funds now available a fine two-masted schooner of eighty-eight tons burden. Piously, though perhaps provocatively of fate, they named it the *Allen Gardiner*.

There now comes into the story the ship's captain who sought permission to quote from FitzRoy's *Narrative*. This was Parker Snow, to whom the Patagonian Mission gave command of the *Allen Gardiner*.

It is not easy to assess the character of Captain Snow. Certainly it was a forceful one. He was not a certificated ship's master or mate—probably few of his like yet were so—but he had been prominent in a voyage in search of the lost arctic explorer, Sir John Franklin. He wrote a two-volume account of his sailings in command of the *Allen Gardiner*, entitled, with the usual lengthiness of those days, *A Two Years' Cruise off Tierra del*

Fuego, the Falkland Islands, Patagonia, and in the River Plate: a Narrative of Life in the Southern Seas.[2] This is a most competent and expressive book, somewhat marred by the author's increasing note of virulent criticism and dislike of his employers, the missionaries. The said missionaries were to accuse him of being vain and of entertaining ambitions to head the mission as well as captain the ship. The relationship does seem a love-hate one on Captain Snow's part, and there are times when he is emulating the missionaries and being almost as pious as they. There are also times when he is reacting like a man almost driven mad with irritation. Undoubtedly, like FitzRoy, he was—as he had need to be on those coasts—a skilful and efficient ship's captain; and, again like FitzRoy and for that matter like most other men in command of sailing ships, he did not easily brook interference and liked his own way on board. The criticism by Captain Snow of the missionaries was in essence that they were guided by an impractical, optimistic and arrogant piety instead of by common sense or even on occasions by common decency. His growing distrust of them was one of the causes of the ensuing tragedy.

After leaving behind in the Falkland Islands the two missionaries he had been commissioned to take out, Captain Snow proceeded, as instructed, to the Beagle Channel in search of Jemmy Button. For Jemmy had been chosen as the most likely Fuegian to respond to the invitation to come to the missionary base and the most useful person if he could be induced to do so. Snow reached the eastern end of the Beagle Channel, and as a first task made a pious visit, with his wife whom he had on board, to the scene of Allen Gardiner's martyrdom. His description of the scene as his wife, with unaffected tears pouring down her face, stood over the lonely graves, is sincere and as yet untouched by his later critical spirit towards the missionaries.

Moving on to Picton Island, where Gardiner had made his last efforts to convert the natives before retiring to the place of his death, Snow met his first Fuegians. Still in the missionary mood, he induced them to pray with him: for a while, he com-

[2] Published by Longman in 1857.

ments, they even stopped their importuning and everlasting cries of '*Yamma scoona*'—which seems to show that they had not changed much since *Beagle* days. After a few more encouraging exchanges Snow then went on to try to obey the main part of his orders.

When, after some difficulties of navigation, Captain Snow did bring the *Allen Gardiner* into Ponsonby Sound and within sight of Button Island, the scene became an almost uncannily precise repetition of that of the farewell visit of the *Beagle*. Just as FitzRoy had stood on the deck and had gazed anxiously about and espied two canoes approaching with shouts of their occupants, so did Captain Snow, and with the same startling result:

> Standing on the raised platform aft, I sang out to the natives interrogatively, 'Jemmy Button? Jemmy Button?' To my amazement and joy—almost rendering me for a moment speechless—an answer came from one of the four men in the canoe, 'Yes, yes; Jam-mes Button, Jam-mes Button!' at the same time pointing to the second canoe, which had nearly got alongside. To down with the helm—throw the ship up in the wind close under the high mountains,—shorten sail,—call all hands on deck, and put the vessel's head in the bay towards Button Island, was but the work of an instant: and, for that instant, so extraordinary did those words in English sound from the lips of a native Fuegian, I was unable to prevent a momentary confusion.

With everyone on the schooner peering over the side, a 'stout, wild and shaggy-looking man' was repeating, 'Jammes Button, *me*!' and enquiring in perfectly recognizable and casual English, 'Where's the ladder?'

> And the next moment Jemmy Button—the very man himself—the *protégé* of Captain FitzRoy—the one upon whom the mission rests so much of its hopes—was alongside, well and hearty, and giving me a welcome in broken words of my own tongue!

Soon Jemmy was on board, shaking hands, while the crew looked on with wonder. Captain Snow had to find an anchorage for the ship before he could turn his attention to Jemmy Button.

Then he did so with an intense and concentrated interest, so forcibly expressed that it deserves quotation:

> Directly I could cease from attending to the ship, I turned my attention to Jemmy. He was easily recognized from his resemblance to the account given of him in Captain FitzRoy's narrative. He was, as on the occasion of that gentleman's second visit in 1834, quite naked, having his hair long and matted at the sides, cropped in front, and his eyes affected by smoke. The same words used by Captain FitzRoy to describe him are applicable now, as well as of his wife, who was also (this being his second wife, and a very young woman) 'good-looking', and seemed to be much attached to Jemmy and the children.
>
> I should mention that by this time we had around us and upon deck most of Jemmy's family and connections: besides many others hovering about the ship in canoes, who appeared as if desirous of claiming relationship with him at the present moment. There must have been at least sixty or seventy persons from various parts (for they were not all of Jemmy's people), surrounding us. But as everything seemed to go on peaceably, I felt no alarm. I merely cautioned my men to be on their guard: and allow no one on deck, except with my permission. This permission I had, at Jemmy's request, given to his uncle, his two brothers and a man about to be married, as I was informed, to the eldest daughter of Jemmy: and, following his good example they conducted themselves with exceedingly great propriety. Surely Jemmy must have taught his people something of the good manners he had himself been taught in 'Ingliss conetree'. No one attempted to get up the ship's side, until permission was obtained from me through Jemmy: and though so many of the natives were around us, and great numbers besides could be observed on shore, they remained as quiet and peaceable as if we had previously obtained some power over them. But I understood from Jemmy that not all the natives I saw were of his 'conetree'. Some 'bad men' were amongst them; and he pointed out one or two of the canoes as belonging to those 'bad men'. I did not, however, notice anything about them worse than the rest: and so long as they remained quiet, save the occasional 'yamma scoona', I only took favourable notice of them.

So Jemmy had not changed in his obsession with 'bad men' and his habit of putting the blame onto them if necessary.

One of the first things Captain Snow did was to find some clothes for his visitor:

> Indeed, Jemmy, directly he got on board, and found an 'Ingliss lady' was in the cabin, asked me for 'clothes to put on'. These I soon gave him: and in putting on the trousers, he said 'want braces' as distinctly as I could utter the words. In fact he appeared suddenly to call to mind many things. His tongue was, as it were, loosened: and words, after a moment's thought, came to his memory expressive of what he wished to say. There was no connected talk from him; but broken sentences, abrupt and pithy. Short inquiries, and sometimes painful efforts to explain himself were made, with, however, an evident pleasure in being again able to converse with some one in the 'Ingliss talk'. That he must have been greatly attached to it, is evident from the fact, that he had not omitted to teach his wife, children, and relations. I could hardly credit my senses, when I heard Mrs Jemmy Button from the canoe calling aloud for her husband to come to her. She seemed most anxious he should not be again taken away.

So again was history repeating itself. After some comments on the missionaries' desire to take away natives for their own purpose to their Falkland Island base (of which more shortly), Captain Snow's narrative continues:

> Much talk, necessarily of a rambling character, had I with this poor man. He was to me personally—if I may separate myself from my official character—an object of much curiosity. I had been amongst numbers of the Aborigines in various lands: but I had never before fallen in with one who had been transplanted to the highest fields of intellectual knowledge, and then restored to his original and barren state. It was therefore with a curious eye that I scanned this travelled Fuegian, when, taking him down into my cabin, I had him alone before me. He was a rather corpulent man, with the usual broad features, and moderately dwarfish stature, his height being about 5 feet 3 inches. My clothes I found were small for him in size: but I think if he had been properly dressed and cleaned, he would have looked not unlike a bold and sturdy man-o'-war's-man. As it was, with his shaggy hair and

begrimed countenance, I could not help assimilating him to some huge baboon dressed up for the occasion.

The first thing I did after his coming down was to put food before him. Poor fellow! There was evidently the germ of good qualities and a refinement of manner in and about him. Seeing my wife, he hesitated; seemed abashed; reflected a moment; and then—for the table had been laid with everything for my tea—asked for 'knife to cut meat, and, and—' but he could get no further. Something he wanted to say he had not the memory of English words to express. When he sat down, I soon saw his agitation and excitement were too great, and I rather think, by some signs in his eye, that his heart was too full, to let him eat. For myself I was also unable to eat. My food was in contemplating the man before me; and some fish bought from the natives in the Beagle Channel went away untasted. I now began to question Jemmy; and to try and draw him out. But he was so confused that, beyond disjointed sentences, I obtained, at that time, very little information from him. One important point, however, I did ascertain; and this was as to the language of his people. Taking from my bookshelves Captain FitzRoy's narrative, I went over several words in the vocabulary, and found that the Tekeenica column was correct. By it, so far as it goes, some communication can be held with the natives in these parts, though not with those in the Beagle Channel or at Banner Cove. The portraits of himself and the other Fuegians made him laugh and look sad alternately, as the two characters he was represented in, savage and civilized, came before his eye. Perhaps he was calling to mind his combed hair, washed face, and dandy dress, with the polished boots it is said he so much delighted in: perhaps he was asking himself which, after all, was the best—the prim and starch, or the rough and shaggy? Which he thought, he did not choose to say; but which I inferred he thought was gathered from his refusal to go anywhere again with us. Of England he, however, spoke with much grateful feeling. 'Yes: me know—Ingliss conetree: vary good—you flag, me know (meaning that he had understood the British Ensign that I had hoisted at the main); yes: much good—all good in Ingliss conetree—long way—me sick in hammock—vary bad—big water sea—me know Capen Fitzoy—Byno—Bennet—Walamstow—Wilson—Ingliss lady, you wife?'

Jemmy was next taken into the Captain's library and shown many things—books, pictures, instruments, firearms—that might remind him of the past. He admired everything—'all Ingliss, vary good!' He wanted the ship's-guns fired—'Capen Fitzoy have gun —make noise—me know'—but Snow cautiously would not oblige. Jemmy told about Matthews and 'bad fellow' York Minster; he explained that he never lived now actually at Woollya where the *Beagle* men had worked so hard, and that there was nothing left of their efforts at cultivation. 'Plenty fight, 'nother countryman come here': again it was the bad man's fault. He ended by sending remembrances to Bo'sun Bennett, Captain FitzRoy and Mr Wilson, but doubted whether he would ever want to cross the ocean again.

'Much water—make sick—planty hammock!' he repeated with distaste—proving incidentally that Darwin's assumption that Jemmy, though sympathetic, had never really experienced sea-sickness must have been wrong.

There now followed what must be regarded as the first significant widening of the rift between Captain Snow and his employers. So far there may have been not very much more than a general disparity of outlook, a growing conviction on Snow's part that the missionaries were pig-headedly inefficient and on the missionaries' that Snow, if efficient, was pig-headed. Snow had been angered at the insistence upon piety as a major criterion when choosing a crew; he had been irritated at such pinpricks as that the missionaries did not think prayers three times a day on board sufficient. But now came the question, should Jemmy Button be induced to sail at least as far as the Falkland Islands? That was the missionary intention. But there had occurred an unexpected difficulty. At Port Stanley, capital town of the Falkland Islands, the Governor had already made it clear that there might be serious difficulties over any importation of natives from the mainland. There was a local 'Alien Ordnance' which might well be held to have been contravened if there was any suggestion whatever that the natives had not come entirely at their own free-will, that they had been 'kidnapped'. Not, the Governor insisted, that he wanted to pour cold water on the missionaries' 'romantic enterprise'. There was also the undoubted fact that any captain of a vessel bringing in natives would be held directly and personally responsible for their welfare and might be chargeable to manslaughter should they die.[3] Though this unexpected development was not to deter the missionaries, it did deter Captain Snow from pressing Jemmy Button too hard. He insists that he did follow out his instructions and ask Jemmy Button. But Jemmy Button declined.

On the *Allen Gardiner* finally leaving, there occurred an incident that strengthened Snow's opposition to the missionaries and all their plans. Jemmy had been loaded with presents, and the cupidity of the Fuegians had obviously been thoroughly aroused. Captain Snow, knowing how untrustworthy they could be, was not happy. Just as he was preparing to leave, two of Jemmy's family did in fact man-handle him, enthusiastically trying to divest him of his coat and waistcoat. There were other natives on board and Snow believed that a serious incident, with bloodshed, might not be far away. The only hope was to convince the Fuegians that they were in danger of being carried out to sea. He gave the necessary orders. The *Allen Gardiner*, however, was in a difficult position of wind and tide: only with agonizing slowness did it move, and convince the natives that they were in danger. It had been a near thing.

Captain Snow returned to the Falkland Islands, without his charge and expecting trouble. The young missionary sent out in charge, by name Garland Phillips, had set up his headquarters in a small, totally uninhabited island of the Falklands, Keppel Island, and had, in spite of Snow's pleadings, insisted upon staying there alone with the only other white man who had come out. Snow half expected on his return to find the two either half starved or half mad, or both, and with himself again responsible to the Governor for the situation.

[3] This is explained to some extent in Snow's book but is elaborated in a letter to *The Times*, appearing on January 10th 1958, from the then Governor, Mr George Rennie, on the occasion of the court case to be later referred to.

His fears were not realized. But now matters came to a head in an unexpected way.

The arrival of a senior missionary to take command had long been expected and Snow had in fact been kept busy making useless trips to Monte Video to meet him. Now at last he arrived. It was the redoubtable G. Pakenham Despard, complete with assistant, wife, several children, including one just born, much furniture, including a piano, and a miscellany of ideas, as difficult for Snow to put into practice as they were by Pakenham Despard immovably held.

Snow was rapidly goaded into desperation. One of the last straws was the insistence that the *Allen Gardiner* should carry, on its trip round to Keppel Island, not only Mr Despard's family and furniture but twenty head of wild cattle. With visions no doubt of wild bulls mixed with new babies, Snow refused. Despard dismissed him.

Tempers had obviously become very high. But whatever the provocation, Despard certainly treated Snow and his wife shabbily. Their passage money home was refused, and when Snow asked if he might at least keep the bedding that he and his wife had been using on board he was told that he could, on the payment of two pounds. Snow managed to procure a passage home, where he set about suing the owners of the *Allen Gardiner* for wrongful dismissal.

Mr Pakenham Despard, energetically and without delay, set about furthering the plans of the mission. He engaged a new and more amenable captain. With his new assistant, Allen Gardiner junior, son of the martyred sailor, he followed Snow's example and made the preliminary ritual gesture of visiting the scene of the martyrdom. He made trips to Rio and Monte Video, to obtain timber for building and to engage a new crew, Snow's crew having refused to accept his terms. He then sent Allen Gardiner junior to fetch Jemmy Button.

This Allen Gardiner was recently down from Oxford and a candidate for ordination, speaking the language of the missionaries. He had none of Captain Snow's fears or inhibitions, and he persuaded Jemmy Button, with his second wife and her three

young children, to come to Keppel Island for a six months'
stay. Where experience had failed inexperience succeeded.

When Jemmy arrived Mrs Despard wrote jubilantly home:
'Rejoice with me, for the Lord has seen fit to give an answer to the
daily prayers addressed to Him, Sovereign Disposer of all hearts,
that He would be pleased to put it into the mind of some of these
poor benighted Fuegians to trust themselves to our hands and
come over to us here.'

So poor benighted Jemmy Button, who had once oiled his hair
and polished his boots and condoled with Charles Darwin about
seasickness, again put on the clothes of civilization and became
the hoped-for blessed tool of human communication. It was
twenty-four years since he had said a last farewell to FitzRoy,
and he was aged about forty-two, for a Fuegian probably already
rather beyond middle age.

Mrs Despard found him as obliging as ever, though lazy. However:'One day I said, "James, God loves good men—good men
no idle. God no love idle men." He nodded in his peculiar way to
show me he understood. A short time after he was hard at work.'
Not only so, but he was polite and grateful. 'For any little trifle
that I gave him, he would go and pick me a beautiful bouquet of
wild flowers, or spear me some fish.' Mr Despard had his practical
purpose in mind. 'We shall set every ear and tongue', he wrote,
'to catch the Fuegian language in these six months, so that when
Jemmy returns we may be able to say something in it, and I pray
God fervently to open their hearts and give entrance to truth.'
He was saddened therefore that, as his wife put it, 'these people
do not like to speak their language before us, and converse with
each other in a whisper.'

A month before the stipulated period was ended Jemmy and
his family were transported back to their home. The plans, however, were going ahead. Mr Despard went with the Fuegians,
took some of his purchased timber with him, stayed a month, and
built a house 'in the English fashion'. He then brought back a
fresh contingent of natives, nine of them including 'Billy', one of
Jemmy Button's grown-up sons, and two young boys. One of these
showed an aptitude and a responsive spirit, a sort of second young

Jemmy, and Despard wrote with loving delight: 'I could not but feel well-pleased to see the little brown boy under the instruction of my children'. The conviction was growing that Fuegian natives were in no way to be feared.

It was felt that a real test could now be made. The young Allen Gardiner having gone home to be ordained, the job was given to Garland Phillips, whom Captain Snow had found so difficult and stubborn. On October 11th 1859 Phillips set sail for Woollya. With him in the *Allen Gardiner* were the second batch of natives being returned to their home and a crew of seven under the command of the amenable Captain Fell. He had his written instructions from Despard. 'Should there be a friendly spirit in Woollya' he was to spend a few days on shore, and if weather allowed he was there to hold 'Sabbath morning and evening services'.

On November 1st the *Allen Gardiner* reached Woollya. The arrival attracted many canoes of natives from the surrounding district. On the first Sunday, five days after arrival, Garland Phillips, with the captain and all the crew but one, the cook, came on shore to hold a service in the 'English' hut. As soon as they were inside natives strolled up to their boats and removed the oars. Then Coles, the cook, heard a commotion coming from the hut. Watching in horror from the *Allen Gardiner* he saw his friends rush out from the hut, pursued by the Fuegians hurling their deadly stones. Only one white man reached the boat and he too was dead before he could escape.

When the *Allen Gardiner's* return was two months overdue Despard sent out a rescue ship, under an American Captain, Smiley. Smiley found the ship still riding at anchor, rifled but intact, and Coles, the cook, living native with the Button family. He returned, with Coles and also with Jemmy Button, who 'impudently climbed on board'. The Governor of the Falkland Islands at once took depositions and reported home to the Colonial Secretary.

This report brings to light some interesting facts. [5] The Reverend

---

[4] Colonial Office Papers, Falkland Islands, 1860, at the Public Records Office.

Despard had, before the *Allen Gardiner* sailed from Keppel Island, insisted upon searching the returning natives because he suspected that they were trying to get away with stolen goods. 'This', the report reads, 'was resented as a gross indignity, and although the assistant missionary, Mr Phillips, strongly protested against it, the natives were forced to submit. The *Allen Gardiner* put into Stanley on her way. The temper of the natives was known here and the Captain and Mr Phillips were warned by several friends to be on their guard.' On reaching Woollya, however, the natives were again searched. 'This time they violently resisted and at last tore off all their clothes and leaving everything on board jumped into the native canoes alongside with their families.' There followed some 'unfriendly intercourse' with Jemmy Button. When the massacre occurred the Englishmen had gone on shore unarmed and had left their boat unguarded.

The deposition made by Coles, the cook, who was twenty-three, made the following additional points and accusations. Two days after the arrival, Jemmy Button had come on board and was much displeased at not receiving the presents he had expected. It was the captain himself who had ordered the second searching of the natives, and it had in fact brought to light stolen property. The natives who had found him (Coles) after his escape into the woods had stripped him naked. Then days later he had fallen in with the Button family, who had clothed him. His first captors had told a story of how Jemmy Button had taken part in the massacre and, the day after, had boarded the *Allen Gardiner* and slept in the captain's cabin. He, Coles, had seen no sign of Jemmy at the massacre, but he did feel certain—he was however watching at from 300 to 400 yards' distance—that he had seen Billy Button throw the stone that killed Mr Phillips. The cause of the massacre was in his opinion Jemmy Button's jealousy at not receiving as much in the way of gifts as he had thought he had a right to, and Jemmy, he believed, was 'at the head of the whole proceedings'.

The next statement to be taken was from Jemmy Button himself. This is a sadly incoherent document: Jemmy's English was not equal to the occasion, nor were his emotions.

Jemmy denied that he went on board or slept in the captain's cabin. He did not have to deny that he was the instigator of the massacre, because nobody except Coles, the cook, appeared to believe that he had been. He sensed, or knew, that his audience— the Governor and his Colonial Secretary, the Colonial Chaplain and Captain Smiley—believed the cause of the outbreak to have been in particular the forcible search of those Fuegians taken to Keppel Island and in general the fact that they had none of them wanted to be taken there at all. Accordingly: 'I staid at Keppel Island four moons with wife and child. Did not like to stop—don't want to—don't like it. Despard says, "Go back Jemmy, you're old, your children stop—would like children to stop at Woollya"—want to go back with you [Captain Smiley]—all like to go back to Woollya.' From this Jemmy wandered off incoherently into talk of fishing at Keppel—'Spear fish at Keppel—no catch seal, no catch big fish'—the point of which is not apparent. There followed an attempt to lay the blame on the *oens* men, the eternal 'bad' men, and then a claim that he buried four of the victims, and a hint that he was terribly upset—'I no sleep in Schooner, run about on mainland, no more sleep, run about. Finally, after a very involved effort to explain the different tribes in the neighbourhood and that his own was the least belligerent of them, he returned to the apparently popular and well received claim that he did not like being at Keppel. He wanted in fact to go home—and would help to identify the graves of the victims if he were taken.

Jemmy Button was in fact taken back almost immediately, by Captain Smiley, who went to identify the graves and to bring back the dismantled *Allen Gardiner*. In order to achieve the latter task with safety Jemmy was kept as prisoner and hostage on board until it was effected. Then he was released, in disgrace and so finally into the white man's oblivion.

The Reverend Despard, who shortly afterwards came home, wrote as follows. 'May the Lord of the harvest send out others to supply the room of those He has taken, and bow to contrition these poor sinners of the Gentiles that they may be prepared for his word.' The Governor of the Falkland Islands, seeing things very differently, held an official magistrate's enquiry into the cause of the disaster and was angered when Despard, sheltering behind the fact that the enquiry was legally a maritime one and that the massacre had not occurred on board ship, refused to give evidence. With the court's findings only stating lamely that the 'abandonment' of the *Allen Gardiner* had caused the disaster, the Governor gave his true opinions in his report. This was unequivocally that the real cause of the disaster was the ill-advised treatment by the missionaries of the natives whom they brought to Keppel Island. There is even a suggestion that the Fuegians had been treated like slaves, which sounds as far from objective truth as are Pakenham Despard's pious elegaics: like servants perhaps, since the missionaries were middle-class Victorians, but like slaves surely not.

At exactly this time the British public were treated to something in the same line of severe criticism of the Patagonian missionaries. The lawsuit of Snow against his employers came up before the Lord Chief Justice; and *The Times*, reporting the case,[5] again took the opportunity to read the missionaries a homily.

Snow lost his case. He had the evidence of Sulivan against him that he had once exclaimed of Despard: 'Do you think I would take orders from a Parson?' and, more importantly, there was the fact that Despard could be legally considered as part owner of the *Allen Gardiner* and therefore entitled to order Snow's dismissal. Nevertheless, the judge was obviously sorry for Snow, whom he called a gallant seaman and an honest man; and *The Times*' leading article seized on the fact that the unhappy captain had been quite unable to control his emotions in court. Were they Turks and monsters, the missionaries, asked *The Times* innocently; and under the heading 'Look before you leap!' accused them of being so 'completely carried away by the romance of their expedition' as to fail to make the necessary preliminary enquiries or prepare for obstacles and difficulties. It was a condescending, at times irritatingly facetious article; but, coupled with the legal report, it did not read well.

[5] Snow *v.* Ramsden and Others, reported on December 8th 1859, with the leading article on the next day.

FitzRoy at this moment was having a wordy war in *The Times* (of which more later) concerning certain antediluvian evidence. It cannot have helped towards equanimity for him to read these reports and criticisms. Two Despards had crossed his path, a soldier in New Zealand and a priest in Patagonia; and he had not had much joy of either of them.[6]

[6] He was at least spared having to read the accusations of a later book. *The Uttermost Parts of the Earth*, by E. L. Bridges, published in 1946, is an authoritative account of the work done in Tierra del Fuego by the author's father (an adopted son of the Rev. Despard) from the late eighteen-sixties onwards. In its opening chapter there is given a short account of the earlier missionary efforts, the 1859 massacre included, and here there is inaccuracy. It is stated that a trial was held at Stanley and that in it Jemmy Button was found guilty of instigating the massacre. There is no evidence for this whatever in the Colonial Office papers. The only approach to a trial was the magistrate's enquiry; and by the date on which it was held Jemmy Button was already back at Woollya. The cook was the only one to accuse Jemmy. FitzRoy's favourite protégé was at least never a villain.

BOOK 4

The New Beginning and the Bitter End

CHAPTER 21

The Pioneer

FITZROY'S half brother, after becoming governor of Australia, received a knighthood; so too did his friend of the *Challenger*, Michael Seymour, and his old lieutenant, Sulivan. Most of FitzRoy's relatives possessed inherited titles and many of his friends in the scientific world had earned them. He may have grieved a little therefore that he remained a commoner, that 'Mrs Robert' remained Mrs Robert. Such is only surmise. What must certainly have saddened and worried him was that the bright promises of 1842 had become so dim a reality, that he was no more than a naval captain without a job but with a young family and a hole knocked into his private fortune.[1]

But FitzRoy had behind him his reputation as a great sailor, a great navigator, surveyor, expert in ships and in the elements in which they sailed. He had not lost that capacity to work and to drive himself which Darwin had noted, nor that capacity which Lord Stanley had recognized, to perform his duty—as he saw it—to the top of his bent.

[1] In Byrnes' Naval Biographies FitzRoy is referred to as having lost £3,000 over the hire and purchase of schooners during the *Beagle* voyage; Darwin—in a letter of October 1853 to his old servant of *Beagle* days and after he had recently dined with his old friend—wrote, 'I am afraid he lost much money by his government of New Zealand'.

FitzRoy, forward-looking in things technical and scientific, if not in things religious, now interested himself in the application of steam to ships. He was certainly not the first to do so, though steam's application to movement over the waters was slower than to movement over land, and its use by the Navy was slowest of all. Brunel had recently ended a tussle with the Lords of the Admiralty, wherein by a marine tug-of-war he had demonstrated that the screw was superior to the paddle, and had then left their Lordships to their own devices. They had not behaved quite so conservatively as Brunel had expected them to do, however, and they had ordered the building of the Navy's first screw-driven steamship, the 360 ton *Arrogant*. To this ship, which some might have said was well named for him, FitzRoy was appointed in the Spring of 1849, having six months previously been given the post of Superintendent of Woolwich Dockyard. His job was to conduct the trials of the new ship.

The records of the trials are scant. During 1849 and 1850 the ship alternated between Woolwich and Portsmouth Dockyards; and she seems to have had to enter pretty frequently for minor repairs and adjustments, as might indeed be likely with such a perfectionist as a captain. A little more is told us by the fact that in the May of 1853 FitzRoy gave a lecture at the United Services Institute on The Application of Steam to Ships of War. The lecture was for the most part highly technical; but it branched out into personal problems of command and of manoeuvre and strategy in war. FitzRoy was modest, and there are few references to the *Arrogant*. It is, however, listed as a ship to which 'it is a pleasure to turn' because of its improvements, and there is talk of a recurring trouble of foreign matter getting under the valves. FitzRoy seems to be sufficiently conservative still to consider steam as only auxiliary to sail, or at least as sail as remaining an auxiliary to steam; and he delivers himself of the aphorism: 'seamanship is as necessary to a naval officer as horsemanship to a rider', having obviously the purely technically-minded engineer officer in view. He shows too his humanity, if perhaps a little naïvely. The engineer should mess with the other officers, he says, in spite of the fact that he may at times arrive a little dirty; the stokers, he thinks, might be given the rather less derogatory name of firemen, as they were in America.[2]

Yet, for all this, FitzRoy had not found his true interest. That lay in something not so new or divorced from all that he had previously experienced, nor so material or mechanical. It lay in a science intimately connected with his days of sailing and one through which he could exercise his passion, his overmastering and wilful passion, to benefit mankind. In 1850 he resigned from active service in the Navy, the stated reason being health and the need to attend to private affairs. That did not seem to presage a promising new start.

The true new beginning was approached when in the following year FitzRoy was elected a Fellow of the Royal Society. In the application form he was described as Captain, R.N., and member of the Royal Geographic Society; author (with Captain King) of the *Narrative of the Beagle*; inventor and improver of a surveying quadrant; distinguished for his acquaintance with the science of Hydrography and Nautical Astronomy; eminent as a scientific navigator and for his chronometer measurements of a chain of meridian distances during his circumnavigation of the globe. He was supported by thirteen fellows, amongst whom were the Naval Hydrographer and the Naturalist of *Beagle* days, Beaufort and Darwin. Beaufort three years previously had taken the opportunity, in a report as Hydrographer to Parliament, to praise FitzRoy's surveying work most highly.

In 1853 two public events occurred, the second somewhat overshadowed by the first. Russia declared war on Turkey, and the Crimean War had become inevitable. This event, whilst affording FitzRoy's one-time lieutenant, Sulivan, the opportunity to show himself a brilliant naval war captain, was to give FitzRoy himself a job of only a few months duration as private secretary to his uncle by marriage, Lord Hardinge, then Commander-in-Chief of the Army—a job, one would imagine, that he was lucky not to have kept.

[2] This lecture was privately printed, 'at the request of esteemed friends' and in order to stimulate discussion. The British Museum holds a copy.

The second and minor event was the holding of a conference by the chief maritime powers at Brussels, on the subject of meteorology at sea. This gave FitzRoy the job which he was to keep for the rest of his life. The British Government, taking its naval responsibilities seriously, as any government wishing to stay in power was well advised to do, voted a sum of money to the Board of Trade wherewith to follow up the conference's recommendations. The Board of Trade, a little hesitant, approached that active and august repository of scientific knowledge, the Royal Society; and this society responded by giving two pieces of advice. The first was short and given promptly, that FitzRoy should be put in charge. This advice the Board at once accepted, giving FitzRoy the title of Meteorological Statist and a staff which, numbering only three, hardly did justice to the title.

The Royal Society's other piece of advice was longer in form and slower in presentation.[3] First it canvassed the opinions of a dozen or so foreign experts. These included Lieutenant M. F. Maury of the United States Navy, who was FitzRoy's slightly earlier counterpart in America, who had in fact been instrumental in getting the Brussells Conference convened, and who was already arousing FitzRoy's envy in possessing a staff of up to twenty. Such opinions as the Society received were then scrutinized by a committee, of which Darwin was a member. Finally, in the February of 1855, there was issued to the Board of Trade the Society's considered recommendations. Their Statist however was already busy and three months later was issuing his first official report.[4]

FitzRoy had by then done or was doing three things. He had circularized captains of British ships, both naval and maritime, and had furnished those willing to help with tested and reliable instruments. He was busy collecting and collating their reports, of winds and of atmospheric pressure, temperature and humidity. He was already, as a start, compiling from this data a series of charts of his own invention which he called 'wind stars'. For an

[3] These reports are to be seen in the Royal Society's archives.
[4] FitzRoy's reports are in Board of Trade papers taken over by the Meteorological Office, Bracknell, Berks.

area of the ocean ten degrees square such a star—the name merely arose from the general appearance of the diagram—showed at a glance the direction and strength of the winds over a stated period of weeks or months. FitzRoy's hope was to produce these ten-square-degree charts for the whole area of the world's oceans.

A considerable part of this first report of FitzRoy's is taken up with such technical matters as his wind stars. But he allows himself space to stress the great advantage of adequate weather knowledge to all those who sail in ships and a plea that no pains should be spared in obtaining it. There is, in fact, an echo of his maritime speech to Parliament. Just as the length of a ship's passage from port to port depended upon its captain's navigational skill, so also it depended upon such adequate and accurate know-ledge as would enable him to do his proverbial duty, which was to 'find a fair wind and fall in with a favourable current'. There next comes a less happy echo, a memory of New Zealand and failure. The ability, asserts FitzRoy, to find that best course would not only result in the saving of money, it might result in the avoidance of misfortune: 'if a frigate, with important despatches, is some days later in arriving at his destination than might be the case, the possible consequences may be disastrous.' Better know-ledge might even result in the saving of lives, if for no other reason than that the time taken on the voyage, wherein risk always existed, had been shortened. Finally there comes in this report a significant pointer to FitzRoy's future activities. Weather information, and particularly barometer readings, he asserts, should be observed and recorded by all ships' captains, for 'comparisons and the judicious inferences drawn from them afford the means of foretelling wind and weather during the next following period.' Soon FitzRoy is to be using not the word 'foretelling', but his own peculiar favourite word, *forecasting*.

In FitzRoy's second year he must have been busy devising better forms or 'logs' for the use of ships' captains who were collecting information for him, and better methods of registering that information. At this time somebody above him at the Board of Trade again wrote to the Royal Society for advice, on the specific question of the form of log to be used. The Royal Society replied circumspectly that this seemed a matter for the head of the department which had been formed, adding, 'It would seem that events have occurred in the conduct of the business of the department in question which appear to Captain FitzRoy to justify his expressing a doubt whether he is really entitled to consider himself as charged with the sole responsibility of carrying the affairs of the department.' That looks like a battle won by FitzRoy: promotion to the rank of Rear Admiral at this time may have helped, if not to give him more authority, at least to boost his morale—he was later to reach the rank of Vice-Admiral. He stated 'we are advancing' in his yearly report, and then turned his attention to what he conceived to be another part of his job and something that was nearer to his heart.

FitzRoy had in mind the fishermen of the coasts of England, and of other coasts, too, if foreign governments would follow him, the little men in the little ships, who suffered as much as any and more than most from the unpredicted storm. What these men needed was barometers and simple instructions on how to use them. FitzRoy was helped by certain private philanthropists, by the recently formed British and Scottish Meteorological Societies, and by the Lifeboat Institution, onto whose committee he was co-opted as a very active member.[5] Soon sturdy barometers —known as the FitzRoy barometer, some still surviving—were being issued to fishing towns and villages. They were followed by a *Barometer Manual* of fifty pages (H.M.S.O., price one shilling), which set out very clearly and simply all that was known on how to use a barometer and other instruments in the art of weather forecasting. It is remembered for the rhyming advice that it gives, compiled by FitzRoy in *Beagle* days:

> When rise begins, after low,
> Squalls expect and clear blow.

And the very useful one:

> Long foretold, long last:
> Short notice, soon past.

[5] He was not, however, as is sometimes stated, Secretary.

Then in time of squalls:

> When rain comes before wind,
> Halyards, sheets, and braces mind!

But:

> When wind comes before rain,
> Soon you may make sail again.

FitzRoy was now well into his stride, so well in fact that for the years 1859, 1860 and 1861 he issued no annual official report of the activities of his department, an action or lack of action reminiscent of his New Zealand days, but one that did not seem to worry anyone unduly at the time. In the autumn of 1859 there occurred an event that set FitzRoy more determinedly than ever on the way he wanted to go.

After a phenomenally dry and hot summer (which caused the Thames to stink phenomenally in the nostrils of Londoners) there came a terrific storm that in particular wrecked the *Royal Charter* onto the Anglesey coast with a total loss of life. This *Royal Charter* storm affected FitzRoy profoundly. It brought to a focus his belief that such calamities could be prevented, and ought to be prevented, by a more bold and more immediate use of the knowledge that was available for forecasting. He was not entirely alone in his convictions, for the British Association's meeting for that year, under the presidency of the Prince Consort, was followed up by two meetings on the subject at Buckingham Palace. But he was the prime mover. The greatest obstacle, he realized, to the effective use of the knowledge available was the slowness of communication: all the information that he was building up from his ships' logs only came to him of course after the ships had reached port. There now existed, however, most conveniently for his service, the new invention of Mr Morse's electric telegraph, which was beginning to be used all over the world as well as in its land of origin, the United States of America. The use of the telegraph could, FitzRoy realized, utterly transform the position.

FitzRoy was convinced of two things. The first, not always so apparent to other scientific users of the instruments available, was that these instruments, the barometer in particular, not only told the user what were the weather conditions at the moment, but what conditions were about to arrive, indeed that they better performed the latter function than the former. The second conviction, also not so clear to less passionately humane scientists, was that this power to foretell or forecast, which the instruments gave, must be used forthwith and without waiting for any further improvements in technique, and that to fail to use it was an unpardonable sin.

Starting in a relatively unambitious, but at least feasible manner, FitzRoy concerned himself only with weather forecasting around the coasts of Great Britain. Laboriously he set up twenty-four stations from which weather information could be telegraphed to him centrally in London. Eighteen of these were on the coasts of England, Scotland and Ireland, and the other six were at Valentia, Copenhagen, Helder (at the entrance to the Zuyder Zee), Brest, Bayonne and Lisbon. Then he began producing what he called and which have ever since been called synoptic charts, charts that showed a synopsis of the weather position for a given area at a given time by means of wind speeds and directions, isotherms and isobars. From these FitzRoy produced and transmitted back his forecast of weather for the next couple of days. In due course he was transmitting these to the newspapers and they, *The Times* included, were issuing for the first time in history a daily 'weather forecast'. At about the same time FitzRoy inaugurated the scheme that was his second major contribution to meteorological advance, a system of warning cones, which were hoisted at ports and harbours and fishing villages when a gale was to be expected.

FitzRoy was in fact by these efforts reaching the peak of his pioneer endeavours. His fame was spreading and he was able in his reports to refer proudly to visits from the representatives of foreign governments and to the fact that Italy, Germany, and France in particular, were copying him. Two events, it may be said, crowned his achievements. The first was to be related ever afterwards, while she lived, by his small and youngest daughter and is recounted by Nora Barlow in the foreword to this book: Queen Victoria's august request for a private weather forecast[6]

The second event, more important if less romantic, was the publication in 1862 of FitzRoy's *Weather Book*. This was a book which, so he told a friend, only took him four months to write, though in fact a good deal of the material had already been prepared: since it comprises 340 pages of text and over a hundred of appendices, together with sixteen maps and diagrams, it seems that FitzRoy was still capable of the phenomenally concentrated effort that had so impressed Darwin.

There are several human touches in this book. There is for instance the reference to the fact that his sailor son had brought back from Japan a curious machine purporting to inform its owner of threatened earthquake. FitzRoy keeps parental pride out of his book, though he does not in letters that he was now frequently writing to his friend from *Beagle* days, the astronomer Sir John Herschel.[7] There is also personal pride in the claim that the special lightning conductors which he had fitted onto the *Beagle* before the second voyage overwhelmingly proved their value, though he was considered very unwise to fit them. There is the rueful confession that want of faith in signs of a coming storm had caused 'a very young commander' to lose two men overboard, this referring to the *pampero* that nearly wrecked the *Beagle* in the La Plata estuary only a few days after FitzRoy had taken command. There is finally related, in the way of significant personal reminiscence used to draw the necessary moral, an episode that occurred on the 'very tediously slow' passage to England by sailing ship back from New Zealand in 1846. Here must have been shown, in spite of all his unhappiness, more than a flash of the FitzRoy of the *Beagle*, in fact of the *Challenger* days.

[6] There was in fact another royal occasion when one of the princesses was making a slightly more extended crossing, Folkestone to Boulogne. FitzRoy's report to the Gentleman in Waiting was: 'Weather on Friday (4th March, 1863) favourable for crossing—Moderate—mild—cloudy, fine, perhaps showery at times.' This correspondence was kept by FitzRoy's widow.

[7] Herschel Letters in possession of the Royal Society.

The ship's captain on this occasion was also a reluctant one, reluctant to make preparations to meet a storm which FitzRoy from interpretation of his own barometers was certain was going to arrive. As midnight on this deceptively calm night approached, and as the barometer fell to nearly twenty-eight inches, FitzRoy took matters into his own hands. 'Aided by a good officer and a few willing hands, the writer (whose family were on board) got the second anchor let go, cable veered, and then waited.' Everyone thought him mistaken, but at about two o'clock a roar was heard and the storm struck. 'Had that ship been taken unprepared, not a soul would have been saved, in human probability; only God's providence could have rescued any one in so desolate, wild, and savage a country.'

The moral of all these three personal reminiscences is the same, that storms at sea can be foretold and guarded against, and that it is criminal not to do so. Here in fact is the belief that informs all FitzRoy's book, a belief as passionately held as that New Zealand must be saved from inter-racial war or that a wrecked crew must be rescued whatever the difficulties, or that salvation lay in the literal truth of the Bible.

The *Weather Book* is in essence: an elementary disquisition on world weather phenomenon and a practical guide to the plain man in weather recording and forecasting; a résumé of FitzRoy's work done at the Board of Trade; a description of great storms, known in history and by personal experience, and an effort to point their significance; a plea for greater effort, national and international, to make forecasting more efficient. The book begins with the striking statement that we all live in 'an ocean of air', a conception that has often been repeated in textbooks, and a stressing of the significant fact that all weather change comes fundamentally from the sun and its rays. Throughout there recurs the fundamental thesis: 'It should always be remembered that the state of the air *foretells coming* weather, rather than indicates weather that is *present*.'

The *Weather Book* deserved to be a success, and FitzRoy must have been pleased when the publishers, Longman, Green and Co., brought out a second edition in the year following publication.[8] Essentially, the book was an effort to get across to the ordinary public the urgent message that his fellow scientists, so he increasingly felt, were annoyingly and frustratingly reluctant to receive: that the real use of meteorological information was not to state the present weather, but to foretell its future.

[8] The publisher's records show that FitzRoy was paid £200 for the copyright, and that the book sold for fifteen shillings.

CHAPTER 22

Senex

THERE was another side to the picture of success, a different picture and one with more than a single aspect.

First, as to meteorology, FitzRoy was doing less and less what it had intended he should do and more and more what he wanted to do; and even there he was experiencing frustration and a feeling of failure.

There were also other unhappy developments. In 1852 FitzRoy lost Mary, mother of his four children, of which the first was still only thirteen years of age and of which the last had in New Zealand brought her near to death. Two years later he had found a step-mother for them in the shape of Maria, the daughter of a FitzRoy cousin who had married into a Yorkshire family of Smyths. In 1856 he lost his eldest daughter, 'a beautiful and charming girl of 16 or 17 years old', wrote the sympathetic Darwin who had suffered a similar loss. These perhaps were no more than the unhappy vicissitudes met by many a Victorian husband and father.

In 1857 FitzRoy applied for the job of Chief Naval Officer in the Board of Trade's Maritime Department, and lost it to his one-time junior, Sulivan—who, however, tactfully asked that the Meteorological Office should not be under him. That perhaps was no more than vicissitude suffered by most men at some time in their careers.

But frustrations, less specific but deeper, were being suffered by FitzRoy. If one were to be saddened and angered by failures to save lives at sea, how much more must one be saddened and angered by failures to save souls at sea. And souls, it must have seemed to FitzRoy, and for that matter to the many who thought like him, were in this decade of the eighteen-fifties increasingly at sea, bewildered by the cross currents of old and new scientific theories, endangered by the rocks of harsh material progress, lost in the broad and trackless ways of atheism.

The years 1859 and 1860 were bad years for FitzRoy. It was in them that he must have read of the tragic and ugly outcome of his Fuegian philanthropy. Events of much wider and deeper impact were also occurring. In 1859 appeared Darwin's *Origin of Species*, the mechanistic, atheistic theory of organic evolution by means of natural selection—if those adjectives now seem excessive they certainly did not seen so at the time. The paleontologists—or as they then more euphoniously called themselves, the antiquaries—were in a similar way making nonsense of a literal interpretation of the Bible, by a demonstration of the vast antiquity of flint-using Stone Age man. In the early December of that momentous year—at the time, as has been stated, of Captain Snow's lawsuit with the missionaries—the antiquary, Sir John Evans (father of Arthur Evans of Minoan fame) was enlarging in *The Times* upon the significance of the art of the 'drift' men, those paleolithic people, that is to say, who had left their beautifully knapped hand-axes on the raised banks of the river Somme where the drift of the last retreating Ice Age had left them.

To him replied one who signed himself 'Senex'. If these flints found on the banks of the Somme were works of human art, how was it that no other works of art had been found? No; they were not made by men of 14,000 years ago 'as Horner'[1] and Darwin pretended', but were left behind by wandering tribes who had *lost* their civilization. 'In what difficulties do not those involve themselves who contend for a far greater antiquity of mankind

---

[1] Presumably Leonard Horner (1785–1864), Scottish geologist and educationalist—who once took Darwin to a meeting of the Royal Society at which Sir Walter Scott presided!

than the learned and wise have derived from Scripture and the best tradition!' John Evans answered in a somewhat condescending vein: it was amusing to see the various opinions of those who steadfastly refused to see the obvious. 'Senex' replied to John Evans. He was also amused—at the clever casuistry, and at the old expedient of 'attacking (not to say abusing) your opponent when advocating a weak cause. Mr Darwin tells us of cliffs in Patagonia', etc.

It was Darwin himself who made the perhaps not very difficult guess that 'Senex' was FitzRoy. Sending copies of the letters to his old friend (and FitzRoy's anathema) Lyell, he commented, 'It is a pity he did not add his theory of the extermination of the Mastodon etc. from the doors of the Ark being much too small!' This reference to the last chapter of the *Beagle Narrative* can hardly be counted as unkind, since it was only meant for a fellow geologist's eyes, yet it does show how far the two friends had drifted apart in their ideas. FitzRoy had visited Darwin at the latter's home in 1853 and 1857, the second time at least being only a stopping-off as he happened to be journeying that way; and these are the last meetings of which there is any evidence.[2] The writings of Sir John Evans were obviously worrying FitzRoy considerably, since he refers to the point twice in his letters to Herschel, in whom he was increasingly confiding. 'There has been much talk of flint (stone) tools in the "Drift",' he writes in 1861, and proceeds to use an argument against their great age which is exactly one used by 'Senex', to wit that *present-day* migratory savages are always leaving stone tools about for others to pick up—thus without any reasonable doubt confirming Darwin in his identification.

Darwin it was, of course, and unhappily, who constituted the greater enemy to all those who were upholding the faith in the inspired truth of the Bible. If FitzRoy was ever to be afforded a chance to refute his old friend he would certainly take it.

[2] The two visits are recorded in Darwin's letters to his old servant, included in Sir Gavin de Beer's 'Some Unpublished Letters of Charles Darwin', reprinted from Royal Society Records, Volume 14, Number 1, 1959.

And such a chance FitzRoy was afforded, and did take, though that he knew it was coming was unlikely.

On June 25th 1860 FitzRoy was writing to his friend General Sir Edward Sabine, President of the Royal Society, that he was proposing to take 'his wind diagrams' to the Oxford meeting of the British Association for the Advancement of Science, in order to place them at the Secretary's disposal. On Friday, June 29th he is reading at that meeting a paper on British Storms. He traces descriptions of storms from the time of Defoe, he enlarges on the *Royal Charter* storm and draws his favourite conclusions; he refers to the opinions of other experts, he touches impersonally and modestly on the fact that France is emulating the British Meteorological Office. It is a good, workmanlike paper. But it is one of many. It is not distinguished, certainly not distinguished by drama.

Not so but far otherwise were two other papers, one on the day before, one on the day after. Their titles are hardly less severely staid: on the Sexuality of Plants, and on the Intellectual Development of Europe. But both have a sting in the tail of their titles—'with references to the views of Mr Darwin', and 'with particular reference to Mr Darwin's work on the Origin of Species'. The one lecture proves a useful advertisement for the other. At the first Huxley tries to keep the argument calm and uncontroversial, but the orthodox Professor Owen tries and succeeds in making it impassioned. Excitement is born. It grows with the rumour that the Bishop of the city that has acted as host to the Association, Bishop Wilberforce of Oxford, son of the slave emancipator, late chaplain to the Queen, brilliant speaker, known nevertheless to some as Soapy Sam, will on the Saturday castigate the Darwinites.

The Saturday lecture, by the comparatively unknown and wholly unoffending Professor Draper of New York, becomes a social occasion, an anticipated entertainment. Such undergraduates as are still up flock to the meeting. So do the local clergy and their wives. The crowd is so large that the venue has to be moved to a bigger lecture room. There is a hum of expectancy; the ladies' handkerchiefs flutter. Henslow, who once got Darwin the *Beagle* job, is in the chair. Huxley is there and Darwin's second great supporter, Joseph Hooker.

Professor Draper drones on for an hour. So say the reports, other, that is to say, than the official and staid *Athenaeum*'s. Probably he did not drone more than most of the week's speakers; but a different standard is being set this afternoon. Then a Mr Dingle rises, and to illustrate the Darwinian argument goes to the blackboard. He has a curious accent and a more curious method. 'Let point A be the man,' he announces, 'and point B the mawnkey.' 'Mawnkey, mawnkey!' cry the undergraduates with delight, and he can get no further. At last the star performer rises, the Bishop Wilberforce. He has been well primed by Huxley's antagonist of the previous meeting, Professor Owen. 'He spoke,' says one account, 'for full half an hour, with inimitable spirit and'—it is an enemy's account—'emptiness and unfairness.' But the speech is being effective. Then Bishop Wilberforce makes his mistake. He tries heavy humour. Turning to Huxley, he asks, may he be informed on which side his friend claims descent from the monkey, his grandfather's or his grandmother's?[3] Huxley, for a moment affronted, sees his chance, slaps his thigh and whispers to Hooker, 'The Lord has delivered him into my hands!'

At last Henslow calls upon Huxley to reply. He begins quietly with a reasoned defence of Darwinism. And then: he was not ashamed to have a monkey for an ancestor, but he would be ashamed to be connected with a man who used his great gifts to obscure the truth! Pandemonium. A lady faints.

Quiet is resumed and the climax has been passed. There are a few more speakers from the body of the hall. One is FitzRoy. FitzRoy 'regretted', said the *Athenaeum*, 'the publication of Mr Darwin's book and denied Professor Huxley's statement that it was a logical arrangement of facts'. FitzRoy, states another account, 'said he had often expostulated with his old comrade

---

[3] No one took down the speeches verbatim, and the *Athenaeum* does not deign to mention this combat of wits. The accounts vary slightly, therefore, but all are agreed on the gist of the exchanges. The *Life and Letters* of both Thomas Huxley and Joseph Hooker cover the incident.

of the *Beagle* for entertaining views which were contradictory to
the First Chapter of Genesis'.

That evening there was a *conversazione* at the house of
Daubeney, the Thursday's speaker, with the excitement continued and Huxley the hero. But FitzRoy would hardly have been
there. He was presumably making his way back by train to his
home in London, in the comfort of First Class no doubt, but not
in much cheerfulness. It was true that the majority at the meeting
had been on his side and not Huxley's, that they had thought the
Bishop not routed but merely abominably treated. It would also
be true, in the light of history, that there was considerable right
on his side in voicing opposition to the over-materialization of the
Darwinian theory, a misrepresentation that was to be increasingly
perpetrated by such as Herbert Spencer and the German,
Haeckel, with their great play with 'the survival of the fittest',
a phrase not of Darwin's invention. But of these two alleviations
to his pain, the second he could not know and the first could not
have cheered him greatly. Though believing himself on the side
of the angels, he may—with the recent activities of the Reverend
Despard on his mind—have not felt very happy when the angels
were represented by a concourse of clergymen. After all, he also
was an active and pioneering scientist, he also was a Fellow of the
Royal Society. It is a hard thing to say; but in FitzRoy's letters to
Sabine and Herschel, making due allowance for his Victorian
and innate elaborate courtesy, there is a slight hint of toadyism
to the famous. FitzRoy would not have been exceptional if he had
desired also to be famous, to be at least somewhere in the front
of the scientific swim.

The severe figure in the railway carriage may be imagined. He
is clothed perhaps in his frock coat, as he is in the photograph of
this time. His strong face has lost the look of exaggeration of
feature of youth, as it has lost too the look of arrogance of middle
age. And if there circled behind the set features thoughts of
disappointment and envy it would have been excusable. Deeper,
however, must have lain the feeling of frustration. He was not, it

must be recalled, the only one of Darwin's friends with a knowledge of the physical sciences who was deeply perturbed. Henslow
would not go much of the way with Darwin; even the great
Lyell would never go all the way. FitzRoy would not go any of
the way. Yet there must have been a lurking fear in FitzRoy's
mind that he was not only not in the swim but that he was on the
losing side. And if that were so, if the iconoclast and the atheist
were going to win, what hope was there for mankind, what use
all his efforts on its behalf? FitzRoy was only fifty-five. But he
had signed himself 'Senex', and on that railway journey he must
have felt it.

But *were* his efforts at the Meteorological Office truly the
work of a scientist? Were they even being really successful? Was
the scientific world, in particular the Royal Society, behind him?
These were the questions that in these later years must have
increasingly worried FitzRoy. We come back to the fact, only
surprising if we forget the compulsive elements in FitzRoy's
character, that, once more, he was largely doing not what he had
been told to do but what he wanted—what he considered it his
higher duty—to do.

'Stones may be shaped, bricks may be accumulated, but without an object in view—without an edifice to be constructed—how
wearily unrewarding to the mind would be such toil, however
animated...by true scientific faith in future results.' So wrote
FitzRoy in his *Weather Book*. Yet the title of the office that he had
been given was, significantly, Statist. We have already seen that
FitzRoy was irked by the Board of Trade's second application for
direction from the Royal Society. But its first direction he had
dubbed, with a hint of impatience 'elaborate'—which in fact it
was. What is most to the point is that this direction concentrated
almost entirely on the *collection* of information. Its application is,
it is true, not altogether ignored: ships' captains, for instance,
'should be able to differentiate between cyclones and storms
accompanied by veering winds.' But this dictum is followed at
once by the direction that the new department should there-

fore *compile statistics* of the position and frequency of thunder-
storms. For the rest, the instruction is directed to collecting and
digesting statistics with the aim of increasing scientific knowledge of the weather over the oceans—no more.

For a year or two FitzRoy had done as he was directed. Then
he had become restive. The reference to the collection of bricks
in the *Weather Book* is preceded by the less oblique criticism:
'Until lately, meterology had been too statistical in practice to afford
much benefit of an immediate and general kind. Indefinitely
multiplied records only tended to make the work of their utilisa-
tion less encouraging, if not impossible.' So FitzRoy felt; and it
was he therefore who made the change, a shift of the accent from
the compiling of records to the using of them. The change was
accelerated, as we have seen, after the wreck of the *Royal Charter*
had shocked his conscience.

It was not so much that he was impatient. It was rather that
he was essentially not a scientist but a humanitarian. To say this
is not to make an invidious comparison. But FitzRoy could never
have waited the twenty years that Darwin waited while accumu-
lating the data that would give overwhelming backing to a
theory. Darwin could never have been stung into action by any
such news as the loss of lives at sea, if his head had told him that
his action would be scientifically premature and would so risk
failure. FitzRoy's heart was never ruled by his head.

He knew the danger. 'Naturally,' he confesses in the *Weather
Book*, 'a truly scientific man inclines to doubt the character of any
treatment of an abstruse and rather complicated subject which is
not defined by number, weight, and measure. Opinions, specula-
tions, and discussions are unsatisfactory to him not based on
facts of which others can be judges rather than a theorist himself,
who may be misled exceedingly. Hence it is, undoubtedly, that
some of the first mathematicians have undervalued the science
of Meteorology, esteeming it almost empirical to foretell atmospheric change, and unwise to attempt more than the observation
of facts, with their registration.' His deduction from this confession is however, and rather humanly, not that he is a theorist
who has been misled exceedingly but that the 'mathematicians'

are wrong and weather forecasting can be made a reasonably scientific occupation.

Nevertheless 'empirical' was a damning word. As a modern actor may be taunted by the accusation of ignoring the Method or an ancient Chaldean of not setting much store by the planets, so was this accusation a taunt to FitzRoy. We find him reacting against it by being at pains in his later official reports to explain the scientific aspect of his methods and by protesting that his forecasts are not 'prophecies' but *informed opinions*. He is also driven to what might seem like protesting too much. He stresses how many letters of thanks and praise he has received and quotes from some of them in his appendices. There was Admiral Evans reporting a sudden gale over the Mersey, for which, however, the Harbour Master was able to make preparations, because he had noted the storm signals. There was the gentleman, crossing to Ireland with an invalid lady, who had had the sense to wait 'though the weather *then* looked beautiful in London.' There was the sad instance of the ship owner who, because an earlier storm warning had proved exaggerated, had sent his captain out to disaster.

Here, FitzRoy realized, was one active source of opposition to him: 'those pecuniary interested individuals and bodies who would leave the coasters and the fishermen to pursue their precarious occupation heedlessly without regard to risk—lest occasionally a day's demurrage should be caused unnecessarily or a catch of fish missed for the London market.' This quotation is from the 1863 report, and in it FitzRoy states roundly that there are no less than four distinct classes of interested opponents to his weather forecasting and system of storm warnings, and that 'they should be known'. As to the other three, there are those who have been trying unsuccessfully to start a daily weather newspaper in opposition and 'who have since endeavoured, by conversation, by letters, and by elaborate criticisms in newspapers and periodicals, to exaggerate deficiencies while ignoring merit in the works of this office.' There are 'certain persons who were opposed to the system theoretically at its origin.' And there are those who, 'whether from lack of time or opportunity, fail to look fully into the matter, continue to undervalue the subject and to call it a burlesque.'

'Burlesque' was worse than 'empirical', or at least must be so in the eyes of the general public. Whether FitzRoy was being thin-skinned, whether he was imagining the opposition and criticism to be more serious than in fact it was, it is impossible to say. The point is he was affected deeply.

Even *The Times*, which had been kind to him, began to grow increasingly critical. A leading article in the issue of April 11th 1862 begins:

> The public has not failed to notice, with interest, and, as we much fear, with some wicked amusement, that we now undertake every morning to prophesy the weather for the two days next to come. While disclaiming all credit for the occasional success, we must however demand to be held free of any responsibility for the too common failures which attend these prognostications. During the last week Nature seems to have taken special pleasure in confounding the conjectures of science.

The article continues, fairly enough, by quoting FitzRoy's own honest confession: 'Certain it is that, although our conclusions may be incorrect, our judgement erroneous, the laws of nature and the signs afforded to man are invariably true. Accurate interpretation is the real deficiency.' It continues with, again, FitzRoy's own finding, that what is needed is more and better observation (which is of course what the Royal Society would have told him, had they again been asked). The article ends with the encouragement: 'Do not give up!'

So FitzRoy does not give up. He works harder than ever, he spares himself less than ever. An ominous sign is that in his letters to his friends Sabine and Herschel, his writing, always a bold and beautifully clear hand, growing larger in his despatches from New Zealand, has now grown enormous. Then comes *The Times* leader of June 18th 1864, covering his latest and last official report. It is not *wholly* unkind:

> 'Whatever,' says Arago, 'may be the progress of the sciences, never will observers who are trustworthy and careful of their

reputations venture to foretell the state of the weather.' Admiral FitzRoy has still to convince the public, and at his task he labours yearly with most praiseworthy assiduity!

FitzRoy, the article continues, himself confesses to some failures. Nevertheless, and at least, 'there can be no doubt that when Admiral FitzRoy telegraphs, something or other is pretty sure to happen', and considering the small cost to the public of his Department, *The Times* could not range itself with FitzRoy's opponents.

But then came the unkindest cut. Perhaps the scepticism that undoubtedly existed was due 'to the singularly uncouth and obscure dialect employed by the Admiral in his explanations.' What for instance did this mean: 'Facts are as the ground; telegraphic wires are roots; a central office is the trunk; forecasts are branches; and cautionary signals are as fruit of this youngest tree of knowledge?' 'What he professes,' the article continues, 'so far as we can divine the sense of his mysterious utterances, is to ascertain what is going on in the air some hundreds of miles from London by a diagram of the currents circulating in the metropolis.'

No man likes to be ridiculed upon the matter nearest to his heart. FitzRoy could only work himself all the harder.

Even the great M. F. Maury had turned against him. FitzRoy had obviously developed mixed feelings about Maury; by 1865, when the American was in this country for a while and suffering financially from the Civil War, the feelings may have even been complicated by ones of guilt for loss of loyalty. In letters[4] to Herschel FitzRoy had accused Maury of 'trumpeting', of not showing sufficient recognition of his predecessors, of being 'solely a politician'. Nevertheless, Maury *was* the great pioneer. And now he was writing discouraging letters which FitzRoy describes sadly in his 1864 report as 'not of a *progressive* character'. 'In discouraging such forecasts as are now drawn in France and England, Captain Maury is unaware how completely he would destroy the scientific foundations of telegraphic *cautionary* notices.'

[4] Herschel correspondence, The Royal Society.

Only cautionary, be it noted, not mandatory. Would no one understand him, not even Maury? Would he never be able to vindicate himself by greater accuracy? He could only work himself all the harder.

In April of 1865 FitzRoy's wife was writing to a relative that her husband's health had been in an unsatisfactory state for some time. 'The Doctors unite in prescribing total rest, and entire absence from his office for a time. Leave has been given him, but his active mind and over-sensitive conscience prevent him from profiting by this leave, as he does not like to be putting the work he is paid to do upon others, and it keeps him in a continual fidget to be at his post, and the moment he feels at all better he hastens back, only to find himself unequal to work satisfactorily when he gets there.'

In another letter the solicitous and frightened wife was referring to 'a severe attack of prostration of strength, threatening paralysis', and was confessing that as far back as the preceding January she had consulted doctors 'with regard to the soundness of his poor mind.'

Suicide always comes as a shock, even when half feared. Reasons can only be guessed at. 'Disturbed balance of mind' is a useless catchphrase.

FitzRoy had been meeting frustration, as on the *Beagle* he had met frustration; and his was not the kind of character that could easily bear it. While on the *Beagle* he had been reasoned and encouraged back to health, and he had been young, now there seemed no hope, and he was 'Senex' and his physical breakdown was greater.

He died by the equivalent of the Roman way, and perhaps he possessed something of the courage of the Roman: he had done what he could with life—let it go! Here follows the widow's description of the last few days before the morning of Sunday, April 30th, 1865, when FitzRoy went into his dressing room and took his razor and cut his throat.[5]

[5] Private papers in the possession of Robert FitzRoy's descendants.

Upper Norwood Friday, April 21st, in bed all day very ill, Saturday April 22nd in bed better. *Most grateful* for recovery. Sunday —up, weak and ill, unable to go out, but came downstairs, asked for his bible and prayer book, while we went to church; told me on my return that he had read as much as his mind was able to take in.

On Monday 24th, still very weak, able to take a short drive with Ad^l. Cary which did him good, and then sat out with me in the garden while the girls played at croquet.

Tuesday 25th. Much better. Would go to London—did no business at his office, came back in the afternoon early, **met** him accidentally near Mrs Thelmson's [?] where we were going to pay a visit, would not come with us, but went home to get a cup of beef tea which I had ordered to be ready for him. Went to see Ad^l. Cary (not at home), waited for us, joined us and then went home. Evening played at whist which he seemed to like.

Wednesday the 26th, he went to London for a short time, not to his office.

Thursday 27th, a hot day, he started directly after breakfast for London in order to be back in time to meet General and Mrs Wood, came back just after 12 very tired out, and lay down to rest, came down to luncheon. Joined us and Colonel Smyth in a walk in the afternoon, had a good deal of conversation with Col. Smyth and myself about our affairs. He met Dr Hetty [?] afterwards and had a ['long' deleted] conversation with him about his health, the last time Dr Hetty had any conversation with him. In the evening he seemed quiet and happy, talking tranquilly with me alone, and seemed to have made up his mind to stay here quietly and really take care of himself. Just before going to bed he received a letter from Mr Tremlett inviting him and myself to come and stay with him from Saturday till Monday to see the last of Capt. Maury. This note seemed completely to upset him, between desire to comply with his request and his just expressed wish of remaining quiet. Of course he did not sleep well that night; the only advice I gave him was to do that which would give his mind the greatest ease. On Friday morning he went to London to his office, came back again relieved at having written and refused the invitation, so he told me. And after luncheon he went to his room to write and called me urgently to come to him; when I came, I found him extremely distressed at the quantity of

unanswered notes and invitations to public dinner which ought
to have been answered long ago. I comforted him and helped him
to answer two or three most pressing, and then he consented
to go out with us for a little while—went to see Admiral Cary,
who came back with him to the door; in the evening he again
played at whist, which he seemed to like. Saturday morning after
breakfast he came to me saying he had got a strong desire to see
Maury again; I told him he had better gratify it if he had; he said
he was totally incapable of exertion, and could only lie down
and rest and asked me to make him comfortable, which I did.
After luncheon he felt somewhat better, and set out to take a
walk with the two eldest girls while I went for a drive, in which
he declined accompanying me, because he thought the walk would
do him more good. When I came home I found that he had left
them, and gone to London, and did not return till nearly 8 o'clock,
worn out by fatigue and excitement and in a worse state of nervous restlessness than I had seen him since we left London (to
live at Norwood]. He seemed totally unable to collect his ideas or
thoughts, or give any coherent answer, or make any coherent
remark. After dinner he recovered a little and mentioned a
circumstance which had impressed him awfully, which had
occurred at Mr Tremlett's and also mentioned Mr Tremlett's
having asked him to come again on Sunday. I expressed my
surprise, as I had myself written to Mr Tremlett on Friday morning by the day post thanking him for the previous invitation, but
telling him that the kindest thing his friend could do would be
to leave him quiet, without tempting him to go up to London, as
he never went there without being the worse, and never remained quiet here for a day or two without being decidedly better.

I offered to have another game of whist in the evening; he said
there was nothing he should like better, but he had had such
exciting conversations with Captn. Maury and Mr Tremlett that
he could not divert his mind to any other subject. He generally
went to sleep after dinner for a little time, but this evening he
did not even close his eyes for an instant. When the girls had
gone to bed he said to me he wished to talk over with me about
his idea of going to London on Sunday to see Maury once again.
I asked him if he had not wished him good-bye: he said he had.
I then said I was very tired and sleepy, and the best thing we
could both do was to go to bed, and talk over that the following

morning. He agreed with me, saying how worn and tired I looked. I went away and than went downstairs again as he had not come up to his dressing-room. He thanked me for coming to see after him, and said he was coming up directly; he was standing up by the table, with the newspaper open before him, and was not long in coming to his room. I was in bed when he came to bed; he came round to the side where I was, asked me if I was comfortable, kissed me, wished me good night, and then got into bed. It was just 12 o'clock. I was soon asleep, and when I woke in the morning I said I hoped he had slept better, as he had been so very quiet. He said he had slept he believed, but not refreshingly; he complained of the light, and I said we must contrive something to keep it out. Just then it struck six. From 6 to 7 neither of us spoke, being both half asleep I believe. Soon after the clock struck 7 he asked if the maid was not late in calling us. I said it was Sunday, and she generally was later, as there was no hurry for breakfast on account of the train at 10 o'clock as there was on other days. The maid called us at $\frac{1}{2}$ past 7. He got out of bed before I did, I can't tell exactly what time, but it must have been about $\frac{1}{4}$ to eight. He got up before I did and went to his dressing room kissing Laura as he passed ['through her little room' added later], and did *not* lock the door of his dressing-room at first.

CHAPTER 23

Vindication and Farewell

*It is much better to serve an ungrateful
country than give up his own fame. Posterity
will do him justice.*

HORATIO NELSON.

THE scene is the anniversary meeting of
the Royal Geographical Society and the President, Sir Roderick
Murchison, is addressing the meeting.[1] He claims Admiral
Robert FitzRoy as an old friend: it was he who had presented the
returned Captain of the *Beagle* with his gold medal nearly thirty
years ago. He continues:

> In deploring the loss of this eminent man who was as truly es-
> teemed by his former chief, the Prince of Naval Navigators, Sir
> Francis Beaufort, as by his successors, I may be allowed to suggest
> that if FitzRoy had not had thrown upon him the heavy and
> irritating responsibility of never being found at fault in any of his
> numerous forecasts of storms in our very changeful climate, his
> valuable life might have been preserved.

That was one opinion, but a responsible one. FitzRoy's widow
seems to have felt the same. What she was determined upon was
that his reputation should not be tarnished by the manner of his
death nor his good work forgotten, that those who thought
differently from Murchison should be refuted and their actions
contained. She collected testimonials and enlisted help.

Though those who write obituaries, particularly on request,

[1] R.G.S. minutes.

285

will seldom say anything but good about the dead, it was nevertheless soon borne in upon the widow that there were those
likely to belittle FitzRoy's achievements. We find her writing
this virulent and impassioned letter,[2] to a Mr Augustus Smith
M.P.:

> Sir,
>
> Not content with hunting a good and noble man almost to his
> grave, you endeavour to depreciate and ruin the work of human-
> ity to which he was so earnestly devoted. But facts speak for
> themselves. If this system of Storm Warnings is so useless and
> defective why do other countries eagerly adopt them? Why is it
> the cry of the wives of fishermen on the Northern coast of
> Scotland, 'Who will *now* take care of our husbands?' and why do
> the boatmen of our Southernmost ports in England say '*We* have
> had a sad loss'—both and many others I could instance alluding
> to that most melancholy and untimely fate of a man who gave
> *all* for his country leaving his family nothing but his reputation.
> You can no longer hurt him—though I do not suppose you act
> from personal malice towards one who never injured anyone.
> Your motive may be to gain a little popularity by being the
> economical Member of the House—but you can add one drop of
> bitterness to the cup of misery already overflowing in the heart
> of his unfortunate Wife who now feels doubly every slur cast on
> *his* work and most gratefully all the deservedly high terms in
> which that work is spoken of by thousands and will be long after
> I am gone and can be no more affected by praise or blame than he
> now is.
>
> > I remain Sir
> > etc
> > Maria I. FitzRoy.

On June 8th of that year, 1865, the House being then in
Committee of Supply, the Member for Truro, Mr Augustus
Smith, had spoken in the debate on the Meteorological Estimates.
Complaining of the diversity of control over the sum concerned,
he asked whether the Board of Trade were going on with weather

[2] The widow's letters are also in the possession of Robert FitzRoy's
descendants.

forecasting, now that the department concerned was without a head. There were returns for the previous year, he asserted, that showed that the 'prophecies'—FitzRoy could have writhed in his grave—were twice as often wrong as right. 'Last Tuesday week what did the Board of Trade prophesy with regard to the weather? Wind S.E. to S.S.W., fresh moderate. What was the fact? The wind did not blow from those quarters; but a tremendous gale, involving great destruction of property, swept across the north of England.' Adding that almost all the great storms had come *before* the warnings, he expressed finally the hope that to fill FitzRoy's post there would be placed 'a gentleman of high scientific attainments'.

The President of the Board of Trade, in reply, did in fact handsomely defend the late head of his Meteorological Department. His Honourable Friend had underrated the reputation enjoyed by FitzRoy in the scientific world. 'He was only speaking the opinion of those best qualified to give one that the late Admiral did a great service in perfecting—in carrying forward —the science of meteorology.' The change made from the collection of statistics to 'a more practical application' of the science had been effected 'very much by Admiral FitzRoy himself, but always with the concurrence of this House and of the Royal Society.'[3]

Nevertheless, in spite of that last assertion, the upshot of the debate was the setting up of a committee, in consultation with the Royal Society, to review the work and consider the future of FitzRoy's department.

The committee's report,[4] appearing in the following year and comprising forty-three foolscap pages plus nearly as many of appendices, ends with the following protestation: 'We should be doing great injustice to ourselves if we were to allow it to be supposed that we undervalue either what the late Admiral FitzRoy attempted or what he effected.' Such an ending was

[3] Hansard, 1865.
[4] Report of a Committee appointed to consider certain questions relating to the Meteorological Department of the Board of Trade, (H.M.S.O. 1866).

somewhat necessary, for the report is critical and sometimes highly critical.

It will be remembered that the Royal Society had had FitzRoy named Statist, or in modern language Statistician. This committee seemed surprised that he had never become one, which to say the least of it is to show a lack of knowledge of FitzRoy's character—as well be surprised if Charles Dickens had not made a success of being John Stuart Mill. The committee found that insufficient use had been made of the data collected in the early years of the department and that latterly the collection of such data from ships at sea had largely ceased. FitzRoy had turned his attention to other things, viz, weather forecasting by means of the use of telegraphic information, and Storm Warnings.

Of the former the committee were forthright in their condemnation. 'We can find no evidence that any competent meteorologist believes the science to be at present in such a state as to enable an observer to indicate day by day the weather to be experienced for the next 48 hours throughout a wide margin of the earth's surface.' As to the Storm Warnings, the committee found that they had become well known and highly prized, and were 'of some use'. They made their recommendation.

With regard to what the committee found, and why they found it, there are two very interesting letters extant. One is from Mr T. H. Babington, who had been FitzRoy's assistant and who carried on after him until the changes recommended were made. The other is by the then Naval Hydrographer, who was consulted on the recommendations.[5]

Babington comes to the defence of his chief against the accusation that the statistical work had been neglected—had in fact and in common parlance, though he does not use the word, been allowed to get into a mess. 'It could not,' he says, 'have been otherwise. Admiral FitzRoy had insufficient clerical assistance. For a considerable period his thoughts were necessarily chiefly engrossed by the origination and organization of an entirely new service which he at length succeeded in reducing to a system and to working order—but at the cost of his own life. For some

[5] Papers in possession of the Meteorological Office, Bracknell.

time before his death his intensely clear and vigorous mind—
clouded and weakened by the continuous strain upon it and the
anxiety he had undergone—was incapable of sustained exertion.
His Office was numerically weak and he had no opportunity of
effecting more than he did. I once heard Maury (on such a point a
competent judge) remark that the only wonder was that he had
effected so much.'

The Hydrographer's letter, or rather memorandum, seeks to
explain how it arose that the original objects of FitzRoy's meteorological department 'may be said to have ceased.' Some curtail-
ment of the original scheme of data-collecting was in any case
right and necessary, for the simple reason that 'the area of observation over most of the ocean tracks' had been in a measure
exhausted. In any case it hardly came within the province of any
government department to superintend the working of a scientific
institution. The Royal Society had never been in a position to
give directions, only opinions and 'the whole disposal of the
Establishment and the nature of the duties to be performed was
left to the discretion of the Superintendent, an officer of acknowledged great scientific attainments, who without doubt discharged them in the way he considered most conducive to the
public interest.'

The Committee's recommendations were (1) that the sea
observations should be properly digested and made available and
should to a degree be recommenced; (2) that the daily weather
forecasts should be discontinued; and (3) that the storm warnings,
'too important, too popular and too full of promise of practical
utility to be allowed to die', should be continued, but on 'a scientific and wholesome foundation'.

Whatever was meant exactly by that word 'wholesome', the
final result was even less satisfactory to the upholders of FitzRoy's
memory than these recommendations might imply. The job of
running this scientific department that had been found so
deplorably unscientific was offered in its entirety to the Royal
Society, or rather to a permanent committee of the Society. The
offer was accepted—but with a change of plan. In spite of the
replies to a questionnaire sent out to the principal ports hoisting

the FitzRoy storm signals, all of which with one exception were highly favourable,[6] and in spite of the recommendation of their own committee, 'the President and Council of the Royal Society are of opinion that, "at present these warnings are founded on rules mainly empirical" and therefore should not be issued under the superintendence of such a scientific body as themselves'. The storm warnings, therefore, besides the daily forecasts, should also cease—though after a few years and when greater knowledge could ensure greater accuracy they might perhaps be resumed.

The Society's stipulation was duly accepted. The deplorers of 'empiricism' in fact had won.

Was FitzRoy hardly done by?

As far as is concerned the last job of his lifetime, he undoubtedly was. The widow retained a letter, which ran:

> Sir,
>
> I have just received your Circular of the 29th ult[mo]. and much regret to learn that the 'Storm Warnings' will be suspended from the 7th instant.
>
> I trust the suspension will not be of long continuance, for the *'warnings'* are *invaluable* on this coast, and I think that if the President and Council of the Royal Society could have witnessed the growing attention paid to the Signals by the sailors and were aware of their general accuracy they would not have recommended even a temporary suspension. Thirty-three warning telegrams have been received at this station during the current year, and in twenty-six instances a gale has followed from the Quarter indicated.

This was from a reverend gentleman who lived at the Parsonage, Siloth, Cumberland and who was a Fellow of the Royal Society—one at least who was not shocked by empiricism. Had the widow had access to Board of Trade files she would have found this opinion backed up by the Liverpool Underwriters, the Manchester Chamber of Commerce, and responsible officers from the ports of Greenwich, Glasgow, Edinburgh, Leith and Dundee,

[6] Page xxxvii of the Report.

the last pointing out that the fact that increased knowledge might give a better service in a few years' time did not seem a valid reason for stopping what was proving very useful in the present. In the following year, 1867, there appeared two pamphlets which were in their titles critical of FitzRoy.[7] Nevertheless both of them, while disagreeing with FitzRoy in some detail of theory, were complimentary to him as a whole, particularly the author of the larger pamphlet, Christopher Cooke. Cooke is at pains to produce statistics to show that the dead man's forecasts had (in spite of what Mr Augustus Smith had said) at least always been more right than wrong. He then becomes at first bitter and then lyrical in defence. 'If a new invention, scheme, or plan is brought to light it seems to be a settled rule of Nature, that the inventor should be misunderstood or maligned by silly and vindictive people.' After stating that comparisons had even been made with astrology by such people, he continues: 'There can be little doubt in the minds of reflecting persons that if Admiral FitzRoy's life had been prolonged his system would have improved and that his predictions would have been verified to a greater extent.' The cost had been less than £45,000 over nine years. 'Surely Britannia, who rules the waves more potently than did Canute, if she deserves to preserve her dominion, should not grudge this national mite in favour of those who do her work.'

FitzRoy in New Zealand may have brought his punishment onto his own head; but, though the pattern of behaviour is remarkably alike, FitzRoy the weather forecaster received not the slightest hint during his lifetime that what he was doing or failing to do on his job was earning the displeasure of his employers as such. He had been, however, premature, rather perhaps as Allen Gardiner had been premature in Tierra del Fuego: both in fact had been willing to sacrifice themselves so that, premature or not, a job on which they had set their hearts might

[7] *Admiral FitzRoy's Exposition of the Solar-Lunar Cyclone Theory with 'R' 's Refutation*, Number V in a series of essays on *The Science of the Weather* (Glasgow); and *Amiral FitzRoy, his Facts and Failures*, by Christopher Cooke, formerly Solicitor to the Astro-Meteorological Society (London).

at least be started—and both in fact had been sacrificed. Such people indeed, in a hard world, are expendable.

FitzRoy of course did *not* know enough. Compared with modern meteorological equipment, his means were pathetically inadequate—he could not for instance even begin to know about the upper air. Nevertheless his basic physical knowledge was good and accurate. He really suffered from the fact that the Royal Society equally did not know enough. It did not know enough to realize that the particular scientific application that they were criticizing had to be empirical, that it would go on during the next hundred years at least being spectacularly empirical but would make spectacular progress none the less.

Was FitzRoy in other ways hardly done by? In his New Zealand governorship, probably not: on that subject enough has already been said.

Of the *Beagle* voyage something more should be said. The manner in which the Admiralty let him down over the matter of supplementary schooners always rankled bitterly with FitzRoy. But FitzRoy was obviously of the open-handed, extravagant type, and the grievance may well have been subconsciously kept alive as a sort of alibi and excuse for being perennially impecunious. The widow continued the cry: her husband's debts at death were met, says Darwin, by some of his friends; and she herself was allowed to occupy a Grace and Favour house by the Queen.

More generally, the great achievements of the *Beagle* voyage may never have been properly appreciated. Though it has been suggested that requested obituaries are likely to err on the side of fulsomeness, yet the one that the widow obtained from the Naval Hydrographer—the same, by name George Henry Richards, who had defended FitzRoy in his memorandum on the Royal Society report—is both so obviously well informed and sincerely expressed that it should be quoted:

> There is and ever has been one opinion among the officers past and present of this department as to the services of the late Admiral FitzRoy. No naval officer ever did more for the practical

benefit of navigation and commerce than he did, and did it too with a means and at an expense to the country which would now be deemed totally inadequate...

In a little vessel of scarcely over 200 tons, assisted by able and zealous officers under his command, many of whom were modelled under his hand and most of whom have since risen to eminence, he explored and surveyed the continent of South America...

The Strait of Magellan, until then almost a sealed book, has since, mainly through his exertions, become a great highway for the commerce of the world—the path of countless ships of all nations; and the practical result to navigation of these severe and trying labours, which told deeply on the mental as well as the physical constitution of more than one engaged, is shown in the publication to the world of nearly a hundred charts bearing the names of FitzRoy and his officers, as well as the most admirably compiled directions for the guidance of the seamen which perhaps was ever written, and which has passed through five editions...

His works are his best as they will be his most enduring monument, for they will be handed down to generations yet unborn.

Over his religious beliefs FitzRoy may also be said to have been hardly done by, it being at once added that such treatment was inevitable and that he was by no means the only victim. Darwin's theory hit him and left him floored—floored, struggling and unnoticed, in much the same way as a modern motor car may leave a cyclist, or to make a stricter analogy, a pathetically old-fashioned tricyclist, by the roadside. None the less, and as has already been suggested, FitzRoy and his like cannot be easily dismissed: such were considerable, and thoughtful men. There is a letter from FitzRoy to Herschel which may be quoted. From his friend's writings, FitzRoy confesses, and from astronomy and physics in general, he has worked out a sort of philosophic theory which, 'helps me to catch faint glimpses of that unapproachable and utterly incomprehensible Power originating and maintaining all that can be seen, felt or known by the mind. In connection with these views *I* find astronomy and geology the *most* convincing proofs of Old Testament *inspiration* (if *fairly* read and thought of).' He was not alone in this.

But this is enough of justification. To stress that FitzRoy was hardly done by will, if carried too far, only belittle him.

What else could he expect? Pioneers are always hardly done by, as Mr Christopher Cooke had said. So too are men who, while being good masters, cannot be good servants. So too are men who are a law unto themselves and will not bow to expediency. So too are men who see their duty narrowly and follow it unswervingly, who do not curb their tongues nor mind what others think of them, who grow as angry with the particular men that thwart them as they are loving towards men in general and those that need their help. It was not an hereditary weakness that destroyed FitzRoy, but rather a toughness—hereditary too maybe —a toughness masochistic in its inability to compromise.

The Times of Tuesday, May 2nd had much in it besides news of the death of Robert FitzRoy. It was still much concerned with the repercussions from the assassination of Abraham Lincoln, which had occurred a fortnight earlier. It told of the Chancellor's speech on the tea duty. Life, in its large things and its small, would goon.

Life in the Meteorological Office (as it was now called) went on, for a while in a somewhat muted fashion, FitzRoy's assistant, Babington, resigning. It picked up again, of course, though it is now considered that the check delayed such fundamental discoveries as that of depressions' warm and cold 'fronts'. The Office now has millions to spend where FitzRoy had hundreds.

In New Zealand, FitzRoy's successor had to deal with a greater Maori war; he became Premier instead of Governor and lived to a good old age. FitzRoy's Secretary of State for the Colonies was, the year after FitzRoy's death, Prime Minister of England for the third time. Jerningham Wakefield, whose castigation had so harmed FitzRoy, returned to New Zealand, but died comparatively young and under a cloud.

There are the young men of the *Beagle*, moulded, according to the Hydrographer, under FitzRoy's hand. Skyring, whom he had replaced in command of the *Beagle*, never lucky apparently, died at the hand of savages on the coasts of Africa. Wickham, became

Governor of Queensland. Stokes, taking over the *Beagle* from Wickham in 1841, captained the ship on another surveying voyage around New Zealand between 1847 and 1851, wrote a book about it and then retired to the life of a country gentleman. Midshipman Mellersh, he of the boast about Byron and self-sufficiency, lived up to his self-assessment by putting pirates in their place in the China Seas and retired the year before FitzRoy died to live on as an Admiral for another thirty years. Sulivan, who crossed FitzRoy's life most often, and who continued his support of the Patagonian Mission to the end of his life, retired from his Board of Trade post in the year in which FitzRoy died and lived on also to ripe old age, loaded with honours.

The ship itself, the *Beagle*, was long-lived. After returning from her fourth and last surveying voyage in 1851, she became a Customs Watch vessel in home waters. In 1870 she was sold by public auction: she fetched £525 and went to the Japanese who used her as a training ship until 1881. Only in 1888 was she broken up.

Jemmy Button died a little over a year before the man who in the waters of the Beagle Channel had made the strange bargain that so altered his life. He succumbed to an epidemic that killed many of his compatriots and was the first of many that in the next hundred years would almost wipe out the Fuegians. The Mission to the Fuegians, however, at length prospered under one of the adopted sons of the Reverend Packenham Despard, Thomas Bridges. FitzRoy may have never heard of the death and certainly never heard of the mission's success. He would have been very happy at the second piece of news, for Bridges was the first fully to follow his advice and master the native language. Darwin too was pleased, though surprised. He wrote, handsomely, that he was 'charmed' at the success of the mission.

As for Charles Darwin himself, it would be super-erogation to sketch his remaining career. He was to outlive his friend by seventeen years, a great and at the end a revered and respected figure who had changed the way of thought of a century.

But Darwin was always a very human man besides being a great one, an essentially kindly and friendly person who understood kindness and friendship and loyalty. It is fitting therefore that he should be allowed to make the final assessment of FitzRoy.

FitzRoy once wrote to Beaufort, the Naval Hydrographer: 'I think you will allow that my messmate has well earned his stowage!' And Darwin wrote to FitzRoy at the end of the voyage: 'I think it far the most fortunate encounter of my life that the chance afforded by your offer of taking a Naturalist fell on me.' His final summing up of character was: 'generous to a fault...and an ardent friend to all under his sway'. Here were two forceful characters discerning enough to see the best in each other, and gracious enough to express it.

FitzRoy may at times have seemed a formidable person, harshly unpredictable, only loving his kind in general and disliking them in particular. But that is not the true and inner character. For that the adjective used by his friend is a better one: ardent. And to have an ardent nature is an admirable, and an enviable, possession.

Darwin's letter to FitzRoy when he was going as Governor to New Zealand shall serve to point the humanity of his friend:

Farewell, dear FitzRoy, I often think of the many acts of kindness to me, and not seldom of the time, no doubt quite forgotten by you, when, before making Madeira, you came and arranged my hammock with your own hands, and which, as I afterwards heard, brought tears to my father's eyes.

Appendix

The *Beagle* in South American Waters

Dates	Chief Moves and Events
28.2.32	Land at Bahia (San Salvador) Brazil.
26.3.32	Examine Abrolhos Islands.
4.4.32	Enter Rio harbour. Ship painted; shore leave.
10.5.32	Return trip to Bahia and back, to check latitude; deaths from malaria.
12.6.32	Regatta at Rio.
23.7.32	Enter La Plata estuary.
3.8.32	Land at Monte Video with armed squad.
7.9.32	Visit Argentina settlement and Punta Alta, Darwin finding fossils.
11.9.32	Two supplementary schooners hired and re-fitted.
Sept–Nov '32	Survey of coast S. of Rio.
4.12.32	Set out for Tierra del Fuego.
15.12.32	First sight of indigenous natives.
23.1.33	Fuegians and Matthews landed near Beagle Channel (at Woollya).
4.2.33	Matthews taken off again.
1.3.33	Reach Falkland Islands.
8.3.33	Supplementary schooner bought, renamed *Adventure*

Dates	Chief Moves and Events
26.4.33	Return to Monte Video.
May–Oct '33	Further surveying of E. Coast, revictualling etc., while *Adventure* re-fitted.
6.12.33	Departure for return visits to Tierra del Fuego and Falkland Is.
25.12.33	Cheerful Christmas at Port Desire.
Jan '34	Off St Julian: search with Darwin for fresh water.
Feb. '34	In Magellan Straits and then Beagle Channel again.
5.3.34	Reunion with and final farewell to Jemmy Button.
March '34	Second visit to Falkland Is.
April–May '34	Return to Patagonian coast. *Beagle* beached for repair; boat expedition up Santa Cruz River.
9.6.34	Finally leave Tierra del Fuego.
22.7.34	Arrive at Valparaiso.
Aug–Oct '34	Captain takes lodgings in Valparaiso, to complete charts etc.; stay a little prolonged because Darwin ill.
Oct '34	*Adventure* sold. Captain ill and threatens to resign.
21.11.34	Arrive at Chilóe.
Dec '34–Jan '35	Surveying of W. coast continues—dreary Christmas.
5.2.35	Leave Chilóe for surveying further North.
20.2.35	The great earthquake.
17.4.35	Leave Concepcion for further North.
16.6.35	News of wreck of *Challenger*—FitzRoy to the rescue.
2.8.35	FitzRoy returns to the *Beagle*.
7.9.35	Small schooner left to survey coast of Peru; *Beagle* leaves S. America for Galapagos Is.

Bibliographical Note

References to sources are made in the chapter notes, as are those to many of the books consulted. For the benefit of those interested, however, there is given below the titles, dates and publishers of the books considered most helpful in a study of Robert FitzRoy.

For FitzRoy's ancestry there is Bernard Falk's *The Royal FitzRoys* (Hutchinson, 1950) and *Robert Stewart, Viscount Castlereagh* by the Marchioness of Londonderry (Arthur Humphries, 1904). For FitzRoy's early days in the Navy, there is *Life and Letters of Admiral Sir B. J. Sulivan*, by Henry N. Sulivan (Murray, 1816), and also *Snotty, the Story of the Midshipman* by G. Penn and *A Social History of the Royal Navy* by Michael Lewis.

For the first and second voyages of the *Beagle* the main source is of course the *Narrative of the Surveying Voyages of H.M.S. Adventure and Beagle* (Henry Colburn, 1839), in three volumes plus an appendix. Vol. I covers the first voyage and is mostly King's account with material by Stokes and FitzRoy. Vol. II is FitzRoy's account of the second voyage, and Vol. III is Darwin's. Only Darwin's volume has been reprinted, under the title of *Journal of Researches*.

Other relevant Darwinian material comprises his *Life and*

Letters in three volumes and *More Letters* in two—all edited by his son Francis and published by Murray, in 1887 and 1903. Darwin's *Diary* of the *Beagle* voyage was edited and published by his grand-daughter, Nora Barlow, in 1933; the diary formed the basis for Darwin's Volume III of the *Narrative* but contains more personal material and is also in chronological order, which Vol. III is not. Lady Barlow has also published *Charles Darwin and the Voyage of the Beagle* (Pilot Press, 1945), which contains all the relevant correspondence, an appraisement of FitzRoy and excerpts from Darwin's rough notebooks, an unexpurgated edition of Darwin's *Autobiography* (Collins, 1958), and an article on FitzRoy in the *Cornhill Magazine* of April, 1932. An excellent and somewhat forgotten biography is *Charles Darwin, the Fragmentary Man* by Geoffrey West (Geo. Routledge, 1937); it pays considerable attention to FitzRoy, the author being able to interview FitzRoy's daughter by his second marriage.

Memoirs of Old Friends, 1835 to 1871 by Caroline Fox (Smith Elder, 1882, two vols.) has two references to FitzRoy; Caroline Fox was a serious minded quakeress and she has much to say on the literary and scientific personalities of her day and gives a good idea of the mental and moral atmosphere of her times. A similarly useful book is the later *Before Victoria* by Muriel Jaeger (Chatto & Windus, 1956).

A useful introduction to New Zealand's early history is *A Short History of New Zealand* by Condliffe and Airey (N.Z., 1954). Baron de Thierry appears in *New Zealand Biographies,* and Paul Blomfield has written a life of *Edward Gibbon Wakefield* (Longman, 1961). Major Thomson's more or less contemporary account, *The Story of New Zealand,* was published by Murray in 1859, and Edward Jerningham Wakefield's *Adventure in New Zealand* was republished by Whitcombe and Tombs, New Zealand, in 1908. By far the fullest account of FitzRoy's governorship is given in *Crown Colony Government in New Zealand* by Dr A. H. McLintock (Wellington, 1958). FitzRoy's own *Remarks on New Zealand* was published by W. & H. White, London, in 1846.

The books concerned with the 'Fuegian Aftermath' are all referred to in the footnotes to that chapter.

FitzRoy's *Weather Book* was also published by Longmans, in 1862. The *Centenary of the Meteorological Office* by Sir David Brunt gives a useful background. Christopher Cooke's *FitzRoy's Facts and Failures* was published by H. Hall, London, 1867.

J. Lort Stokes's account of the later voyages of the *Beagle* is *Discoveries in Australia* (T. & N. Boone, 1846, two vols.)

Index

303